Beleaguered Poets and Leftist Critics

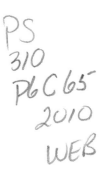

Beleaguered Poets and Leftist Critics

Stevens, Cummings, Frost, and Williams in the 1930s

Milton A. Cohen

The University of Alabama Press
Tuscaloosa

Typeface: Bembo

∞

The paper on which this book is printed meets the minimum requirements of
American National Standard for Information Sciences—Permanence of Paper
for Printed Library Materials, ANSI Z39.48-1984.

Library of Congress Cataloging-in-Publication Data

Cohen, Milton A.
    Beleaguered poets and leftist critics : Stevens, Cummings, Frost, and Williams
in the 1930s / Milton A. Cohen.
        p. cm.
    Includes bibliographical references and index.
    ISBN 978-0-8173-1713-3 (cloth : alk. paper) — ISBN 978-0-8173-8445-6
(electronic) 1. American poetry—20th century—History and criticism. 2.
Politics and literature—United States—History—20th century. 3. Right and
left (Political science) in literature. 4. Poets, American—20th century—Political
and social views. 5. Stevens, Wallace, 1879–1955—Political and social views.
6. Cummings, E. E. (Edward Estlin), 1894–1962—Political and social views.
7. Frost, Robert, 1874–1963—Political and social views. 8. Williams, William
Carlos, 1883–1963—Political and social views. I. Title.
    PS310.P6C65 2010
    811'.5209—dc22

                                                                    2010017778

In memory of Gail
and Frank Gettleson

Contents

Acknowledgments

A "Special Faculty Development Assignment" from the School of Arts and Humanities of The University of Texas at Dallas provided time for much of the research and writing of this book. I wish to thank Dean Dennis Kratz for his additional support. Dr. Michael Webster kindly read the Cummings chapter and made several helpful suggestions. The anonymous readers who evaluated this book for The University of Alabama Press also made several very useful suggestions for revision. Dr. Morgan Swann, research librarian of the Beinecke Library, Yale University, provided valuable assistance. Finally—and as always—I am grateful for the unfailing support and editorial assistance of my wife, Florence Chasey-Cohen.

Beleaguered Poets and Leftist Critics

Introduction

The pressure of the contemporaneous from the time of the beginning
of the World War to the present time has been constant and extreme.
No one can have lived apart in a happy oblivion. . . . We are preoccupied
with events, even when we do not observe them closely. We have a sense
of upheaval. We feel threatened.

    —Wallace Stevens, 1936

[P]olitics was placed at the center of the times to the extent that even
writers who were apparently unaffected by it felt the moral necessity of
justifying their indifference.

    —William Phillips and Philip Rahv, 1937

Imagine you are a modernist poet, and it is 1931. In the 1920s you were a
critical success: you enjoyed the approbation of your peers, a small circle
of poets and critics—the cognoscenti. Now, almost overnight, everything
has changed.

In the face of growing hordes of the unemployed, the breadlines and
soup kitchens, the bank failures and foreclosures, the utter confusion of
business moguls and the paralysis of the White House, many of your colleagues—very many—have concluded that capitalism is crumbling in this
deepest of all crashes (just as Marx had predicted) and that the future,
the only viable foreseeable future, belongs to communism, a worthy and
promising economic system. A massive conversion is under way, a mass
migration to the left: friends and fellow writers have left the sidelines and
joined the struggle. In addition, a younger generation of writers and critics is arriving—more each day—who need no converting, who already
accept the tenets of Marxism. And those tenets, applied to literature, discussed and debated in countless articles and symposia, have utterly changed
the direction of literary effort.

Modernism is out; proletarian literature is in. Freud is out; Marx is in.
Babbitt is no longer the subject; Paris is no longer the refuge; "pure art" or
"art for art's sake" is no longer a credible aesthetic philosophy; 1920s despair, nihilism, and elitism are now unwelcome attitudes. *The Dial* and *The
Little Review* are defunct. *New Masses* and *The New Republic* are what the
intelligentsia now read. Now the subject is the American working class,

unemployed or striking for decent wages or better working conditions. The mood is upbeat. The artist's social stance is no longer amused detachment or indifference, but involvement and activism. And "pure art"—*your* art—must now recognize social realities in a style no longer esoteric but comprehensible, even inspiring, to the working class. The pressure is on. Critics and reviewers (recent converts themselves, many of them) increasingly judge literature by these new criteria. If your writing is still grounded in the aesthetics of 1920s modernism, you are going to be scalded in reviews, at best considered "confused" or, worse, dismissed as outmoded, a bourgeois decadent. And if you refuse to bring your politics and aesthetics in line with the new realities, you can expect even harsher judgments: counter-revolutionary, fascist.

Such was the approximate experience, oversimplified to be sure, of three of the four modernist poets in this study: Wallace Stevens, E. E. Cummings, and William Carlos Williams. The fourth, Robert Frost, differed only in being a popular as well as critical success in the teens and twenties.[1] All four felt the pressure of the times, of the politicized literary scene, and all four saw their reputations critically challenged in the early and mid thirties. This book examines the dynamics of their literary experience in the 1930s: what they wrote; what they believed politically and aesthetically; how critics, particularly leftist critics, reviewed their work; and, most important, how these poets responded to this leftist pressure and often negative criticism. None of these topics yields a fixed answer; all—beliefs, poetry, reviews, literary standing, the poets' responses to the pressure, and the pressure itself—were in flux, shifting and changing as the times and literary politics themselves changed over this turbulent decade.

These four poets were chosen for several reasons. First, all four are major poets, whose work rewards close critical scrutiny. More important, all four reacted strongly in the 1930s to the juggernaut of leftism,[2] whether expressed radically in communism or in the liberal New Deal, and to leftist demands for politically engaged poetry. All four wrote significant poems, even whole books of poems, in response to these pressures, as well as letters, essays, and lectures. In short, the leftist times and literary influence got under their skins more so than for other poets, for example Marianne Moore.[3] The central thesis of this study is that, individual and distinctive as it is, the 1930s work of each of these four poets can yield new insights when seen as a complex interaction with the literary-political pressures of the period, and when placed against comparable experiences and poems of colleagues who were reacting to the same pressures. Scholars have studied the poets individually in social and political contexts,[4] but the four have never been grouped together to reveal comparable patterns in the exertion of and responses to these pressures. Yet in a decade so politically agitated, so rife and riven with belief and counter-belief as the 1930s, we can scarcely hope to grasp the full import of their political poetry without understanding the political milieu in which they wrote it and the complex ways in which each poet responded to this milieu in his life and work.

They had much in common, these four poets. By the end of the 1920s, each enjoyed a distinctive status in the literary community: three as "difficult" but important avant-garde poets, one as a popular poet with an "easy" style that concealed complex themes and techniques. Significantly, none of the four joined the early migration to the left in 1930–32. All, therefore, were caught in the paradigm shift of poets who continued to write in the early thirties with styles and subjects they had evolved in the teens and twenties, while all around them literary styles, standards, and criticism were changing. But neither were they indifferent to these changes: they scarcely could be when critics and reviewers now questioned the poets' literary importance and suggested they might be passé. They expressed their responses variously: Frost, Williams, and especially Stevens aired their political thoughts extensively in letters; Stevens and Frost gave lectures that addressed the times (and Frost provocatively read some of his most explicitly political poems to audiences he knew would be leftist and unsympathetic); Frost also gave interviews expressing his political views; Williams wrote letters to leftist magazines and wrote fiction (more of it, in fact, than poetry in the 1930s) that empathized with his working-class characters. Most important for this study, they wrote poems—some forgettable, but others quite significant—with explicitly political themes. This was a relatively new experience for most of them;[5] only Cummings was an old hand at political poetry, and even his satires changed markedly in the thirties.

Their political poems reveal comparable patterns of rejection or accommodation of the Left, but are also as individual as the poets themselves. Even the two poets most similar in their rejection of leftism, Frost and Cummings, differed significantly in the tone and mood of their rejections. Frost, focusing more on the New Deal, was more buoyant, assertive, and provocative as he offered in poem after poem his own counterphilosophy to what he saw as the prevailing national mood. Cummings was more personal, more bitter and defensive, suffering more directly, he felt, in the rejections (personal and literary) of his colleagues. Increasingly, he became more closed in on himself as Frost became ever more the public poet. By contrast, Stevens and Williams approached the Left in their views and poetry of the mid-thirties, but in quite different ways. Stevens, secure in his executive position and comfortable in his everyday life, nonetheless came to feel that, under the pressure of the times, his own philosophy of pure poetry was increasingly untenable. Accordingly, he felt obliged to acknowledge and come to terms with leftism in his poetry, but he expressed that obligation in his own characteristically complex manner. Williams's experience was paradoxical: he felt the ravages of the Depression more directly than Stevens as he dealt with its working-class victims—his patients—every day. Impelled by both his personal feelings and his long-standing aesthetic interest in poetry of the locality, he wrote empathetically about these struggling individuals in fiction and poems. Far more involved than Stevens in the left-literary world of magazine publishing, petitions, committees, and causes, Williams nonetheless distrusted communism and let the comrades know it on several occasions. His frankness and sometimes maladroit involvements alienated him from leftist power centers, even as the proletarian focus in his fiction and poetry aligned with their agendas.

Chapter 1 provides a contextual overview of the period, focusing on the various waves of leftist migration (especially 1930–33), the Left's proletarian aesthetics, and its prominent magazines and critics, whose names recur in the quoted reviews of subsequent chapters. Chapter 1 also examines how all of these elements changed as the Left evolved from the enthusiasm and idealism (but also sectarian infighting) of the early thirties, to the Popular Front period of the mid-thirties, to the increasingly diverse and divisive leftism of the late thirties.

Chapters 2 through 5 examine the 1930s experience of each poet in detail. One important facet of this experience emerges in the literary reviews and criticism their work received: Who reviewed their books? How did the reviewer's political orientation affect his or her evaluations? How did each poet's work and reputation fare with leftist critics? And most important, how did the poet react to the critic and the criticism? (Stevens responded to one leftist review with a major poem, while Frost at one point engineered a hatchet job on his critics.) Accordingly, chapters 2 through 5 will discuss reviews, particularly from leftist critics, for each major book of the four poets. Another side of their experience concerns publishing opportunities during the Depression. Who was willing to publish poets like Williams and Cummings, when major publishers were not? How did these opportunities—or lack of them—affect the poets' productivity and outlook? And how did one mysterious publisher with half a dozen aliases intercede in the creative lives of Stevens and Williams with important book commissions and also develop Stevens's political thinking? Chapters 2 through 5 will consider these questions as they explore each poet's individual relationship with the Left.

The conclusion pulls these four stories together to consider their emergent patterns. The poetic responses of all four poets to the Left describe a kind of bell curve of political involvement and disengagement, moving in roughly parallel stages from indifference (for Stevens) or lesser engagement (for Williams, Frost, and Cummings) in the early thirties, to a peak of involvement for all four (including active resistance) in the mid-thirties, to separation in the late thirties. It is not coincidental that the great majority of writers and intellectuals attracted to the Left in the thirties experienced this same pattern at roughly the same times with one notable exception: As chapter 1 will show, engagement with the Left for the first wave of the intellectual converts (1930–33) was not tentative, but intense. Moreover, even though Frost, Cummings, and Williams were beginning to respond to that "first wave" conversion (e.g., Frost's long poem "Build Soil" in 1932, Cummings's *Eimi* in 1933, Williams's coeditorship of *Blast*), the collections of poems that all four published in the early thirties (Stevens's second version of *Harmonium,* Frost's *Collected Poems,* Cummings's *ViVa,* and Williams's *Collected Poems, 1921–1931*) contained almost no poems responding to the Depression and leftism; hence the critics' impression that these poets were indifferent to their times. The high point of leftist appeal, generally, came in the mid-thirties,[6] spurred by the Popular Front against fascism and the outbreak of the Spanish Civil War. Accordingly, with leftist pressures at their most intense, the political poetry of these four poets correspondingly reached a high point in Stevens's *Ideas of Order* (1935) and *Owl's Clover* (1936), Frost's *A Further Range* (1936), Cummings's *No Thanks* (1935), and Williams's *An Early Martyr* (1935). Finally, as the Left experienced dissention and disaffiliation in the late thirties and leftist influence declined, the political poetry of the four poets also diminished. This disengagement was not total, however, for as the conclusion will also describe, their political responsiveness in the thirties transformed itself into social and political concerns in the decades following the Depression.

CRITICAL CONTEXTS

The past twenty-five years have witnessed an upsurge of critical interest in 1930s poets and poetry formerly excluded from or barely represented in the literary canon formed after World War II. The pioneering work of

Cary Nelson and Alan M. Wald, supplemented and expanded by more recent studies by Walter Kalaidjian, Michael Thurston, Constance Coiner, Paula Rabinowitz, James D. Bloom, and several others, have "recovered" the work of such poets as Edwin Rolfe, H. H. Lewis, Ruth Lechlitner, Sol Funaroff, and Joseph Kalar and of prose writers like Meridel Le Sueur, Tillie Olsen, and Grace Lumpkin.[7]

Equally important, these studies have challenged our assumptions about how we read poetry, what we value in it, and how we assume poets operated. The explicitly political dimension of much 1930s poetry—its immediate aim to heighten the reader's political consciousness, inspire political action, and engage in dialogue with readers and other poets over contemporaneous issues, rather than to strive for an isolated, timeless, and perfect work of art—not only distinguishes this decade's most characteristic poetry but largely accounts for why it has been ignored by a critical tradition that denigrates the timely, the didactic, and the dialogic[8] as it elevates formal perfection, individual subjective expression, and transcendental themes (Thurston 37–39). As Cary Nelson has pointed out, this critical tradition, arising from the New Criticism of the 1940s and 1950s, is itself "contingent" and inappropriate for reading this ideological poetry ("Poetry Chorus" 40–41).

Inevitably, however, in the course of this much-needed expansion of the poetic landscape and challenging of our aesthetic assumptions, the older focus on canonical poets has come in for much criticism. Even distinguishing between "major" and "minor" poets (as I have done above) now raises eyebrows and charges of elitism. Nelson, for example, asserts that as a result of canonical studies, "we no longer know the history of the poetry of the first half of this century; most of us, moreover, do not know that the knowledge is gone" (*Repression and Recovery* 4). And Walter Kalaidjian dismissively describes the Pound-Stevens debate between Hugh Kenner and Marjorie Perloff: "The clash between two 'great' white patriarchs is symptomatic of how criticism exploits historical framing to prop up disciplinary authority, institutional force, and canonical power" (1).

But if "canonical" poets—Stevens, Frost, Cummings, and Williams in this instance—were also grounded in the historical moment, why should they be excluded from these cultural studies, especially since their political involvements were largely ignored by earlier formalist critics? In responding to what Williams called "the dialectic necessities of [the] day,"[9] these four poets demonstrate a dialogic interchange with their times quite different from what Nelson describes of far-left poets of the 1930s. These four did not remain aloof from their times, nor did they consider their poetry as always timeless and above the fray of contemporary politics. Although their audience was diverse, these four often wrote for the readers of Kalar, Rolfe, and Funaroff. They published poems and letters in leftist magazines (*New Masses, Partisan Review, Contempo, The New Republic, The Nation,* and many more). They engaged leftist audiences on college campuses and at writers' conferences. And Williams even joined leftist groups, organized leftist committees, helped edit leftist magazines, and went to major leftist conferences.

To be sure, their political participation differed significantly from that of the far-left poets. These four did not write from within the leftist movement; even Williams, the most politically involved, maintained skeptical distance and independent aesthetics. Hence they did not enjoy the inspiring (and comforting) "sense of a common mission" shared by leftist poets (Nelson, "Poetry Chorus" 39). Their outsider status is best captured in Stevens's poem "Mozart, 1935" (*CPP* 107). The poet plays alone at the piano while the crowd outside throws stones upon the roof; yet the poet realizes he cannot remain aloof and must respond to the present. Another difference that separates these poets from leftist poets of the 1930s is stylistic individuality. All four had formed their mature styles in the 1910s, and even when those styles changed in the 1930s (as Stevens's did in *Owl's Clover*), they remained idiomatic to each poet (and in Stevens's case even more opaque). Williams, for example, deeply distrusted what he considered the propagandistic in leftist poetry. His poems sympathetic to working-class individuals (rather than to the abstract class) are typically Williams-esque: imagistic, compressed, unrhymed, rhythmically irregular, in abbreviated, often syncopated line lengths. While the styles of the far-left poets were certainly not identical, they were sufficiently similar in political stance and in adhering to social realist demands for directness and transparency to form a kind of choral interchange, as Nelson has demonstrated ("Poetry Chorus" 46–51). Applied to Frost, Cummings, Williams, and Stevens, such a collective collage would serve only to demonstrate their stylistic individuation.

These differences, however, should not preclude our reconsidering these four poets in their political relationship to the times. Indeed, it might well be argued that the very success that scholars have achieved in "recovering" forgotten poets of the 1930s suggests that it is no longer necessary to rob Peter to pay Paul in our scholarly attention, that canonical poets, rather than being scorned for the supposed sins of earlier critics who focused on them exclusively, now deserve renewed attention, reconsideration within the same political and social contexts that have been applied to the "forgotten" poets. As noted above, scholarly work has already progressed in this direction on the poets individually. My book builds on this research, expanding and integrating it to accommodate the experiences of four poets, so as to reveal larger patterns of political challenge and engagement.

Finally, a word about the title of this book. When I began my research, I assumed that for three of the four poets (Williams excepted) relations with leftist critics, and with the Left generally, were oppositional and defensive. As so often happens, research and closer examination revealed a more complex, less binary picture, particularly with Stevens and Williams, who were both attracted and repulsed (sometimes simultaneously) by aspects of the Left and whose poetic responses to it were complicated. "Beleaguered," therefore, does not simply denote that these poets were under attack—although all experienced harsh critical attacks from leftist critics at various times in the thirties—but that they were under pressure: from these reviewers, to be sure, but also from the entire leftward movement of writers, artists, and intellectuals, which permitted few writers to remain in "happy oblivion." The epigraphs above were chosen to illustrate this point. Stevens is perhaps the perfect example of someone whose poetry seemed supremely indifferent to the everyday world in the 1910s and 1920s—"I was the world in which I walked"[10]—but whose ethical and artistic sensibilities during the Depression would not allow him to continue this indifference, and who increasingly felt that "the pressures of the contemporaneous" demanded some response. This book is a study of those responses.

1

"Leftward, Ho!"

Migrations of Writers, Critics, and Magazines in the 1930s

There is much excitement in this country today about the increasing radicalization of the American intellectual.
—V. F. Calverton, 1932

[Writers now show] increasing anxiety . . . [and] determination to be on one side or other of the fence, not sitting on it. . . . To join no party seems, now, a sign of weakmindedness.
—Frank Chapman, 1936

LITERARY CONVERTS IN THE EARLY THIRTIES

By all accounts, the 1930s were tumultuous years for writers—angry, hopeful, confused, hard-up, disillusioning years—but most of all social: writers formed groups, signed petitions, attended meetings, made speeches, marched in rallies, started little magazines, responded to surveys and symposia in literary magazines, criticized other writers' responses. And the direction of this socializing—so different from the sense of isolation typically imputed to the 1920s[1]—was political: "The atmosphere of American literature became more political than at any time in its history," write William Phillips and Philip Rahv, who, as editors of *Partisan Review* in the later 1930s, had much to do with that politicizing.[2] More specifically, writers went left, toward communism, a few joining the Party, many more becoming fellow travelers: sympathizers of the Soviet Union, joiners of the Party's many front groups in America, readers of and contributors to its official literary magazine, *New Masses,* and a host of evanescent leftist mags. The catalyst of this leftward migration in the early thirties was the Depression. To be sure, a small circle of writers—John Dos Passos, John Howard Law-

son, Mike Gold, Joseph Freeman, and a few others—continued the leftist literary agitation of *The Liberator* and *Masses* of the war years into the
1920s with the formation of *New Masses* in 1926 and in the New Playwrights Theatre the following year. The Sacco and Vanzetti executions
of 1927, moreover, were an international cause célèbre and a politicizing
event for writers like Edna Millay and Katherine Anne Porter. But not
until the Depression had really taken hold in late 1930 and 1931—when,
as Edmund Wilson wrote, there was "no sign of any political leadership
which will be able to pull us out . . . no sign of a [Teddy] Roosevelt or a
[Woodrow] Wilson to revive our political vision"—did writers like Wilson, who previously had been tepidly liberal or apolitical, conclude that
"what has broken down, in the course of one catastrophic year, is not
simply the machinery of representative government but the capitalist system itself"—just as Marx had predicted it would.[3]

Two Exemplars

Wilson's essay containing these passages, "An Appeal to Progressives," is a
seminal document in the psychological conversion of writers to radicalism,
and it deserves close scrutiny. Its venue, *The New Republic,* had long been
the bastion of progressivist liberalism under its late editor, Herbert Croly.
But with Croly's death in 1930 and the Depression's worsening, the remaining editors, including Wilson, were moving the magazine's position
far beyond liberalism.[4] In addressing the typical reader of *The New Republic,* "the contemporary progressive," Wilson's tone is restrained and rational, avoiding militancy and assuming an almost professorial formality
in his rhetorical questions: "May we not assume . . . ," "It may be true
that . . . ," "Doesn't this program today seem rather inadequate?"

His argument unfolds logically, but with increasing force. First, amidst
this present crisis, liberalism is no longer a viable political position: "It seems
to me impossible today for people of Herbert Croly's general aims and con-
victions to continue to believe in the salvation of our society by the gradual
and natural approximation to socialism which he himself called progressivism, but which has more generally come to be known as liberalism. . . .
[It] has not [brought on socialism or] been able to prevent a national economic disaster of proportions which neither capitalists nor liberals foresaw
and which they both now [are] . . . unable to explain" (521–22). Wilson
then presents his key surmise: that the Depression marks the breakdown
of capitalism and "one of the turning-points in our history" (524). "[I]t
may be true that with the present breakdown, we have come to the end

of something, and that we are ready to start on a different tack" (529–30). This new tack is a planned society on the model of Russia. As will be developed below, Russia in the early thirties—the Russia of the first Five-Year Plan—seemed to most Western intellectuals the rational antithesis of a reckless, materialistic, now shattered capitalism: "It may be that the whole money-making and -spending psychology has definitely played itself out, and that the Americans would be willing, for the first time now, to put their traditional idealism and their genius for organization behind a radical social experiment" (530).

Then Wilson proposes something unexpected: don't just adopt Marxism, Americanize it:

> I believe that if the American radicals and progressives who repudiate the Marxist dogma and the strategy of the Communist Party still hope to accomplish anything valuable, they must take Communism away from the Communists, and take it without ambiguities, asserting that their ultimate goal is the ownership by the government of the means of production. . . . If we want . . . to demonstrate that the virtue has not gone out of American democracy, if we want to confute the Marxist cynicism . . . predicated only on an assumption of the incurable swinishness and inertia of human nature—. . . an American opposition must not be afraid to dynamite the old conceptions and shibboleths and to substitute new ones as shocking as necessary. (532–33)[5]

The "Appeal" concludes on a hopeful note. Observing that in the Republican twenties, liberals felt increasingly discouraged by their failure to be heard, Wilson asks: "Who knows but, if we spoke out now with confidence and boldness, we might find our public at last?" (533).

Wilson's "Appeal" epitomizes the thinking of writers of his generation who went left in the early thirties.[6] It assumes that capitalism is crumbling, that liberalism cannot deal with the crisis any more than have the captains of industry or the government, that Russia presents a model of social planning that the United States can and should adopt, and finally, that liberal intellectuals can find something to counteract their own malaise, something hopeful, *if* they are not "afraid to dynamite the old conceptions . . . and to substitute new ones as shocking as necessary." Bold declarations, and coming from a highly respected scholar, critic, and author, Wilson's views were doubly impressive because this bookish intellectual seemed the least likely candidate for radical political involvement.

The essay's date, January 14, 1931, is also a bellwether. Observer-participants like Malcolm Cowley and Granville Hicks point to the summer of 1930, following the second stock market crash, as the time when it became clear that the Depression was not ephemeral and that "Hoover's optimistic pronouncements . . . were little more than incantations."[7] By mid-1930, however, "the revolutionary movement has not yet produced a strong and unified literary group" in Joseph Freeman's assessment.[8] Two years later, however, V. F. Calverton could confidently declare in his leftist magazine, *The Modern Quarterly,* that "literary radicalism had become 'a mainstream affair'" ("Leftward Ho!" 27). Thus 1931 seems to have been *the* conversion year for writers and intellectuals in the early thirties, and Wilson's essay stands at the threshold of this migration. In 1931, moreover, with unemployment doubling from six to twelve million and banks failing at an ever-increasing rate, there was nothing on the horizon—certainly nothing from the Hoover administration—to suggest that government could cope with the plummeting economy. Failure and paralysis were the norm, and Wilson's conclusion that it was time for liberals to jettison a failed system and work to replace it with a radically different one seemed reasonable.

If the rhetoric of Wilson's essay was logical and restrained, the editorial statement for the first issue of the radical magazine *The Left*—also published in early 1931—proudly asserts militancy and brash confidence:

LEFT!

There exists among intellectuals a steadily increasing awareness of the disintegration and bankruptcy of the capitalist system and its accompanying social order and culture. The intellectual tradition which held its political faith in democracy, progressivism, or the evolutionary approach, . . . and its artistic credo in the paradox of "art for art's sake" is crumbling—capitalist democracy is in world-wide chaos and bourgeois philosophy and literature are becoming emasculate anachronisms.

The more intellectually honest are becoming convinced that the capitalist system must be replaced by a collective state, dictated by the proletariat. . . . They are not avoiding the realities of the social struggle by following the alternative course of escapism and defeatism.

They accept the coming of the new order . . . and realize that the valid, significant art of today and tomorrow finds its impetus, substance and sincerity in the emergence of the proletariat through the revolutionary movement.

The LEFT [quarterly] . . . is born of this revolutionary move-

ment and will provide a new medium for its expression in the arts—
present the work of proletarian and revolutionary writers—and attempt to win over to the movement those artists who have hitherto
found their material and ideology in the bourgeois tradition. . . .

The LEFT calls the intellectual and artist from his blind bourgeois psychology, his pathological introspection, his defeatism and
futile liberalism. Only in the world revolutionary movement to over-
throw capitalism and build a co-operative, classless society is there
new ground for talent, new strength in affirmation, new ideology,
new courage.

Left![9]

The message is almost an echo of Wilson's (no coincidence, since it was
the typical rhetoric of radical recruitment): capitalism is finished; progressivism won't work; the twenties' attitude of "art for art's sake" is over; the
"intellectually honest" are coming over to communism and "the social
struggle," trading their defeatist bourgeois mentality for proletarian affirmation. The editorial's perspective, however, is altogether different from
that of Wilson's essay: This is a manifesto of the already-converted, calling across the divide to bourgeois intellectuals: "Join us!"

Both styles were common in the early thirties, but the direction was
the same: Left! The hopeful migration of writers and intellectuals, however, was not always greeted with open arms. As will be discussed below,
Communist Party functionaries distrusted them as unreliable and gave
them a chilly welcome. Others, like Lillian Symes, looking back in *The
Modern Monthly* a few years later, depicted their conversion with detached
amusement:

Into a political labor movement, which still lacked a substantial foot-
hold among the American masses, . . . moved a new army of enthusiastic, confused, politically uneducated but highly articulate individuals ready to serve—and to direct—the revolutionary movement
immediately with pen and voice and to take part in political controversies about which they frequently knew nothing. . . . [F]or every one of these [who had studied the labor movement for years]
there were dozens who passed directly through the experience of
emotional conversion into the orbit of Communist activity, surren-
dering their souls in an ecstasy of self-abasement to the high priests
of proletarian culture. Party membership was, in most instances, too
sacrificial a step to take and the bulk of the leftward-moving liberal

army camped in the intellectual outskirts of Party headquarters. Still
clinging to the protective coloration of the "liberal" label, many of
them functioned as genuine "innocents" or as conscious "stooges"
in those numerous Committees, Groups, Leagues against this or that
which constitute the Party periphery and which permit the leftward
liberal to dabble safely in the class struggle.[10]

Who were these writer-converts? Many came from Wilson's generation, which had come of age during World War I or slightly later, and many
spent at least part of the twenties as expatriates and aesthetes: Malcolm
Cowley, Waldo Frank, Edna St. Vincent Millay, Matthew Josephson, Slater
Brown, Gorham Munson, Alfred Kreymborg, Maxwell Bodenheim, Horace
Gregory, Kenneth Fearing, Lola Ridge, Granville Hicks, Genevieve Taggard, Witter Bynner, Isador Schneider, George Dillon, Eda Lou Walton,
and Wilson himself. A few had achieved prominence even earlier, for example Theodore Dreiser, Sherwood Anderson, and Lincoln Steffens. But
only a few had been strongly leftist before the Crash, such as John Dos
Passos, John Howard Lawson, and Mike Gold, all coeditors of *New Masses*
in the late 1920s, as well as Joseph Freeman, Edwin Seaver, and Newton
Arvin.

A younger generation, who had come of age in the Depression, did not
need to covert: they had learned their economic lessons firsthand in employment agencies, and radicalism was a natural response. As Alfred Kazin, one of their number, recalled,

The "new" writers looked as if they had been born to trouble—as in
fact they had been, for they were usually products of city streets, factories and farms. More than the age of the ideologue . . . the Thirties
in literature were the age of the plebes—of writers from the working
class . . . the non-literate class. . . . What was new about the writers
of the Thirties was not so much their angry militancy, which many
shared, as their background; writers now came from anywhere. . . .
[They] wore a proletarian scowl on their faces as familiar as the ciga-
rette butt pasted in their mouths. . . . [My friends] were all radicals
as a matter of course.[11]

Some of these younger writers achieved literary prominence beyond the
thirties: Richard Wright, Muriel Rukeyser, James T. Farrell, Erskine Caldwell, Kenneth Patchen, and Kazin himself. The stars of many others faded
when political literature faded—they became scholars, critics, and histo-

rians, and patiently waited for doctoral students and literary historians to rediscover them: Meridel Le Sueur, Robert Cantwell, Jack Conroy, Stanley Burnshaw, Edwin Rolfe, H. H. Lewis, Ruth Lechlitner, Sol Fun-aroff, Joseph Kalar, and Joy Davidman, to name a few. During the early thirties, however, it was primarily the older "converts" who seemed to occupy center stage; moreover, they provided the generational context for the reactions of Stevens, Frost, Cummings, and Williams. In approaching the converts' complex experience, several questions arise: What did they leave behind? What did they gain in becoming political? How did they view Russia? What were the historical way stations along the path of their conversion? What kind of new literature did they create?

Losses and Gains

The first two questions are obviously complementary. What the converts left behind includes both modernist aesthetics and the 1920s literary ethos, both of which received a thorough bashing not only from the younger 1930s writers, as one would expect, but also from the older converts themselves, who had once subscribed enthusiastically to "the revolution of the word" and to what Malcolm Cowley called "the religion of art."[12] Modernist aesthetics that gloried in abstraction and difficulty was now damned for the very elitism its practitioners once proclaimed and for appearing, in Horace Gregory's words, "'arty,' pretentious or distracted."[13]

Accompanying modernist elitism (as Cowley describes in *Exile's Return*) were writers' isolation from and cynicism toward mainstream American society and their consequent self-absorption, attitudes branded neurotic and decadent in the thirties. Edwin Seaver, for example, refers to "the counterfeit after-the-war cynicism. . . . Morally, spiritually, politically, socially, aesthetically—this generation was bankrupt by the end of the last decade. Sooner or later it would have to be liquidated and make a new start, for ahead lay only complete inanity and despair, only sterility."[14] Now, however, the prospect of allying themselves with the proletariat, or even just joining with other writers in leftist causes, gave writers a new sense of purpose. As Granville Hicks opined in describing the advantages of communism, "alliance with the proletariat is the only escape from the narrow individualism that leads so inevitably to futility and decay. . . . The sense of a cause, of something to affirm, is of tremendous value" ("Whither the American Writer" 19). Cowley agreed in a more comprehensive discussion of the advantages that joining the revolutionary movement could offer (listed here):

• An end to the desperate feeling of solitude and uniqueness that has been oppressing artists for two centuries.

• A sense of comradeship and participation in a historical process vastly bigger than the individual.

• An audience . . . larger and immeasurably more eager than the capitalist audience and quicker to grasp essentials.

• Once [the writer] knows and feels the struggles of the oppressed classes all over the world, he has a way to get hold both of distant events and those near at hand, and a solid framework on which to arrange them.

• Values exist again, after an age in which they seemed to be lost; good and evil are embodied in the men who struggle. ("Art Tomorrow" 61–62)

Cowley concludes: "Artists used to think that the world outside had become colorless and dull in comparison with [their] bright inner world. . . . [Now] it is the inner world that has been enfeebled as a result of its isolation; it is the outer world that is strong and colorful and demands to be imaginatively portrayed. The subjects are waiting everywhere. There are great days ahead for artists if they can survive in the struggle and keep their honesty of vision and learn to measure themselves by the stature of their times" (62). Other writers described the same camaraderie and sense of purpose in different ways. For Sherwood Anderson, "[t]he artist . . . needs to feel himself a part of the struggle" ("Whither the American Writer" 12). And Josephine Herbst recalled: "[T]he beauty of the thirties was its communion among people—its generosity—its willingness to be guilty of folly and its chance to get out of the constricted *I* in what seemed a meaningful way."[15]

Beyond the personal gains that converted writers might realize, there were broader ideals to work for: building a new, egalitarian society on the ruins of capitalism, a society based on the working class rather than the bourgeoisie or the wealthy. If the theorist of this ideal was Marx, the model was the Soviet Union; and in the early thirties, the overwhelming consensus was that the Soviet Union was rising economically in diametrical opposition to the plummeting Western economies. Arthur Koestler summarizes:

In the West, the anarchy of *laissez faire* was drowning the capitalist system in chaos and depression; in Russia, the First Five Year Plan was transforming, by a series of giant strokes, the most backward into the most advanced country in Europe. If History herself were a fellow-traveler, she could not have arranged a more clever timing of events than this coincidence of the gravest crisis in the Western world with the initial phase of Russia's industrial revolution. The contrast between the downward trend of capitalism and the simultaneous steep rise of planned Soviet economy was so striking and obvious that it had led to the equally obvious conclusion: They are the future—we, the past.[16]

Edmund Wilson made a similar point in his "Appeal": "The apparent success of the [Five-Year] plan has had its effect on all classes in all the rest of the world. . . . In the course of this winter of our capitalist quandary, the Soviets have been emerging from the back pages of the New York newspapers . . . and . . . even in the reactionary papers, one feels as much admiration as resentment" (531). He adds that "the great Communist project" had qualities Americans cherished: efficiency, economy, "the ideal of a Herculean program . . . to be put over by concerted action to the tune of impassioned boosting" (531). In Daniel Aaron's apt phrase, Russia appeared "a hive of happy industry—not only to its well-wishers, but also to a large number of unideological observers" (169).

Visiting Russia to see its accomplishments firsthand became almost a fad among American intellectuals moving left.[17] While a few who went—Cummings and, significantly, Dos Passos—did not like what they saw, the majority agreed, if in more measured phrases, with Lincoln Steffens's famous apothegm of 1921: "I have seen the future, and it works." Of course, in viewing Russia as "the Revolutionary Holy Land," as Lillian Symes quipped (8), American writers were partly seeing what they wanted to see—or were permitted to see—and naïveté was inevitable. Cowley, for example, made the astonishing prediction in 1933 that if three thousand bourgeois marchers had descended on the Kremlin (as the Bonus Army had marched on Washington in 1932), "[t]hey would be efficiently suppressed (not executed; the day of mass executions has passed in Russia). What would happen if 3000 proletarians marched on the Kremlin? They wouldn't do so, because the Soviets are their own government. But if they ever did march, the government would yield to them, or cease to be communist."[18] It would take several more years of Stalinist betrayals—the Moscow Trials, Soviet ruthlessness in Spain, and ultimately the Nazi-Soviet pact of 1939—before real disillusionment with Russia took hold in the American Left. Even in the mid-thirties, as Alfred Kazin recalled, "the fascination of the [Russian] Revolution was still great, the wild hope of a totally new society that it had inspired in the minds of people like [Max] Eastman was dying hard. For these [anti-Stalinist] thinkers . . . [there was still] more belief in the Revolution than not; its positive value was not yet in doubt" (70).

BECOMING ACTIVISTS: SIGNAL EVENTS IN THE EARLY THIRTIES

The process of political conversion transcended ideology—it was also a conversion from apathy to activism. And the early thirties did not lack for events and issues to galvanize intellectuals to political action. In 1930, rallies demanding jobs, supporting workers, and protesting anti-Soviet propaganda attracted thousands, while petitions against the recent arrest of workers obtained 135 signatures of prominent writers, including Edmund Wilson, Sherwood Anderson, and even H. L. Mencken (Klehr 74).[19] The arrest of the Scottsboro Boys in Alabama in 1931 became a major communist cause and produced the Emergency Committee for Southern Political Prisoners, chaired by Theodore Dreiser with Dos Passos acting as treasurer. That committee evolved into the National Committee for the Defense of Political Prisoners in May 1931, issuing statements signed by Dreiser, Dos Passos, Lincoln Steffens, Malcolm Cowley, and Burton Rascoe, among many others.

Several of these writers boldly moved from signing petitions to becoming eyewitness participants when Dreiser's committee investigated conditions in coal-mining camps, most notably the strike in Harlan County, Kentucky, in late 1931 and again in February 1932 under Waldo Frank. Dreiser, Frank, Dos Passos, Cowley, Edmund Wilson, Mary Heaton Vorse, and Samuel Ornitz were among those who participated in one or more of these investigations, and their experiences in Kentucky—interviewing miners, being arrested and prosecuted, and in one instance being beaten up at night by deputy sheriffs—were both radicalizing (for Cowley) and somewhat disillusioning (as both Dos Passos and Wilson felt the Communist Party was trying to use them and refused to become martyrs). As Cowley observed much later:

> The missions were widely reported and, though they did not win strikes in Kentucky or elsewhere, they helped to raise funds for the strikers (and for the party). . . . [W]riters [other than Dos Passos and Wilson] resigned themselves to being used since they thought it was for the common good. They committed themselves to a new life not merely by accepting opinions . . . but . . . by their own actions. . . . I

found myself committed to "the movement" by working and speaking for it. . . . [but also] by the hungry, ragged, but clear-eyed look of the miners' wives, by the talk of shooting men in cold blood, and by the machine guns pointing at me from the Pineville courthouse. This was another war, . . . and I knew which side I was on. (*Dream* 75–76)

So did hundreds of other writers. By the spring of 1932, several of them—Waldo Frank, Edmund Wilson, Lewis Mumford, Sherwood Anderson, Dos Passos—issued a manifesto urging a "temporary dictatorship of the class-conscious workers" (Klehr 79). But a far more defining moment was the public declaration of more than fifty prominent writers rejecting both major political parties and supporting the Communist Party's candidate for president in the 1932 election, William Z. Foster. "The League of Professional Groups for Foster and Ford" grew out of the National Committee for Defense of Political Prisoners. Its manifesto, a pamphlet titled "Culture and the Crisis: An Open Letter to Writers, Artists, Teachers, Physicians, Engineers, Scientists, and Other Professional Workers," appeared in the summer of 1932. Drafted by Matthew Josephson, James Rorty, and Malcolm Cowley, it decried conditions under Hoover, predicted no improvement under Roosevelt, called the Socialists a "do-nothing party," and lauded the Communists as the only active fighters for the dispossessed. In their conclusion, the signers declared their partnership as "brain workers" with the "muscle workers," the working class:

It is our business to think and we shall not permit business men to teach us our business. It is also, in the end, our business to act.
. . . As responsible intellectual workers, we have aligned ourselves with the frankly revolutionary Communist Party, the party of the workers. In this letter, we speak to you of our own class—to the writers, artists, scientists, teachers, engineers, to all honest professional workers—telling you as best we can . . . why we think that you too should support the Communist Party in the political campaign now under way.[20]

The signers stated that their endorsement of the Party was "an act of protest" against the limited alternatives offered by the Democrats and Republicans and, as Josephson later noted, was intended "to call attention to the severity of the crisis."[21] Though given scant attention in national newspapers, the manifesto was taken seriously by liberals and leftists as a trenchant discussion of national issues and an attempt to expand that discussion beyond leftist circles. Daniel Aaron called this proposed alliance of workers and professionals "unprecedented in American history" (214). But looked at differently, "Culture and the Crisis" reflects a fundamental fissure of the Left between the strongest supporters of the Communist Party at this point, bourgeois intellectuals, and those whom the communists tirelessly championed as the revolutionary vanguard, the working class. The only problem was that class wasn't producing many revolutionaries in 1932; and the intelligentsia reflected more than a little uneasiness about its own middle-class roots in reaching out to the workers. Note, for example, the unwitting condescension of the manifesto referring to them as "muscle workers" as opposed to the professional "brain workers." More important, how could middle-class writers create the proletarian literature that the leftist magazines kept calling for? A more immediate problem emerged for the signers after the presidential election in determining the future direction of the League of Professional Groups (whose title had now dropped "for Foster and Ford"). Would it be open to all groups on the left and function independently, or would it act as an auxiliary of the Communist Party and, following the Party's "Third Period" factionalism, exclude all non-communist groups? The tensions arising from these questions led to the resignation of the League's leader, James Rorty, and eventually to the dissolution of the League itself. In Harvey Klehr's view, the League became "a victim of the Party's need to control with an iron fist any organization associated with it." Klehr concludes that the Communists bungled a huge opportunity: "Not until 1935 was the Party able to organize another large, broadly based cultural auxiliary, the League of American Writers—and even then only a handful of the 1932 group of intellectuals—notably, Cowley, Hicks, and Josephson—could be persuaded to go along" (84).

The Party's maladroit handling of the League was symptomatic of its distrust and mixed messages regarding its new allies, middle-class writers and intellectuals. At the same time that the Kharkov conference of 1932 called for the CPUSA, Communist Party of the USA, "to enlist all friendly intellectuals into the ranks of the revolution" (qtd. in Aaron 238), and Mike Gold, editor of *New Masses,* was boasting there that "the best known writers in America, the cream of the American intellectual world, is [*sic*] oriented today toward the Revolution and toward the Soviet Union,"[22] the Party was deeply suspicious of intellectuals—independent thinkers were unreliable and uncontrollable, after all. Moreover, the Party's Third Period doctrine attacked all other parties and individuals on the left as "social fascists": writers would have to toe the Party line or be branded enemies. Even in personal dealings with would-be members, Party functionaries were notoriously unfriendly and made joining difficult. Thus, despite his buoyant description of the Party attracting prominent writers, Gold had to accept the stinging criticism of the International Union of Revolutionary Writers that the *New Masses* was too soft on social fascists (Aaron 246). Attacks on intellectuals soon followed. *The Daily Worker* called Edmund Wilson a fascist, and radical mavericks like V. F. Calverton and Max Eastman were constantly vilified. As a result of these contradictory policies, relatively few writers actually joined the CPUSA, preferring to remain fellow travelers; many of those who did join soon dropped out; and the Party's membership actually *declined* after the 1932 election from 18,119 to 14,937 by June 1933 (Klehr 91–92). The conclusions of historians are scathing: "Imprisoned by its own dogma, [the Party] had squandered a historic opportunity to enlist allies" (Klehr 84); "Before a Left literary movement could begin to sprout, it was smothered in politics. Had a free and autonomous Communist movement developed in the United States or had *New Masses* and the John Reed Clubs remained politically unattached, the middle-class malcontents would undoubtedly have entered the Left movement in larger numbers and stayed longer" (Aaron 247). But as Aaron also acknowledges, the Party's bungling did not keep writers from going left or becoming fellow travelers, even if they did so "because of the social and political crisis, rather than because of party persuasion" (247).

RADICAL AESTHETICS: PROLETARIAN LITERATURE AND DOCUMENTARY REPORTAGE

Once converted to the Left, what could writers do for it besides writing radical manifestos and pamphlets? Complicating this question was the class issue mentioned above: the writer-converts in the early thirties came predominantly from the middle classes. Yet, all the discussion in leftist literary journals in these years was about a proletarian literature, written about, for, and preferably by the working class. Could bourgeois writers create proletarian literature?[23] What should such literature consist of? How oriented toward the Left should it be: Blatant propaganda for Marxism? "Realism" that depicts proletarian life without preaching? Something in between? Another issue was writers' attitudes toward modernist experimentation of the teens and twenties. Many, perhaps most of the older writer-converts had written within this loose rubric (it was not a style); but, as noted above, the current leftist view was that modernism was bourgeois, esoteric (hence, inaccessible to the workers), isolated (typically concerned about the author's personal issues), and pessimistic or defeatist. It must be replaced by an altogether new, revolutionary literature. Were former modernists, then, simply to repudiate their previous practice?

The question of proletarian literature dates back to the Russian Revolution, but soon it appeared in the United States in an article that the future Mike Gold (née Irwin Granich) published in *The Liberator* in 1921, "Towards Proletarian Art."[24] Gold called for "the creation of a distinctly and militantly working-class culture," but he was short on specifics. When he helped create *New Masses* in 1926, he solicited and published correspondence from workers and invited "diaries . . . letters from hoboes . . . poetry from steelworkers," and so forth (Homberger 123, 126). "Tell your story," Gold encouraged worker-writers. "It is sure to be significant. Tell it simply and sincerely, in the form of a letter. Don't worry about style, grammar or syntax. Write as you talk. Let America know the heart and mind of the workers."[25] Indeed, by 1928, *New Masses* described itself as "A Magazine of Workers' Life and Literature" (Foley 88). But fully developed fiction, especially as novels, was slow to emerge from working-class writers, as Gold complained at a conference of John Reed Clubs in 1932 (Foley 89). And limiting such literature to working-class writers obviously excluded the talents of bourgeois writers who were now flooding into the Left. The solution was obvious: at that same conference, the draft manifesto declared: "Allies from the disillusioned middle-class intellectuals are to be welcomed," although primary focus should still be on the working class (qtd. in Foley 90). This grudging "welcome," typically conditioned by provisos that bourgeois writers reject their class perspective and completely identify with the proletariat (Foley 93; Homberger 134), vastly expanded into an open-arms greeting once the CPUSA had adopted its Popular Front stance in 1935.

So middle-class writers could participate; but what should their—or anyone's—"proletarian" fiction consist of? In September 1930, Gold attempted to define some characteristics of what he called "Proletarian-Realism."[26] Some of the points were vague and question-begging, for example, "Away with all lies about human nature. We are scientists; we know what a man thinks and feels." The others, pared down, amount to this:

• Proletarian literature "must have a social theme" and deal "with the *real conflicts* of men and women" (i.e., social class conflicts, Gold's emphasis).
• In contrast to modernist ambiguity and complexity, it must have "swift action, clear form, the direct [thematic?] line."

• It must avoid the "verbal acrobatics" of modernism (exit Joyce, Eliot, Cummings, Faulkner, et al.).

A few months earlier, Gold had elaborated his contempt for "style": "Style and content cannot be separated into watertight compartments. Technique has made cowards of us all. There is no 'style'—there is only clarity, force, truth in writing. If a man has something new to say, as all proletarian writers have, he will learn to say it clearly in time."[27]

Gold could find little guidance from Russia on what proletarian literature should be. As Eric Homberger notes, the newly formed International Union of Revolutionary Writers (IURW) paid "surprisingly little attention . . . to the meaning of the term" at its second congress in Kharkov in November 1930 (132–33). What the IURW did offer was a list of requirements that established strict Party control of "proletarian" writers, for example: "(1) Artists are to abandon individualism and the fear of strict 'discipline.' . . . (2) Artistic creation is to be systematized, organized, 'collectivized,' and carried out according to the plans of a central staff like any other soldierly work. (3) This is to be done under the 'careful yet firm guidance' of the Communist Party. (4) Writers and artists of the rest of the world are to learn how to make proletarian art by studying the experience of the Soviet Union."[28] Such restrictive discipline would obviously grate against the creative independence bourgeois writers were used to enjoying.

Gradually, however, as numerous articles and symposia in America took up the issue in the early thirties, other criteria emerged. V. F. Calverton's article "Can We Have a Proletarian Literature?" states:

• Its political ideal is democratic (. . . once the stage of the proletariat dictatorship has passed. . . .)
• Its attitude towards religion and mysticism is hostile.
• It should expose . . . the inadequacies and mendacities of bourgeois culture.[29]

And Granville Hicks added more requirements in discussing what a Marxist critic looks for in literature:

• [It] would lead the proletarian reader to recognize his role in the class struggle. . . . [T]he theme must deal with . . . the central issues of life. Obviously, the novel must, directly or indirectly show the effects of the class struggle, since, according to Marxism, . . . no novel that disregarded it could give an adequate portrayal of life.

• It must have intensity. The author must be able to make the reader feel that he is participating in the lives described. . . .
• [The author's] identification with the proletariat should be as complete as possible. He should not merely believe in the cause of the proletariat; he should be, or should try to make himself, a member of the proletariat.[30]

Synthesized, these prescriptions tell the would-be proletarian writer to

1. View human conflict from a social perspective (as opposed to personal, psychological, or universal) and see society in terms of economic classes.
2. Portray these classes in conflict (as Marx described them): workers versus bosses, sharecroppers versus landowners, tenants versus landlords, have-nots versus haves.
3. Develop a "working-class consciousness," that is, identify with the oppressed class in these conflicts, rather than maintaining objective detachment.
4. Present a hopeful outcome to encourage working-class readers. Other outcomes are defeatist, pessimistic, or "confused."
5. Write simply and straightforwardly, without the aesthetic complexities of formalism.
6. Above all, politicize the reader. Revolutionary literature is a weapon in the class struggle and should consciously incite its readers if not to direct action then to a new attitude toward life, "to recognize his role in the class struggle."

This synthesis, however, never emerged in any one place as an agreed-upon program. Even the role of Marxism, as Barbara Foley notes, remained unspecified; hence, "critics' grounds for judgment appear to have shifted from text to text" (117, 95).

The fourth item of this synthesis proved the greatest stumbling block for serious writers. If one presented a class conflict realistically, as Gold insisted upon, the "haves" by definition held power—hired the strikebreakers, controlled the police, the courts, and the politicians—and should logically prevail. How, then, to overcome their power without violating realistic plausibility? When Meridel Le Sueur published her powerful documentary piece "Women on the Breadlines" in *New Masses* (January 1932), the editors added a disclaimer that her depiction "is defeatist in attitude, lacking in the revolutionary spirit and direction which characterizes the usual contribution to *New Masses*" (qtd. in Foley 114). On this same point, John Dos Passos, for one, refused to compromise. Once considered (in Gold's words) "the hope of our left-wing literature in America," after the final volume of his great *U.S.A.* trilogy, Dos Passos now seemed misanthropic to Gold in his bleak characterizations and relentlessly pessimistic outcomes: "Dos Passos hates Communists because organically he seems to hate the human race. It is strange to see how little real humanness there is in his book."[31] Other proletarian novelists and playwrights resolved the problem of the ending by keeping it open and making the protagonists' newly radical understanding of their situation their main achievement. The cabbies realize they can act without Lefty to lead them and finally vote to strike in *Waiting for Lefty;* the protagonists in *The Disinherited* finally realize the hopelessness of going it alone and light out together as leftist agitators. And Tom Joad carries on Jim Casey's battle into an indefinite future in *The Grapes of Wrath.*

The early thirties witnessed many proletarian novels, but only a few, like Conroy's *The Disinherited* or Cantwell's *Land of Plenty,* gained an enduring critical esteem. Well before the decade was over, critics like William Phillips and Philip Rahv were declaring: "It is time to realize that the revolutionary trend of the thirties did not profoundly transform the literary consciousness of America" (175). The problem, they felt, was that "Marxism . . . one of the highest manifestations of Western consciousness, can be readily turned into a scholastic formula when applied to a low level of awareness. Its fecundity in art does not lie in a point by point utilitarianism" (179). "The basic failure" of the revolutionary trend, they continue, was "the tendency to reduce men to parts of themselves. . . . [The new political works] merely substituted social behaviorism for individual behaviorism" (175). While this critique goes beyond proletarian literature, that genre was increasingly criticized for its mechanistic and formulaic handling and began fading in popularity by the mid-thirties.[32]

Writers who felt they could not create proletarian literature had a less radical alternative: to bear witness to the times and document the conditions of individuals in all parts of the country. This reporting gradually evolved into its own genre, documentary reportage. One impetus for it was the widespread belief that the newspapers were intentionally underreporting the worst aspects of the Depression to avoid discouraging their readers still more. Edmund Wilson helped establish this genre when he traveled cross-country in late 1930 and 1931, sending back reports to *The New Republic* on his findings in such places as Detroit; Ward, West Virginia; Bellamy, New Mexico; and San Diego. The articles became a book, *The*

American Jitters: A Year of the Slump, one of the most interesting documents of the times. Wilson did not try to conceal his growing radicalism, but rather sought to move readers toward it by emphasizing the exploitation of workers at the hands of big business. In "Detroit Motors," for example, he quotes extensively from factory line workers who describe how Ford more than compensated for its innovatively high wages by speeding up the line, cutting break time, and cutting hours, as well as instituting an extensive spy network that even looked into the workers' home lives. As William Stott points out, this narrative slanting was typical of documentary works in trying to arouse public indignation and action to remediate the conditions reported on.[33]

Several other writers produced books or articles documenting the United States in the thirties, including Theodore Dreiser's *Tragic America* (1931), Moritz Hallgren's "Unemployment in the United States" (*The Nation* 1932), Sherwood Anderson's *Puzzled America* (1935), James Rorty's *Where Life Is Better: An Unsentimental American Journey* (1936), Nathan Asch's *The Road: In Search of America* (1937), Louis Adamic's *My America* (1938), Erskine Caldwell's *Say, Is This the USA?* (1941), and John Steinbeck's articles on migrant labor in California for the *San Francisco News* in the mid-thirties, which became the basis for part of *The Grapes of Wrath.* The most celebrated work in this genre was also the most idiosyncratic: *Let Us Now Praise Famous Men* (1941), combining an emotive, highly subjective and poetic text by James Agee and seemingly objective and emotionally detached photographs by Walker Evans.[34] On assignment from *Fortune* magazine (Agee) and from the Farm Security Administration (FSA) photographic unit (Evans), they spent several weeks in 1936 living with three families of white sharecroppers in Alabama. Regrettably, the book, growing far beyond its original intent, was not published until 1941, well after public interest in the fate of migrant workers had faded.

The collaboration of writer and photographer to approach documentation from two perspectives was noteworthy in other books as well. *An American Exodus* (1936) featured unforgettable photographs of dust bowl émigrés in California by Dorothea Lange and a statistics-laden text by Paul Taylor, a professor of economics. Erskine Caldwell and Margaret Bourke-White collaborated on *You Have Seen Their Faces* (1937), which presented glimpses of the lives of southern sharecroppers with caption-comments by the authors. And both Archibald MacLeish and Richard Wright drew on photographs from the FSA to accompany their own texts, poetic in MacLeish's *Land of the Free* (1938), and documentary (a Marxist-tinged history of blacks in the United States) in Wright's *12 Million Black Voices* (with photos selected by Edwin Rosskam, 1941). Arguably, the FSA photographs themselves, apart from any accompanying text and numbering in the thousands, provided the most remarkable and complete documentation of everyday life in the thirties.

LEFTIST MAGAZINES AND MAGAZINE WARS

Paralleling and resulting from the political transformation of writers in the early thirties, little magazines, that most essential showcase for the work of new writers and established ones as well, markedly changed in the early thirties. By 1934 nearly all the modernist giants were gone: *The Dial, The Little Review, the transatlantic review, This Quarter, The Exile,* and in 1934 *Hound & Horn.* Replacing them were magazines with an obviously leftist political agenda and colorful names like *Cauldron, Blast, Dynamo, Unrest, Anvil, Hammer, Red Pen, The Left, Left Front, Leftward, Left Review, The Partisan, Contempo, New Leader,* and *Trend,* as well as the two radical mainstays, *New Masses* and (in the second half of the thirties) *Partisan Review.* Some, like *Blast* (which William Carlos Williams helped edit) and Jack Conroy's *The Anvil,* limited themselves to proletarian literature; others welcomed radical literature from all types of writers. And as with earlier little magazines, some of the leftist mags limited themselves to a single genre: *Blast* published only short stories; *Dynamo* was "A Journal of Revolutionary Poetry."

Their particular political slant, of course, was crucial. *New Masses,* the oldest and clearly the most important of these magazines, was the official literary journal of the CPUSA and could be counted on to express the Party line in all matters of aesthetics and politics. When it was founded in 1926, however, it was more receptive to writers of all political persuasions (including D. H. Lawrence, Robinson Jeffers, and Alan Tate) and, like its predecessor, Max Eastman's *Masses,* tried not be doctrinaire (Homberger 125). But as the magazine became increasingly committed to proletarian writing (chiefly defined by class conflict) in the late 1920s and following a stinging rebuke by the IURW in 1931, it came to reflect more rigidly the Comintern's "Third Period" factionalism.

At the other fork of the leftist divide, *The Modern Quarterly* (which became *The Modern Monthly* in 1933) welcomed writing from a wide range of unaffiliated and anti-Party radicals. It was edited by V. F. Calverton, a radical gadfly who had been expelled by the Party and was now its constant target along with other mavericks. As Alfred Kazin (one of this group) observed, "*New Masses* could not mention Calverton, Norman Thomas,

Max Eastman, [and] Sidney Hook . . . without accusing them of literary plagiarism, sabotage against the Soviet state . . . and all other crimes necessary and logical to miscreants opposed to Stalin" (66). Later in the thirties, *Partisan Review* would assume this role of Antichrist, conducting a bitter rivalry with *New Masses.*

Several leftist magazines were published by the various John Reed Clubs the Party had created: *Partisan Review* began this way in 1934 in New York (though it soon assumed a more independent stance). Other John Reed Club magazines were *Left Front: Revolutionary Art of the Midwest* (Chicago), which published Richard Wright's early poems and stories; *The Partisan* (Hollywood); and *Red Pen* (Philadelphia). A few good ones came out of England: *Left Review,* which non-leftist Morton Zabel praised as having higher "literary quality . . . than most of its rivals in the U.S.," and *New Verse,* which Wallace Stevens considered "the best poetry magazine"—at least until it was taken over by the "propagandist" Geoffrey Grigson and his "social revolution" group.[35]

These magazines had a small, devoted readership and, like little magazines in all periods, a short life expectancy. Not so the two major liberal-leftist journals in America: *The New Republic* and *The Nation.* These long-lived liberal stalwarts had, as Lillian Symes observes, "an influence out of all proportion to their circulations" because "to most [subscribers] . . . the two liberal weeklies—in contrast to the 'capitalist press' and the frankly propagandistic revolutionary press, represented factual integrity and intellectual independence" (7). For Alfred Kazin, they meant even more: *The New Republic* "was not merely a publication but a cause and the center of many causes" (10). Before 1930, their liberalism was progressivist but certainly not radical; Symes wryly describes their support of Russia but not of American communism: "[T]hey took their revolution vicariously . . . [and] displayed the typical liberal intellectual's romantic palpitations over violence at a safe distance" (7). As noted above, when the longtime editor of *The New Republic,* Herbert Croly, died in 1930, the new editors (particularly Edmund Wilson) shifted the magazine's political stance much further to the left. The same shift, though less dramatic, applied to *The Nation.* Symes summarizes with just a trace of leftist bias:

> The leftward swing of the intellectuals . . . and the sudden scramble among them for the currently fashionable water-mark of proletarian art, were reflected immediately in the *Nation* and the *New Republic,* for among them were most of the contributors and some of the editors of the two weeklies. . . . But neither journal could afford to sacri-

fice, by the frank espousal of a revolutionary position, the right-wing liberal support, the academic prestige it had built. . . . [B]oth straddled the dilemma by clinging to the political irresponsibility of its liberal past while actively participating through articles, editorials and books reviews, in radical politics. On this ground they were forced to complete with *New Masses* for left-wing patronage. (8)

When Malcolm Cowley became literary editor of *The New Republic,* he took the magazine even further left, promoting proletarian literature and expressing in his editorials and reviews "a polite echo of the Party line," despite "a pretense of non-partisanship within the radical movement" (Symes 9). At its most extreme, this Party line questioned the critics of the Moscow Trials and led those critics to brand Cowley a Stalinist. Daniel Aaron writes that "until 1939, when he left the movement, Cowley quite consciously but somewhat uneasily allowed himself to be used as a front man by the party. He spoke for it, defended it, encouraged its writers, yet he never gave himself completely to it" (348). Kazin is less forgiving: "[H]e could not separate himself from the Stalinists with whom he identified the future. To Cowley everything came down to the trend, to the forces that seemed to be in the know and in control of the time-spirit" (19). But as Alan Filreis observes, Cowley also carried over from the twenties his "love of good writing" and published several distinctly non-leftist poems by Wallace Stevens and William Carlos Williams in the mid-thirties (15, 182).[36]

By contrast, *The Nation* was less extreme and less definite in its migration left. From a leftist perspective, it "has attempted to maintain a more neutral position in the radical movement by blowing first this way and then that (sometimes in the same issue). . . . [Its editorial board] has been more intellectually mature and intelligent than that of the *New Republic,* but it has been also far more divided. . . . And the color of its editorial comment has depended not so much upon a definite policy as upon which of these individuals happened to write it" (Symes 9). But like *The New Republic,* "[e]ven as [its] feature essays, and book reviews, and editorials demonstrated unbroken commitment to radical causes, the verse published in 1935 and 1936 did not particularly support or disavow its editorial policy" (Filreis 32).

One other source of leftist reviews should be noted: the books section of the *New York Herald Tribune.* Editors of other magazines characterized the *Herald Trib*'s reviewing policy rather snidely. Morton Zabel, an editor of *Poetry,* referred to "their usual practice of describing new publications, un-

troubled by scruple or objective" (172). And Margaret Marshall and Mary
McCarthy, in a satire of the proletarian critic, wrote: "The obligations of
the *Herald Tribune* reviewer are simple: . . . to write, in fair English, more
or less favorable reviews of the book presented to him."[37] But the *Herald
Tribune* published a sizable number of Marxist and leftist reviewers, including Willard Mass, Ruth Lechlitner, Genevieve Taggard, Horace Gregory,
and Babette Deutsch. One might wonder why a major New York newspaper, liberal but certainly not radical, would print reviews by these leftists. Filreis offers a simple explanation regarding Ruth Lechlitner's reviews:
"[S]he hid the extent of her radicalism from . . . her *Herald Tribune* editors," and "they cut and rewrote [her] reviews in such a way as to suggest
a political toning down" (283).

Though the modernist journals had faded, the most important poetry
magazine from the teens, *Poetry,* persevered through the thirties under
its founder, Harriet Monroe, until her death in 1936, then briefly under
Morton Zabel, followed by George Dillon. Monroe steered *Poetry* clear of
the growing radicalism around her, and for that, of course, she was attacked
continuously, sometimes viciously, by the Left. Through much of the thirties, a continuous sniping between the two sides existed. Orrick Johns, for
example, fired off this letter to Monroe in the summer of 1932:

> I think the poetry published in *Poetry* including my own lately is
> tripe. I think *Poetry* ought to end its career. Why? Because it cannot
> see the turn. The turn has come. In what direction is the turn? In
> the direction of positive social necessity. . . . My poetry, all my life,
> has at least been incitation to action. The men of fame of my time
> have always been Professors of Triviality, masters of false gods, seek-
> ers of cold, passionless finesse, Yeats, Eliot, whoever. They are dead. And
> well dead. And dead with Pound on top of them. . . . I will outlive
> you all. Why? . . . Because I am still young and can sing the work-
> ing class!!![38]

Monroe held her fire publicly until her 1934 editorial "Art and Propaganda."[39] In it she distinguishes between the message that "insinuates itself unconsciously into [the poet's] art" and "comes from the artist's spirit"
and one that is "driven or hammered" into his or her art from an "effort
of individual will or . . . collusion with mass sympathy or class prejudice."
The latter is debilitating propaganda: "[T]he deliberate propagandist rarely
achieves art, and the artist, though possessed by a cause, can rarely become
a successful propagandist" (211). This distinction leads to her key point:

"[W]e cannot believe it is our duty to accept and spread before our readers such half-baked efforts at class-conscious poetry as *The New Masses,
The Anvil, Partisan Review, Dynamo, Blast,* and other enthusiastic organs of
the Left groups . . . may perhaps legitimately use" (212). She then devotes
several paragraphs to a lecture by Stanley Burnshaw, poetry editor of *New
Masses,* reported secondhand by one of her readers: "Mr. Burnshaw would
strike out of the modern picture not only *Poetry* but all the poets, living or
dead, on our records who are not 'aware of this changing world'—that is,
who are not idealizing the Russian system and anathematizing our own"
(213). Monroe concludes by quoting Yeats—"It is not the business of a poet
to instruct his age—he should be too humble [for that]. . . . His business is
merely to express himself, whatever that self may be." Provocatively, she
draws a line between the leftists ("*New Masses,* Mr. Burnshaw, Mr. Cowley, *et al.*") and "*Poetry,* Mr. Yeats, Mr. MacLeish, and Mr. Tate" (215).

Burnshaw lost no time in responding to Monroe's editorial in both published and private letters to her. The published one, aptly titled "The Poetry Camps Divide," appeared in *New Masses* and reiterates the leftist argument for socially engaged literature:

> [I]sn't it rather clear to you that honest writers aware of the intensi-
> fication of the class struggle during the past five years have found it
> increasingly difficult to write about themes removed from the break-
> down of society and its amelioration by proletarian revolution and
> socialism? . . .
>   . . . [S]how me the poet worthy of the name who can be excited
> into writing about ["fields and streams, gallant gentlemen and la-
> dies, spots on a butterfly's wing"] . . . when the entire social system
> in which he believed is bursting apart in chaos. Revolutionary po-
> ets are no less fond of . . . [these things] than are reactionary poets—
> but these things cannot interest them when hundreds are dying daily
> of starvation at the same time that food is destroyed by legislative
> ordinance; when a government curtails education and appropriates
> the largest sums in the history of mankind for war materials; when
> workers are shot. . . . In such times as these a poet's themes are the
> record of his sense of values.[40]

Burnshaw acknowledges that "[a] poet allied with the proletariat may
write about any theme that interests him. . . . [But h]e will see the implications of the class struggle in numberless events and objects ignored

by bourgeois poets. . . . Not every one of his poems, obviously, will explicitly call for revolution, but the totality of his work will be a weapon fighting on the side of the revolutionary proletariat" (22). Finally, Burnshaw agrees that Monroe has drawn the line between the two sides "with admirable clarity."[41]

Despite the seeming intransigence of both sides, there was more discourse between *Poetry* and the Left than at first appeared. To cite just one example, a major review of Williams's *An Early Martyr*, by the Marxist critic T. C. Wilson, appeared in *Poetry* (May 1936). And when George Dillon took over the editorship in the later thirties, *Poetry* began to publish more left-wing poets, like H. H. Lewis, and reviewers, like Ruth Lechlitner, as well as featuring a special "Social Poets" number in 1936 and a "Federal Poets" issue in 1938.

CRITICS, REVIEWERS, AND RADICAL AESTHETICS

Since the same leftist reviewers of poetry regularly reappear in the chapters that follow, it would be useful to note who they are and to consider the evaluative criteria that Marxist critics applied to literary works. Virtually all the reviewers were poets themselves, and, like the literary magazines they wrote for, they can be very roughly divided into three overlapping groups: (1) radical to Marxist (including Nathan Asch, Newton Arvin, Stanley Burnshaw, Mike Gold, Geoffrey Grigson, Granville Hicks, Philip Horton, Rolphe Humphries, Ruth Lechlitner, Fred Miller, Philip Rahv, Edwin Rolfe, Muriel Rukeyser, Isador Schneider, Edwin Seaver, Dorothy Van Ghent, and T. C. Wilson); (2) liberal to leftist (Malcolm Cowley, Babette Deutsch, Henry Seidel Canby, F. W. Dupee, Alfred Kazin, Raymond Larsson, Sherry Mangan, Gorham Munson, Louis Untermeyer, and Eda Lou Walton), with Kenneth Burke, Horace Gregory, and Genevieve Taggard bridging these two groups; and (3) apolitical or anti-Communist (William Rose Benét, R. P. Blackmur, Harriet Monroe, Paul Rosenfeld, Alan Tate, Yvor Winters, and Morton Zabel).[42] Of these, I wish to focus on three critics: Eda Lou Walton (briefly), because her reviews of the four poets appear so often in this study; Stanley Burnshaw, because of his prominence in establishing Marxist critical theory and his importance to Stevens's poetry; and Horace Gregory, both because his reviews were especially perceptive and because they show how he evolved from liberal-leftist to radical.

First, however, some words about Marxist aesthetics and style. Granville Hicks seemed to sum up the Marxist critical perspective when he listed the qualities of fiction that a Marxist critic should look for (listed above). In addition, Hicks qualified the Marxian dictum that, as a weapon in the class struggle, literature should lead to direct action: "[E]xperience actually convinces us that books seldom have such an effect. . . . [Rather, a] great work of art will change the reader's attitude towards life" ("The Crisis in American Criticism" 4–5). Two other documents about the period, however, depict the Marxist critic from quite different perspectives: Stanley Burnshaw's retrospective reflections in his 1961 article "Wallace Stevens and the Statue," and a satirical sketch of the proletarian critic by Margaret Marshall and Mary McCarthy in 1935.

Burnshaw's memoir, prefacing a reprint of his important review of Stevens's *Ideas of Order*,[43] might well have been titled "Confessions of a Marxist Critic." Somewhat ruefully, he explains the attitudes and pressures underlying the cocksure, often arrogant tone of Marxist criticism: "[T]entativeness and humility were unthinkable; the world was separating into two enemy camps and time was running out! One had to act in behalf of mankind, and for anyone with a brain there could be no choice. Like the rest of the intellectual Left, [*New Masses* writers] moved in the serenity of certainty" (358). He continues: "[I] had also been advised that formal analysis could lead to futile complexities, and that a too-temperate stance was simply a foolish timidity" (360). Political doubts or reservations the Marxist critic was to keep to himself: "[A]ny number of these writers were troubled or torn, each for his private reasons; but the tendency was to keep one's reservations under control, for what mattered was the task at hand—ending the material miseries of the many, extinguishing the dangers of Fascism" (361). Burnshaw then presents a concluding list of attitudes (excerpted here), glossing such politically loaded words as "confused" and "middle ground" used in his Stevens review,

1. The world . . . is divided according to one groundplan only: We (Left), They (Right) and You (Left, Right or Middle), with Escapists in limbo. . . .
2. Caveat with respect to irony, Marxist reviewers were often stupendously literal, earnest, humorless. . . .
3. [T]hese critics held the naïve belief that a book could or would affect directly and even shape the minds of readers; hence, in a war between classes, each "nonconfused" book was an instrument for either the Left (*read* Good) or the Right (*read* Bad). . . . Authors of "Middle-ground" books were, of course, confused and in need of direction,

which was often generously offered by the reviewer. It requires no ex-
pertness in Freud to perceive that the present reviewer's concern with
Stevens' confusion was at least in part a projection of his own.
4. At times one might make broad statements which one would not
normally make, simply because they were supposedly required by the
Ultimate Good. . . . The over-riding concern—the greatest good for
the greatest number—was also a principle whose morality was beyond
question, regardless of what might be required in its name. (362–63)[44]

Marshall and McCarthy published their article on the proletarian critic
in *The Nation* in 1935. Its irreverent satire, aimed directly at the *New Masses,*
anticipates McCarthy's move in the later thirties to *Partisan Review,* where
she contributed regularly to that magazine's vigorously anti-Stalinist leftism. The article feigns sympathy in describing the Marxist critic's obligations and dilemmas (listed and excerpted here):

1. He must . . . applaud any proletarian novel, no matter how inept, on
political grounds. . . .
2. As a corollary . . . , the Marxist critic must, willy-nilly berate the
bourgeois. . . .
3. [T]he *New Masses* critic . . . must also hew to the party line, accom-
modating himself swiftly and dexterously to its every shift. . . . Thus,
in 1934 *Man's Fate,* a real revolutionary novel, is slighted because it
accepted Trotsky's view of the Chinese Revolution. (653–54)

The authors then gleefully point out examples where *New Masses* critics had to reverse themselves on individual authors (Sinclair Lewis, James
Rorty, Ezra Pound, Theodore Dreiser, Sherwood Anderson, and Morley
Callaghan) according to that author's current political acceptability. For
example, Archibald MacLeish "was denounced by a *New Masses* critic as
a 'dirty Nazi' "; but after he publishes his play, *Panic,* he becomes "America's most splendid singer" (655).
      The reviewer's style is also a problem because he or she writes for two
audiences simultaneously: intellectuals and the "more or less untutored"
working class. Thus, "[t]he Marxist critic, already self-conscious, has been
obliged to deal with abstract problems in over-simplified sentences, to mix
'plebian' with 'fancy' words and melodramatic name-calling with scholarly analysis, and finally, to dot his most intellectual discourse with 'god-
damns,' 'hells,' and 'stinkings.' . . . [Though the proletarian may feel pa-

tronized,] it gives the intellectual the feeling that he is right in the midst of the class struggle" (654).

Aesthetics also poses a problem, since "[q]uestions of content and form can be taken up only within the framework of Marxian dialectics: faults of style or construction are still 'minor' faults." Hence, "[t]his curious internal warfare between Marx and aestheticism . . . gives to left-wing reviews of bad proletarian and good bourgeois books . . . a hybrid, muddy quality" (654).

Finally, the authors feel the proletarian critic cannot support his multiple roles: "Subjected to pressures from within and without, the *New Masses* critic has developed a lively inferiority complex. . . . [He is] aware that there has not yet been any great proletarian writing. . . . [He] must, therefore, act as missionary for the revolutionary movement. He must court young writers of talent, lure them into the proletarian camp" (655). The conclusion continues this mock-sympathy: "If we are to have any sensible Marxist criticism, this critic must be relieved of some of his responsibilities. It may be that the new united front will disembarrass him of a few of sectarian obligations and so reendow him with critical and revolutionary dignity" (655). The authors never explain what "revolutionary dignity" means.

These Marxian obligations were not a problem for the first of our representative critics, Eda Lou Walton, since she largely kept her politics out of her reviews for the *New York Times Book Review* and *The Nation,* and focused on the poet's style and themes. This formalist focus is noteworthy since she was, in Filreis's description, "a poet motivated by an urban liberalism that soon turned toward radical activism (and possibly Communist Party membership)" (59). Like Malcolm Cowley, she urged Harriet Monroe (without success) to publish proletarian poets in *Poetry,* but her own reviews were free of Marxian cant. Her review of Stevens's 1931 *Harmonium,* for example, points out its modernist style, as any leftist critic would in 1931, but she rejects the reductive depiction of him as a "dandy" and does not dwell on what Gregory called his "highly polished surfaces"; to her credit, she recognized that Stevens's irony is too complex to be labeled.[45] While she had little patience with Cummings's apparent repetitiveness in *ViVa* ("more of the same roses and locomotives") and even less with Robinson Jeffers's *Such Counsels You Gave to Me,* calling it decadent romanticism and antisocial,[46] her description of the political shift in Stevens's *Ideas of Order* is perceptive. Noting that Stevens is "arguing with himself" in these poems, she observes: "Today he is certainly taking account of a world in which this [Epicurean] philosophy [of *Harmonium*] is antiquated. He is trying to evaluate the position of the artist in a world of struggle, of action. If this means, for a time, that his poetry is less surely perfect, it means also that his later poetry may be more significant than his earlier work. Stevens is trying to put aside mood and dream clothed in fine rhetoric for reality."[47]

Stanley Burnshaw cut a much wider swath in leftist criticism than did Walton. As poetry editor of *New Masses* in the mid-thirties, he engaged in a number of free-swinging debates with other editors, critics, and poets. We have already looked at his exchanges with Harriet Monroe in 1934 about proletarian poetry and *Poetry* magazine, as well as his revealing comments in 1961 on being a radical critic for *New Masses*. In chapter 2 we will consider in detail his review of Stevens's *Ideas of Order* and Stevens's response in "Mr. Burnshaw and the Statue." Here, however, we should consider his role as the Far Left's chief theorist for poetry. Burnshaw is often depicted as a firebrand of Marxist aesthetics, but his articles in *New Masses* often assume a pedagogic, sometimes pedantic stance as lectures to other radical critics and poets on how to evaluate and write revolutionary poetry. Two articles, in particular, stand out: "Notes on Revolutionary Poetry" (February 1934) and " 'Middle-Ground' Writers" (April 1935), both published in *New Masses*.[48]

Superficially, "Notes" sounds like other pieces on radical aesthetics from the early thirties. It takes its pro forma swipe at modernism: "[L]et ... [revolutionary] poets free themselves from the modes of expression of the poets of despair and decay. Such models are not in our direction. . . . [L]et us turn our backs on oversubtle, overdelicate, oversophisticated, obscure writing" (22). And it construes poetry as a weapon in the class struggle: "Let us forge a clear, sharp weapon of poetry . . . which can be understood by multitudes" (22). Further, it echoes Mike Gold's demands for simplicity, clarity, and directness (versus modernist obscurity) and confidently asserts that, armed with Marxist social analysis, the poet "burns through all the obfuscations of contemporary society" (22).

But Burnshaw cannot quite shake his modernist roots (Harriet Monroe had teased him about this in "Art and Propaganda," recalling his earlier "Eartha" poems in *Poetry* that praised solitude), and he advocates a number of positions modernist poets would approve of.[49] One key point sounds very much like what the New Critics would maintain in asserting the "inseparability of form and content" and that the poem be seen as a whole. In arguing that "a poem is an entity growing out of a configuration of words" (20), that form "must be . . . looked for in the mode of expression" and that "poor art is poor propaganda" (20, 21), Burnshaw sounds

very much like William Carlos Williams, writing at the same time.[50] Even
the much reviled T. S. Eliot echoes in Burnshaw's concession that "a large
part of the writing of the past remains as valid and significant today as
when it was first written. . . . To deny to contemporary revolutionary poets the right to use certain modes of expression used by revolutionary poets of the past is to deny the continuity of revolutionary thought" (21).
And like such right-wing modernists as Pound and Eliot, he calls for "the
creation of a vital mythopoetic literature" (22).

If recycling modernist aesthetics-in-disguise to criticize revolutionary
poetry sounds like bad faith, it also points up internal conflicts (or, to use
the Marxists' preferred word, "confusions") that Burnshaw was experi-
encing at the time. A letter to Alfred Kreymborg the same year as "Notes"
confides that "I shall not be able to continue at the New Masses" because
literature there was becoming "an excrescent act rather than a compulsion."[51] Such doubts were not to be made public, however, as he acknowledged in "Wallace Stevens and the Statue," and he cautioned Kreymborg
that his feelings were "strictly *entre nous.*"

Those contradictions seem to have faded (or were more skillfully repressed) the following year, when Burnshaw wrote "'Middle-Ground'
Writers." In the fourteen months since his "Notes," a new aesthetic philosophy reflecting Popular Front politics had taken hold in the Far Left,
and Burnshaw's article was in the forefront,[52] instructing other leftist critics on the care and feeding of this liberal animal, the "middle-ground"
writer. Where once the Far Left would have dismissed such writers as social fascists, now "[w]e need every ally who can be enlisted. And we can
afford to drive away no one who can be turned into a friend of the revolutionary movement." Who were these middle-ground writers? They were
"the waverers—confused writers who believe themselves to be standing in
a supposed middle ground between capitalism and revolution" (19). Burnshaw encourages leftist critics to understand their dilemma and "guide
[them] by critical analysis" rather than attack the "anti–working class element" in their work (19). His key point is that middle-ground writers
cannot remain in this anxious no-man's-land: they must resolve their dilemma by going right or left: "[T]here is no [future] middle ground. . . .
[H]e can be[come] a revolutionary writer or a fascist writer" (20). Curiously, Burnshaw assumes that the latter choice—going right—is more
intrinsic for such writers, since he refers to them as "incipient fascists,"
not future Marxists. But this gravitation can be headed off: "The confused writer . . . when he is sincerely striving toward ideological clarification, acts in a manner incompatible with fascism. It is for this reason that

he must be regarded as a potential ally against fascism" (21). Such writers, therefore, must be given understanding and guidance: "[T]he incipient fascist may be honestly struggling to find a way out of the crisis"; therefore, Marxist critics must show these writers that "[e]ven on your own terms . . . fascism is an unthinkable alternative" because it opposes your values (peace, fraternalism, opposition to race hatred, opposition to terror and mass murder); "that fascism and declining capitalism are basically identical in their strangulation of life and art"; and that "[f]ascism and literature, therefore, are contractions in terms" (20–21).

To win over confused writers, revolutionary critics must avoid "the skull-cracking method" of criticism (Mike Gold's attack on Thornton Wilder is the supreme example): "Bludgeoning criticism may accelerate [the writer's movement left or right]. . . . But he will not be a genuine part of either the revolutionary or counter-revolutionary forces until he has entirely understood his position and adopted it through choice." Thus, "the better they see where they are going [i.e., toward fascism], the more eager they are to reverse their course" (19, 20).

That same year, 1935, Burnshaw applied his prescriptions to the "confused" poet Wallace Stevens in a controversial review of *Ideas of Order* titled "Turmoil in the Middle Ground."[53] But as he so candidly admitted in "Wallace Stevens and the Statue," "the present reviewer's concern with Stevens' confusion was at least in part a projection of his own" (362). Perhaps to clarify that confusion, Burnshaw broke with the Party and *New Masses* in the summer of 1936.

Horace Gregory presents the example of a longtime liberal-leftist poet and critic drawn to doctrinaire Marxism by the mid-thirties (perhaps enticed with the status of serving on the editorial staff of its most prestigious journal), then disaffiliating and later denying much of his involvement. Because he was a respected poet as well as a thoughtful critic, Gregory was highly influential in the 1930s. His books of poems, *Chelsea Rooming House* (1930), *No Retreat* (1933), and *Chorus for Survival* (1935), were praised, particularly by the Left, and by 1937 Gregory seemed, at least to another Communist critic, Willard Maas, to hold "sole dominance in . . . the left-wing poetry movement."[54] But this did not prevent him from locking horns with Party leadership on several occasions.

In a semi-confessional article in *New Masses,* "One Writer's Position" (1935), Gregory describes his leftist sympathies as long-standing: "Ever since 1924 my poetry has contained social implications that can be resolved only by the success of the Communist Party in America. . . . I was one of the small group who founded the John Reed Club; I have served as a member of the staff on the editorial board of *The New Masses.*"[55] More-over, "the Communist Party has proved to me again and again that it is the only group retaining a hope for the future that I find necessary for living through these times of terror and destruction" (20). This presentation of leftist credentials, however, was a prelude to frank expressions of doubt—in itself a rather remarkable document for *New Masses* to publish. Gregory describes himself as essentially a loner by temperament, standing "some-where outside of the circle of all groups" (20). This separation enables him, he feels, to achieve a more objective viewpoint: "I believe my value as a writer depends upon a gift of observation. . . . I must remain in a posi-tion to observe. . . . For me to leave that position would destroy my unique value. Others can write, do write in the heat of conflict; I can't. I must witness the conflict, then walk away and gain perspective. If I ignore that rather delicate balance of my relationship to the Party and to America . . . my sensitiveness to an entire situation would become dulled" (20).

What he observes regarding the Party's attitude toward poetry is un-settling and highly reminiscent of Burnshaw's private reservations; but Gregory commits a Party member's mortal sin by confessing his doubts in public: "The Party line . . . of that moment . . . becomes a matter of first importance. . . . Tomorrow, however, the Party line may change. . . . I believe that all important works of art *do* change in meaning, but within Left cultural groups, aesthetic standards undergo daily revision. One day we may be told to read Proust and the next to drop him. . . . [T]he instru-ment of dialectical materialism is being made to function as a political tool, not as a standard by which we measure works of art" (21). Moreover, Gregory acknowledges that his own poetry lacks the necessary Marxian optimism: "[S]omeone might well ask me why my own poetry has no celebration of victory and why in the very cadences I write does one dis-cover music broken and the truncated image? . . . I do employ a deliberate technic, but its origin lies in emotional conviction, and shows something of the way I feel as well as the way I see and hear. . . . There has been no revolution in America and all my work would be one eloquent, scream-ing emotional lie if I shouted victory in this dark hour" (21).

For this candor, Gregory was sternly rebuked. In its next two issues, *New Masses* published long letters excoriating him. The letters are reveal-ing for the absolutist mentality of what Eric Hoffer called "the true be-liever." Edwin Seaver accused Gregory of being no "true Communist poet," only a Communist sympathizer, and wrote that Gregory lacked the "integrated philosophy which enables [a Communist poet] to see beyond defeat and 'this darkest hour.'" "The literary honeymoon is over," Seaver

warned, "and the time is fast approaching when we will no longer clas-
sify authors as proletarian writers and fellow-travelers, but as Party writers and non-Party writers." In short, you are either with us 100 percent
or you are against us.[56] Meridel Le Sueur published a letter the following
week, asserting that Gregory suffered from a "middle-class malady": the
fear of joining. "[I]t seems very dangerous to me to want at the same time
to be in and to be out. . . . [to] accept the discipline of the party and . . .
[to] be objective and individual and outside." Such a stand was equivocal
and hypocritical. Le Sueur acknowledges: "It is difficult [to maintain full
belief] because you are stepping into a dark chaotic passional world of
another class, the proletariat." But the creative artist "will create no new
form of art . . . for that new hour out of that darkness unless he is willing to go all the way, with full belief into that darkness."[57] This was not
the first time Gregory was hauled over the coals. In "One Writer's Position" he mentions being previously attacked in a *New Masses* editorial and
having been called a "right deviationist" (20). In his autobiography, *The
House on Jefferson Street,* he recalls that when "the editor of the *New Masses*
lightly scolded me for translating a 'dead' poet like Catullus, I held my
temper, while others in the [John Reed] Club assured me that the man
was a kindly fellow who meant no harm" (183).

Though for a time estranged from the *New Masses* after "One Writer's
Position," Gregory was reinstated and became poetry editor in 1937. By
this time his reviews reflected his renewed status and radicalism: "[A]ny
work of the imagination," he wrote in the introduction to *New Letters in
America,* "must always be retranslated into political ideas by the political
critic."[58] His 1931 review of Stevens's *Harmonium* had been mixed, criticizing the poetry's "polished surfaces" that were "still unbroken" but also
calling Stevens "a trained observer who gazes with an intelligent eye upon
the decadence that follows the rapid acquisition of wealth and power."[59] By
1937 he felt that Stevens's vision was "now dimmed by the effort to explain his 'position' in a medium ill-suited to the demands of exposition"
and that "The Man with the Blue Guitar" was "convincing only when
Mr. Stevens recreates what he would call the 'anti-poetic' image [in describing "Oxidia," an industrial suburb]."[60] In 1931 he called the Cummings of *ViVa* "a bit old-fashioned today" and "static" in a review tellingly titled "Adolescent Songster."[61] By 1938 his opinion of Cummings
had not really changed—"The very latest of Mr. Cummings's new poems
are fixed in rigid attitudes of youth, which now seem to show signs of
weariness"—but now he saw Cummings's immaturity as symptomatic of
his generation (which, ironically, was Gregory's also): "The same charge

of seeming adolescent beyond their years may be brought against many American writers who had reached the age of twenty-one between 1914 and 1924. The desert of our 'wasteland' period in both prose and verse is white with the bones of those whose careers may be best described as a lingering adolescence followed by a long senility."[62]

This twenties-bashing, already a tired exercise by the late thirties, continues in Gregory's articles in 1937:

The period of wholesale experimentation, with its high mortality rate, came to an end in 1929. ("Introduction" 10)

The 1936 edition of the "[American] Caravan" is very, very dead, a pathetic last tribute to the America *that was* (anytime from 1930 back to 1912). ("Firsts" 8)

[T]he newer poetry is . . . no longer concerned with mere verbal experiment. ("Firsts" 103)

But at the same time, like Burnshaw, Gregory was concerned that leftist poets and critics were downgrading technique and artificially separating it from content (note in the following that the effective writer should be "useful," presumably to the Party or the movement): "It was forgotten, for the moment, that the useful writer cannot divide his intelligence by ignoring the way he says a thing in favor of what he has to say. The unperceiving writer will always betray his blindness by the very words he uses, and if he is careless his usefulness becomes extremely limited. . . . When some of our Liberal critics dropped the thing they had called art (which to them had become associated with art for art's sake) they also found that they could not live long on a diet of depression literature for depression's sake" ("Introduction" 11, 12).

Finally, Gregory used his position to promote younger poets: "[A] group of new names have [*sic*] appeared. . . . The poets of *New Letters in America* and of the *New Masses* represent the majority of the influences now at work in changing the picture from one of a single 'waste-land' generalization to another that promises a new phase in American poetry" ("Poetry in 1937" 12). Among this new group were Ruth Lechlitner, Muriel Rukeyser, Elizabeth Bishop, T. C. Wilson, Robert Fitzgerald, and Edwin Rolfe.

As a postscript to Gregory's active career on the left, it is interesting to note its partial erasure in his 1971 autobiography, *The House on Jefferson Street* (the narrative ends at about 1936). Around 1934, "I was beginning to note that almost every poet of stature was being dismissed [by the Party] as politically 'wrong.' ... Without my being conscious of the change, I had begun to lose interest in Left Wing literary opinions, and ... I saw a wide gap between transient Left Wing sentiments and works of art."[63] While "One Writer's Position" candidly expresses this discomfort with the Party's "transient" opinions, *House* makes it seem that Gregory soon opted out: "When during 1936, an editor of the *New Masses* phoned me demanding that I sign a statement approving the verdicts in the Moscow Trials, at last I found it easy to say: 'No' ... I was shown, clearly enough, that Communist editors merely followed orders from Moscow—that these orders had no relationship to truth as I saw it, or to the arts" (257–58). The narrative is silent about Gregory's service as *New Masses* poetry editor in 1936–37, another instance of the "political amnesia" that Alan Wald describes in *The New York Intellectuals.*[64]

THE MID AND LATER THIRTIES: A BRIEF OVERVIEW

Given the Communist Party's contradictory and hostile responses to would-be converts in the early thirties, an observer in 1933 or 1934 might have predicted that writers' flirtation with communism would be brief. After all, with the beginning of Franklin Roosevelt's New Deal, key props in the Marxist conversion argument—capitalism's failure and governmental paralysis—had collapsed. The New Deal did not eradicate the Depression, but it did present from its beginning a federal government actively engaged in confronting the Depression's worst features: unemployment, hunger, bank failures, and, perhaps most important, hopelessness. Capitalism teetered with the massive bank failures of 1932–33, but it did not collapse—indeed, Roosevelt later boasted with some justification that, despite being vilified by Wall Street and big business, he had rescued capitalism. Under New Deal work programs, unemployment declined from approximately 25 percent of the workforce in 1932 to 16.9 percent in 1936; industrial production in 1936 doubled that of 1932; farm income nearly doubled, despite the dust bowl; banks had stopped closing; home foreclosures (about a thousand a day in 1932) diminished.[65]

Moreover, it was clear by 1933 that there would be no revolution in the United States. In fact, there had been little likelihood of one even during the Hoover years, as Edmund Wilson discovered in his travels across the country. Unemployed workers at the time were frequently described as stunned and largely passive, not filled with revolutionary anger. And whatever the New Deal's failures and reversals, the unemployed could at least feel that under Roosevelt the government cared about their problems and was *trying* to help them. The revolutionary climate simply was not there.

But rather than fade, the CPUSA flourished in the mid-thirties for two interlocking reasons: the rise of fascism and the Soviet Comintern's decision in 1934, in response to that rise, to abandon its Third Period policy of world revolution and sectarian infighting and to form a Popular Front of all parties and factions on the left to oppose fascism. Where in 1934, American intellectuals could witness the ugly spectacle of the Communists breaking up a socialist meeting at Madison Square Garden—an action that contributed to the disillusionment of a number of fellow travelers like John Dos Passos—by the following year the Party was *welcoming* socialists (at least in theoretical statements).[66] And where liberal writers would be routinely branded as social fascists in the early thirties, they were now, in Burnshaw's term, "middle-ground" writers to be courted and freed of their proto-fascist confusions. As early as April 1933, Mike Gold declared: "Every anti-fascist is needed in this united front. There must be no base factional quarrels."[67] Most telling of all, communism and the Soviet Union now represented a bulwark against rising fascism. As Daniel Aaron observes: "[F]or a large number of American intellectuals after 1932, [Russia] had assumed the leadership in the world struggle against the menacing power of international fascism. . . . Until the Nazi-Soviet pact in 1939, hatred of world fascism brought writers and intellectuals into the Left orbit who otherwise might never have affiliated with the movement" (172).

With the outbreak of the Spanish Civil War in the summer of 1936, that leadership was put to the test: as the Western powers embargoed arms to Spain and watched passively as Germany and Italy sent planes and pilots, troops and munitions to help Franco's forces win battle after battle, the Soviet Union was the only country to actively aid the Spanish Loyalists. Of course, as Alfred Kazin pointed out in his memoir, it would not do to look too closely at Russian tactics in Spain: "I did not want to dwell on what the Stalinists were doing in Spain. I wanted only to see Fascism destroyed" (137).

The results of the Popular Front were striking: Party membership in the United States, having declined after Roosevelt's election in 1932, began to rise steadily again. The *New Masses* circulation jumped from six thousand as a monthly to twenty-four thousand as a weekly in early 1935, actually surpassing *The New Republic*. Fellow travelers, once deeply distrusted by the Party, were now encouraged—and thousands of intellectuals and writers gravitated *toward* the Party without thinking seriously of joining. In fact, it became chic. As Alfred Kazin recalls:

All the cleverest and most dynamic people I met now gave authority to Marxist opinion—especially if they were from the upper echelons that I had waited so long to see. When the iron laws of history were pronounced in upper-class accents, it was hard not to be impressed. . . . So many editors and publishers were now fellow travelers and complacently intellectual about Marxism, preening themselves on being pathologists of their class "in decay," that I tended to miss the emotionalism of working-class commitment. The cool-looking types I now met at cocktail parties never seemed to find it odd to express the most "revolutionary" opinions against the most luxurious backgrounds. (87)

"Name" writers were now courted by *New Masses,* and many were eager to respond, as Stanley Burnshaw recounts: "More and more writers, some from unexpected places, were knocking at the door and asking to be let in. In 1934–36 *The New Masses* printed work by Hemingway, MacLeish, Saroyan, Dos Passos, Elmer Rice, Erskine Caldwell, Richard Wright, Waldo Frank, . . . Nelson Algren, Edward Dahlberg, Horace Gregory, Kenneth Burke. . . . [T]he world of books had suddenly become alive with excitement" ("Wallace Stevens and the Statue" 359). He adds sardonically: "[T]he traffic in and out of the literary Left was surely the heaviest in American cultural history" (361).

The romance was not to last. For once again, the CPUSA and its Soviet masters committed blunders small and large that alienated writers and intellectuals almost as quickly as they were attracted—hence, Burnshaw's "traffic in *and out* of the literary Left." For openers, the CPUSA, in turning toward established writers in the mid-thirties, turned its back on younger, unknown ones by closing the John Reed Clubs in 1934—at a high point in their popularity—in favor of holding an American Writers' Congress limited to well-known literati (Klehr 351).[68] Granville Hicks, a power at *New Masses,* even opposed disbursing money and effort to the numerous radical magazines—"more than a dozen," according to Daniel Aaron— arguing that all literary and financial resources should be used to improve *New Masses* (Aaron 311). Both moves were vigorously opposed by those harmed: the New York chapter of the John Reed Club, in fact, refused to disband, and its magazine, *Partisan Review,* eventually turned into the most important *anti*-Party journal on the left.

The move at first seemed to pay dividends. Young, unpublished writers devoted to the movement found outlets for their radical verse and prose other than John Reed Club publications. And the Writers' Congress of

1935 appeared to be a major success. It attracted four hundred delegates, including many prominent writers, and was easily controlled by the communists. While Malcolm Cowley spoke on the advantages to a writer of belonging to the revolutionary movement, the congress's chief topics were the political struggle against war and fascism and the literary "problem of presenting America in a revolutionary context" (Aaron 299). In addressing the latter issue, however, many speakers were highly critical of reductive proletarian aesthetics, which "damned everything bourgeois and praised all expressions of the working class life" (Aaron 303). Waldo Frank, the congress's chairman, bluntly asserted that "the place of the artist in the revolutionary movement was not in the oversimplification of propaganda, the necessities are far more complex than that."[69] His speech impressed William Carlos Williams, who was more a curious onlooker than a delegate. James T. Farrell attacked ideological criticism—a sign of his growing disenchantment with the Party. Thus, while the participants were generally united about the need to fight fascism and create a revolutionary literature, they were not about to become Party hacks churning out proletarian propaganda. They did, however, form the League of American Writers with about 125 members, which eventually included Thomas Mann, John Steinbeck, Ernest Hemingway, Theodore Dreiser, James T. Farrell, Archibald MacLeish, Lewis Mumford, Van Wyck Brooks, Lillian Hellman, William Carlos Williams, Nelson Algren, William Saroyan, and Nathaniel West (Klehr 353).

The logic of the Popular Front made it inevitable that its inclusive appeals to writers and intellectuals would attract many who might consider themselves revolutionary in some way, and certainly opposed fascism, but who would not march with the Party if they disliked the orders and who felt free to criticize those orders. This became clear at the Second American Writers' Congress, held two years later, in 1937. While it attracted about the same number, this time including visual artists, the CPUSA played a much smaller role in stage-managing: "[T]he openly pro-Communist tone of 1935 meeting had disappeared. The call [for the congress], dominated by the theme of combating fascism, lacked the revolutionary language of its predecessor" (Klehr 354). Moreover, the most famous speaker at the second congress, Ernest Hemingway, fresh from covering the Spanish Civil War, spoke only about the need to fight fascism. And in his book on that war, *For Whom the Bell Tolls*, the protagonist, Robert Jordan, pointedly says he is not a communist, but an anti-fascist.

The Spanish Civil War might have solidified the Popular Front not only as anti-fascist but as pro-communist had it not been for Soviet persecu-

tion of other leftist groups in Spain—apparently the Popular Front concept did not pertain there. Even more damaging at the same time were
the Moscow Trials of many of the Party's founders. Both of these actions,
particularly the blatantly trumped-up trials, created profound cognitive
dissonance among the Party faithful and fellow travelers. As Daniel Aaron
summarizes: "At the moment when the party seemed to have succeeded
brilliantly in its united-front campaign, the arraignment and execution
of old Bolsheviks blurred the sharp distinction between Communism and
fascism the party had been so assiduously fostering. . . . [T]he Comintern
at one stroke alienated a large number of its American allies and obliged
its still-loyal adherents to defend an insupportable position" (324).

Opposition to the Party from former supporters intensified: John Dos
Passos, on learning that the Soviets in Spain had executed his friend and
translator, José Robles, broke with the Party once and for all. James T. Farrell continued to criticize Marxist aesthetics and *New Masses* critics until
he, too, left the Party. Edmund Wilson's 1935 trip to Russia to gather material for *To the Finland Station* left him more sympathetic to American
democracy. Most damaging of all, the John Reed Club magazine that the
Party had failed to close down, *Partisan Review,* became a gathering point
and influential forum for all leftists opposed to Stalinism when it was re-
vived in 1937 by Philip Rahv and William Phillips. Even in its earlier incarnations beginning in 1934, *Partisan Review* under Rahv and Phillips had
challenged the Party's narrowly schematic concepts of proletarian literature, arguing for a more complex aesthetics that did not arbitrarily separate form and content and that did not scorn modernist techniques (Wald
78). By 1937 such maverick intellectuals as Dwight Macdonald, F. W. Dupee, and Mary McCarthy had joined the staff and, with Rahv and Phillips, maintained a running battle with *New Masses* and with Stalinists such
as Malcolm Cowley during the last years of the thirties over such issues as
the Moscow Trials and the fate of Leon Trotsky.[70] By 1937, then, the influence of the CPUSA among radical intellectuals was slowly waning: "[I]t
clearly had lost its role as cultural pacesetter. . . . [Now] it had a dedicated
band of intellectual opponents" (Klehr 364). Mike Gold could only complain that "intellectuals are the most unstable and untrustworthy group
in modern society."[71]

For most fellow travelers and many members, the coup de grâce for allegiance to the Party was the Nazi-Soviet Nonaggression Pact of August
1939. In one blow, Russia destroyed its Popular Front argument, its status
as the bulwark against fascism, and enabled the hated enemy, Germany,
to invade Poland with impunity. As Russia proceeded to occupy eastern

Poland and the Baltic States, it clearly shared in the spoils. Fellow travelers were appalled when the *Daily Worker* did a complete about-face from urging all-out opposition to fascism to now calling for non-involvement in the imperialists' war. Some disillusioned writers followed Granville Hicks's lead and publicly disaffiliated from the Party in the weeks following.[72] Many more did so privately. For those on the left who had been conflicted in their allegiance by the Moscow Trials and other Soviet actions, the pact finally resolved their dilemma, while it confirmed the views of anti-Party leftists like Kazin: "Day after day I followed the *Daily Worker* with savage joy at its confusion as [it] . . . now tried to explain the secret contribution that the noble Stalin, the great Stalin, the all-wise and farseeing Stalin, had made to the cause of world peace" (141). While some, like Richard Wright, stayed in the Party a few more years, the death knell of allegiance had clearly sounded, marking the counter-migration of writers and intellectuals away from radicalism.

Silhouetted in miniature against these sweeping movements and migrations are the experiences of four American poets, each of whom reacted sharply to the literary-political pressures of this decade and to the Left's waxing and waning influence. Each poet's response was individual, evolving, sometimes muddled and contradictory, and conditioned by a complex of particulars. Nonetheless, their stories describe patterns of attraction and repulsion, involvement and resistance that say something about the experience of the poet in a political age. It is to these complementary and contrasting trajectories that we now turn.

2

Wallace Stevens

No More Arpeggios

Nineteen twenty-three was a banner year for modernist American poetry. In addition to William Carlos Williams's pathbreaking *Spring and All,*
the year witnessed the first books of poems by E. E. Cummings (*Tulips
and Chimneys*) and Wallace Stevens (*Harmonium*). For Cummings it was
a major breakthrough, for, outside of *The Dial* and a few issues of *Broom,*
his poetry had not appeared much in print.[1] Stevens, however, was well
known and highly regarded by readers of little magazines like *Poetry, Others,* and *The Little Review,* where his poems had appeared often in the preceding nine years. In fact, several reviewers of *Harmonium* echoed Mark
Van Doren's observation that since the mid-teens "he has continued . . . to
dance like a tantalizing star through magazines and anthologies. But there
has been no volume until now."[2]

When *Harmonium* finally did appear, it received several favorable reviews,[3] but these reviews established a stereotype that would haunt Stevens
the rest of his career: he was the "dandy," the aesthete par excellence, whose
finely tuned rhythms, occasionally esoteric diction, and whimsical humor epitomized the "art for art's sake" ethic of modernism and were completely detached from the poet's political and social world. Descriptors like
"exotic," "fastidious," "exquisite," and "elegant" appear repeatedly in reviews of Stevens's poems in the 1920s and 1930s. Typical of these reviews
is Edmund Wilson's in *The Dial:* "Mr. Wallace Stevens is the master of a
style: that is the most remarkable thing about him. His gift for combining
words is fantastic but sure: even when you do not know what he is saying,
you know that he is saying it well."[4] Wilson goes on to identify two other
qualities that subsequent critics would reiterate: his whimsical titles and his
seeming lack of emotion: "When you read a few poems of Mr. Stevens,
you get the impression from the richness of his verbal imagination that he
is a poet of rich personality, but when you come to read the whole volume
through you are struck by a sort of aridity. Mr. Stevens, who is so obser-
vant and has so distinguished a fancy, seems to have emotion neither in

abundance nor in intensity. . . . Emotion seems to emerge only furtively in the cryptic images of his poetry, as if it had been . . . disposed of by being dexterously turned into exquisite amusing words" (63).

Other reviewers of the 1923 *Harmonium* offered variants of Wilson's appraisal; their vocabulary expresses the tenor of Stevens criticism for years to follow. Several observed his "love of magnificence" (Moore), the "scenery of luxuriant and intricate design" (Seiffert), his penchant for the exotic (Tate). Equally noted were his "pure phrasing" and "deliberately enunciated melody" (Van Doren), the "music of his words" (Josephson), the "sheer beauty of sound, phrase, rhythm" (Monroe). Even a reviewer put off by Stevens's "determined obscurity" recognized his "verbal elegance" (Untermeyer). One critic, however, John Gould Fletcher, noted the social costs of Stevens's aestheticism: "Stevens is an aesthete. . . . [He] is definitely out of tune with life and with his surroundings, and is seeking an escape into a sphere of finer harmony between instinct and intelligence."[5]

Probably, the early review that most memorably characterized Stevens's persona as a poet was Gorham Munson's 1925 essay in *The Dial,* "The Dandyism of Wallace Stevens."[6] Two years after publishing a penetrating essay on Cummings, Munson defined Stevens as America's first poetic dandy, in whom "impeccability is primarily achieved by adding elegance to correctness. . . . Elegance he attains in his fastidious vocabulary—in the surprising aplomb and blandness of his images" (79). Stevens, Munson continues, "is a connoisseur of the senses and emotions. [His] imagination comes to rest on them. . . . The integration achieved is one of feeling; in the final analysis, it is a temperate romanticism" (80). In contrast to Baudelaire's dandyism, which defied a society he despised, "tranquility enfolds Mr. Stevens. . . . The world is a gay and bright phenomenon and he gives the impression of feasting on it without misgiving. . . . [a] well-fed and well-booted dandyism of contentment" (80–81). Munson concludes: "No American poet excels him in the sensory delights that a spick-and-span craft can stimulate: none is more skillful in arranging his music, his figures, and his design. None else, monocled and gloved, can cut so faultless a figure standing in his box at the circus of life. . . . No one has . . . more perfectly exemplified to us the virtue of impeccable form" (82). This image of Stevens as the self-satisfied connoisseur, elegantly crafting his rhythms and selecting his "fastidious" diction as if with tweezers, while the noisy and scruffy world of events passes by unnoticed, would shadow him for many years to come.

The dearth of Stevens's poems between 1924 and 1931 did nothing to alter this image. Day-to-day responsibilities of marriage, fatherhood, and solidifying his executive position at Hartford Accident and Indemnity Company occupied virtually all of his time. As he recalled in a letter to Ronald Lane Latimer in May 1937: "[A] good many years ago, when I really was a poet in the sense that I was all imagination . . . , I deliberately gave up writing poetry because, much as I loved it, there were too many other things I wanted not to make an effort to have them. . . . I didn't like the idea of being bedeviled all the time about money and I didn't for a moment like the idea of poverty" (*Letters* 320).

HARMONIUM (1931)

When Stevens published his next book of poems, eight long years after *Harmonium,* it proved to be virtually a reissue of that book, with the same title, a few poems dropped, and several poems added.[7] The new poems included one long poem, "Sea Surface Full of Clouds," and the excellent "Death of a Soldier"; but none of the added poems were written after 1924, and they marked no change in his style or technique: he still appeared the dandy. But just as Frost, Cummings, and Williams were to discover in the early 1930s, though they had not essentially changed from the 1920s, many critics and reviewers had, joining in the leftist migration of 1930–33. The same impatience that would color reviews of Cummings's *ViVa* (1931) and Frost's *Collected Poems* (1930) began to creep into some reviews of the 1931 *Harmonium.* Stevens's biographer Joan Richardson summarizes: "While his reputation had been growing steadily through the twenties, as illustrated by the various articles written between 1924 and 1929, . . . most of the reviews of the 1931 edition of *Harmonium* denounced his esotericism and his finely polished style."[8]

"Denounced" seems too strong a characterization of these reviews, for many were favorable or at least mixed. On the left, however, some critics were less willing to tolerate the image of Stevens as the unchanging dandy. Raymond Larsson's review in *Commonweal* was the most dismissive. Although he acknowledges that certain of Stevens's poems "wear" well and will be "one of the distinct values of contemporary poetry," Larsson considers the poet's dandyism—"fastidious, elegant, the 'beau with a muff' "—as grounds to dismiss him as a "minor poet," a superannuated imagist who finds "in the world of things something akin to security, one fancies." "Security," here, alludes to the insecure present and Larsson's leftist distaste for what he sees as Stevens's preciousness.[9]

Horace Gregory's review in the *Herald Tribune* is more ambivalent in both charging Stevens with stasis even as it attempts to refigure this value in social terms. Acknowledging that Stevens's "subterranean reputation has been steadily growing" since the 1923 *Harmonium,* Gregory accedes to Munson's stereotype of Stevens as dandy: "the immaculate top hat and stick are always there." Curiously, however, he tries to find a place for Stevens in the contemporary world by turning him into "a trained observer who gazes with an intelligent eye upon the decadence that follows the rapid acquisition of wealth and power." "Decadence" and "rapid acquisition of wealth" sound more like 1928 than 1931—or like a leftist reviewer balefully looking backwards—and Gregory never explains how a dandy who "remains static" and "will not allow himself to grow beyond the limitations which he has imposed upon his talents" can become, willy-nilly, a social observer of decadence. The review's title and most quoted sentence simply reinforce Stevens's sameness: "The general impression [of the new poems] remains the same and the polished surfaces are still unbroken."[10]

Eda Lou Walton, writing in *The Nation,* is more consistently positive in her review, but arrives at a similar conclusion in seeing Stevens as the epitome of the twenties modernist. For Walton, however, this modernism expresses itself not in dandyism but in irony, and Stevens's "deflation of the emotions" is "the very extreme of the Wasteland [*sic*] theory. . . . No feeling is more than acknowledged before it splays out into a dozen different and antithetical feelings. No intensity mounts to its climax without the insidious question at its center." Walton concludes: "Stevens persists in being a poet of moonlight who in the end pricks the bubble of the moon itself. . . . The poet is sincere in being insincere."[11] If Walton saw a destabilizing irony as Stevens's key feature, it was "balance" and "poise" for Morton Zabel, poetry harmonizing "richness" and "simplicity," "indulgence and austerity," a "disciplined individualism."[12] Like Walton, he rejects the "dandy" label.

In sum, none of the reviews of the 1931 *Harmonium* attacked Stevens on explicitly political grounds; indeed, most praised his poetry. But the consensus that his poetry has not changed clearly had a political undercurrent. Never a compliment, "stasis" by 1931 was anathema to reviewers like Larsson and Gregory, whose leftist ideology demanded change. Regardless of whether the critics accepted or rejected the "dandy" label, they largely relied on the vocabulary of the earlier critics with subtle refinements: ironic undercutting, antithetical feelings, balances of opposed sensibilities—all of which describe Stevens's poems as self-contained entities quite detached from a collapsing world.

"HEADED LEFT": RONALD LANE
LATIMER AND *IDEAS OF ORDER*

Something rather remarkable happened to Stevens in late 1934 and 1935. The dandy shed his top hat and cane; the ivory-tower aesthete climbed down and began to reflect on the world around him; the fundamentally conservative business executive—the least likely person to change his political stance or even to acquire an interest in politics—now began to describe himself as sympathetic to leftist politics and, more important, began expressing political themes in his new poems. In October 1934 he had still declared himself politically unaffiliated, at least in response to an "Enquiry" by the left-wing magazine *New Verse:* "Do you take your stand with any political or politico-economic party or creed?" "I'm afraid that I don't," Stevens replied. He even provocatively confided in this survey (in response to the question "As a poet what distinguishes you, do you think, from an ordinary man?") that he was unable to "see much point to the life of an ordinary man."[13]

Likewise, the poems Stevens wrote between 1932 and 1934—while they often reflect darker moods apposite to these worst years of the Depression (for example, "Autumn Refrain"), show no real change in his political attitudes. In fact, two poems he composed in the summer of 1934 (and left out of *Collected Poems*)—"The Drum Majors in the Labor Day Parade" and "Polo Ponies Practicing"—are explicit in their lack of sympathy for the working class (*CPP* 562–63). In "Drum Majors" the speaker complains that these parade leaders don't "make the Dagoes squeal" by doing fancy tricks with their batons. He calls them "prigs" and wonders if they (as workers) really fit the Marxist stereotype as "Toys of the millionaires, / morbid and bleak." Instead, they should be "muscular men, / Naked and stamping the earth, / Whipping the air"—a pagan echo of the "ring of men" in "Sunday Morning" and the "muscular one" who "whips" curds in "The Emperor of Ice Cream." The two lines immediately following seem almost a parody of proletarian parades: "The banners should brighten the sun. / The women should sing as they march." At least, these clichés would elicit some emotion. But the parade fails both as entertainment and as rabble-rousing. Hence, the speaker's disgust: "Let's go home."

"Polo Ponies Practicing" exudes a complementary joy in watching "the world of movement / Fitted by men and horses / For hymns." The speaker is quite aware that polo is a rich man's sport played now in a time of widespread poverty; he even begins the poem by defensively referring to "The constant cry against an old order." But he dismisses these cries first by be-

littling them as "old and stale" and by subordinating the political issue altogether to the sensuous joy of the moment:

> Beyond any order,
> Beyond any rebellion,
> A brilliant air
>
> On the flanks of the horses, . . .
> On the shapes of the mind.

This poem closely resembles the first eight stanzas of William Carlos Williams's "The Yachts" in aesthetic admiration for particular sports of the
rich; but where Stevens's poem ends with this pleasure, Williams's "Yachts"
twists into a shocking and political conclusion (discussed in chapter 5).

Given these predictable political attitudes in 1934—Stevens was by now
a vice-president at Hartford and had just purchased a large home—it is
more than a little surprising that just a year later he declared in a letter that
he hoped that he was "headed left" (*Letters* 286). What accounts for this
astonishing change? What did he mean by "headed left"?

Of course, by 1935 Stevens was well aware of the changes in the literary-
political landscape. He kept abreast of the increasingly leftist discussions
in *The Nation* and *The New Republic;* in fact, he published several poems
in both magazines, and "The Men That Are Falling" won *The Nation*'s
prize for the best poem of 1936. He had been reading *Partisan Review* since
its inception in 1934 (Richardson 95), and he also read books of poetry
and prose by radical leftists. In March 1933, for example, he read Horace
Gregory's book of poems *No Retreat,* which reflected the poet-reviewer's
Communist sympathies. Stevens did not care for the book (*Letters* 265).
By 1935 he was even reading *New Masses.* Indeed, as he commented in a
letter, it would be impossible to remain oblivious to the radical changes in
the literary world: that world was too small to miss them (*Letters* 286–87).
But such changes in themselves did not mean that Stevens had to change.
He might well have been expected to ignore the whole thing or to react
to this new politicization of literature as Frost and Cummings did: by rejecting and satirizing it.

Three motivating factors, at least, prevented Stevens from taking that
route. The first was utterly mundane: he read the newspapers every day
and closely followed the turbulent events of the early and mid-thirties:
the ever-worsening news of the Depression, Roosevelt's election and his
rapid creation of New Deal programs, the rise of Hitler, and Mussolini's

invasions of Abyssinia and Ethiopia (Filreis 20).[14] In the early thirties he
was keenly aware of the growing disparity between his prosperity and the
widespread destitution around him, prompting both concern for the safety
of his family and also guilt over his ability to spend money on exotic trifles
like Chinese tea or on artwork from abroad. One passage from a 1933 letter expresses his worry facetiously: "[B]ecause of the depression, there are
so many burglars about that, instead of living in a neighborhood that is
poorly lighted, the neighborhood is in reality brilliantly lighted. People
actually go to bed leaving lights burning all over the house in order to fool
the bums. . . . Holly and Mrs. Stevens have been trained, in the event of a
break[-in], to offer to make breakfast and show any visitors round, whether
I am absent or not. I am afraid that, if I hear burglars in the house, no one
will be able to determine whether I am absent or not" (*Letters* 266–67).
He jokes in the same letter: "If things go from bad to worse, I am either
going to move to a farm in Sweden or a houseboat in Key West Harbor."
A hint of guilt appears in another letter to a business colleague that things
like "collecting *object d'art* 'are not permissible subjects now-a-days. . . .
Everything is overwhelmingly real now-a-days.'"[15]

   Closely related to what he read, his job at Hartford Accident and Indemnity often required Stevens to deal with the Depression's brutal effects
on businesses; he traveled to other states, settling bankruptcies of companies, breach of contract cases, foreclosures. As Richardson concludes:
"The changes in the outside world were too great to be ignored. As one
directly connected to the economic workings of that world, Stevens could
not avoid being affected by what they meant" (72–73). Indeed, he pon-
dered the same questions that his leftist fellow writers had a few years earlier: how should one respond in these catastrophic times? What is the role of
poetry—and the poet—when "reality" is bearing down hard? But merely
reading and thinking about these hard times, even being professionally involved with them, do not inevitably lead one to change his or her politics and poetics. Something more was required to engage Stevens's mind
in the reflections that led to his political transformation.

   That impetus was as curious as the first two were ordinary: the entrance
into Stevens's life and career of Ronald Lane Latimer (alias J. Ronald Lane
Latimer, alias James G. Leippert, alias Mark Jason, alias Mark Zorn, alias
Martin Jay, alias Jay Martin).[16] A glance at Stevens's published letters in
the 1930s shows that Latimer was his primary correspondent between
1934 and 1938, the years when Stevens became politicized; in fact, many
of his letters to Latimer express political observations, mostly in answer

to Latimer's questions.[17] At times, for example November 1935, this correspondence was so prolific that Stevens was writing him lengthy letters more than once a week. Latimer was not just a correspondent, however; he became Stevens's publisher in this period. His magazine, *Alcestis Quarterly*, solicited poems from Stevens, Williams, and other modernists, while, at the same time, his Alcestis Press published lavish limited editions of their work—this at a time when, as Stevens quipped, "selling poetry . . . must be very much like selling lemonade to a crowd of drunks" (*Letters* 284).[18]

By all accounts, Latimer was a queer duck: the aliases and multiple addresses he used reveal his elusiveness or even paranoia. And, as Alan Filreis has discovered, many of the questions he put to Stevens were ghost-written (on Latimer's orders) by his assistant, the Communist poet Willard Mass, a fan of Stevens (12–13, 121–22). But even if slippery and weird, Latimer provided Stevens—and posterity—two essential services that have earned him a small niche in literary history. He published Stevens's next two books of poems, *Ideas of Order* (August 1935) and *Owl's Clover* (November 1936),[19] which contained the most explicitly political poems in Stevens's oeuvre; and he drew from the poet in their correspondence political opinions and self-assessments that might otherwise have stayed silent, providing readers and critics some rather remarkable insights into Stevens's thinking at the time. More than this, Latimer's questions almost certainly spurred Stevens to reflect on his political views much more than he had previously, reflections that pushed those views leftward.

Stevens was probably unaware of his first published mention of Latimer. In April 1934, he writes to his friend the poet Witter Bynner: "To hell with Leippert" (*Letters* 270). Apparently, Bynner had been upset by his dealings with Leippert/Latimer, and Stevens advised: "I don't see why you should pay any attention to the thing. Ordinarily when one has been played for a sucker one forgets it. Of course, I don't know that Leippert is all that you say he is; I don't know anything at all about him, and don't care."[20]

Not a promising beginning. But seven months later, Stevens is delightedly responding to *Latimer's* proposal to bring out a new book of poems: "I cannot imagine anything that I should like more" (November 28, 1934, *Letters* 271). The book would become *Ideas of Order*, and that proposal, along with Latimer's solicitation of poems for *Alcestis Quarterly*, helped spur his muse and in a new direction. As Stevens acknowledged gratefully, "One of the essential conditions to the writing of poetry is impetus. . . . While poems may very well occur, they had very much better be caused. If all this is true, then it may be that in a few weeks time my imagination will

be such a furnace that I can stroll home from the office and fill the house
with the most iridescent notes" (January 8, 1935, *Letters* 274). Later, he
observed: "I owe a very great deal to him. I don't mean to say because
he published some of my things, but because he started me up to doing them."[21]

The 1935 *Ideas of Order* presents a much-changed Wallace Stevens from
the *Harmonium* poems: the new poems are more somber, far less playful.
Some of their themes are familiar from "Sunday Morning" and "A High-
Toned Old Christian Woman": that the sustaining spirit for this poet comes
from the natural world ("what spirit / Have I except it comes from the
sun?"—"Waving Adieu, Adieu, Adieu"); that for the isolated climbers at
the "heroic height" "There was neither voice, nor crested image, / Nor
chorister, nor priest" ("How to Live. What to Do"). Another major theme
continues Stevens's lifelong fascination with the imagination; only now, he
characterizes the poet as a shaper of imaginative order as much as a medium of inspired words:

> It was her voice that made
> The sky acutest at its vanishing.
> She measured to the hour its solitude.
> She was the single artificer of the world
> In which she sang. And when she sang the sea,
> Whatever self it had, became the self
> That was her song, for she was the maker.
> ("The Idea of Order at Key West," *CPP* 105–6)

Stevens emphasized the poet's ordering function both in the book's title
and in his description of it to Latimer: "The arrangement is simply based
on contrasts: there is nothing rigid about it. Not every poem expresses a
phase of order or an illustration of order; after all, the thing is not a thesis"
(March 26, 1935, *Letters* 279).[22]

An altogether new theme, however, emerges in several poems: How can
poetry survive in this time of economic catastrophe?

> Who can think of the sun costuming clouds
> When all people are shaken
> Or of night endazzled, proud,
> When people awaken
> And cry and cry for help?
> ("A Fading of the Sun," *CPP* 112–13)

And what is to be "the status of the poet in a disturbed society"?[23] The dust jacket of the 1936 Knopf edition of *Ideas of Order* carries this statement of Stevens's:

> We think of changes occurring today as economic changes, involving political and social changes. Such changes raise questions of political and social order.
>
> While it is inevitable that a poet should be concerned with such questions, this book, although it reflects them, is primarily concerned with ideas of order of a different nature, as, for example, the dependence of the individual, confronting the elimination of established ideas, on the general sense of order; the idea of order created by individual concepts . . . ; the idea of order arising from the practice of any art, as of poetry. . . .
>
> This book is essentially a book of pure poetry. I believe that, in any society, the poet should be the exponent of the imagination of that society. *Ideas of Order* attempts to illustrate the role of the imagination in life, and particularly in life at present. The more realistic life may be, the more it needs the stimulus of the imagination. (*CPP* 997)

Clearly, the last paragraph captures Stevens's primary purpose and belief, but the dependent clauses of the second paragraph are revealing. A few years earlier he would never have agreed that "it is inevitable that a poet should be concerned with such [political and social] questions"; nor would he have conceded that his poetry "reflects them."

In the poems that address these questions of the poet's—and poetry's—role in difficult times, Stevens's attitudes and tones are complex: a piquant entangling of regret for a lost past, disgust at the tawdry present, recognition of the demands for change, and resolution, albeit grudging, to face these demands. "Botanist on Alp (No. 1)" (*CPP* 109–10) regrets the loss of a world of serene order and perspective, symbolized by the pillars and arches of Claude Lorrain's painting: "Panoramas are not what they used to be. / Claude has been dead a long time." The culprit, however, is precisely the fellow whom leftist writers were identifying as the savior: "Marx has ruined Nature, / For the moment." In response to Latimer's question about this line, Stevens provides a painfully obvious answer: "as any Marxian would know, . . . I am not a Marxian poet" (November 15, 1935, *Letters* 294). But what was he in 1935?

If "Botanist" seems bitter, its conclusion is upbeat: "Yet the panorama of despair"—that is, Claude's world in ruins—"Cannot be the specialty /

Of this ecstatic air." "Sad Strains of a Gay Waltz" (*CPP* 100–101) is more complex: nostalgic for the time, now lost, when the waltz was "a mode of desire" and despairing that now

> There is order in neither sea nor sun.
> The shapes have lost their glistening.
> There are these sudden mobs of men,[24]
>
> These sudden clouds of faces and arms,
> An immense suppression, freed,
> These voices crying without knowing for what,
>
> Except to be happy, without knowing how,
> Imposing forms they cannot describe,
> Requiring order beyond their speech.

The poem is also prophetic, predicting that "The epic of disbelief / Blares oftener and soon, will soon be constant" and that

> Some harmonious skeptic soon in a skeptical music
>
> Will unite these figures of men and their shapes
> Will glisten again with motion

Could Stevens become that "harmonious skeptic"? Not in 1935. But what he could do was recognize and *acknowledge* that the "epic of disbelief" was now "blaring." "Mozart, 1935" (*CPP* 107–8) conveys this theme masterfully, as well as combining the other themes and attitudes discussed above. It was this poem that Stevens said "expresses . . . the status of the poet in a disturbed society" (*Letters* 292). Mozart's music represents for Stevens—as listeners then so often misconstrued it—the untroubled art of an aristocratic age: the "unclouded concerto," "that lucid souvenir of the past, / The divertimento." It is caviar for the elite—much as Stevens's critics saw his own poetry as being. But now the times are grim:

> If they throw stones upon the roof
> While you practice arpeggios,
> It is because they carry down the stairs
> A body in rags.

Clearly, this is no time for practicing arpeggios. Even if the poet seated at the piano—Stevens himself, of course—wants to keep doing so (or keep writing the playful poems of *Harmonium*), the times won't let him: the crowd is throwing stones upon the roof. The speaker therefore urges the poet: "Play the present" with all its cheapness and vulgarity, and, in response to "the body in rags," to "Strike the piercing chord," to be "The voice of angry fear, / The voice of this besieging pain."[25] Running all through this grudging recognition of the deteriorating present is regret for the lost Mozartian past, a past when art could be "pure" and the artist untroubled by his times: "He was young, and we, we are old." But the poem ends in a clear assertion that the poet must somehow respond to the times, must indeed become its voice: "The snow is falling / And the streets are full of cries. Be seated, thou." It is fitting that Stevens published this poem in a magazine once politically liberal, now radical under Malcolm Cowley's aegis, *The New Republic*.[26]

In "Mozart, 1935" Stevens recognizes that art can no longer be "pure," detached from ephemeral reality, that poetry—his poetry—must change with and in some meaningful way respond to its time, even when those times are hateful and ugly. He expressed the same sentiments in a letter to Latimer: "When *Harmonium* was in the making . . . I then believed in *pure poetry*, as it was called. I still have a distinct liking for that sort of thing. But we live in a different time, and life means a good deal more to us now-a-days than literature does. In the period of which I have just spoken, I thought literature meant most. Moreover, I am not so sure that I don't think exactly the same thing now, but, unquestionably, I think at the same time that life is the essential part of literature" (October 31, 1935, *Letters* 288, Stevens's emphasis).

Stevens's willingness at least to recognize this "different time" partly explains one of his most astonishing declarations in another letter to Latimer a few weeks earlier: "I hope I am headed left, but there are lefts and lefts, and certainly I am not headed for the ghastly left of [*New*] *Masses*." He continues: "These professionals lament in a way that would have given Job a fever. . . . *Masses* is just one more wailing place and the whole left now-a-days is a mob of wailers. I do very much believe in leftism in every direction, even in wailing. These people go about it in such a way that nobody listens to them except themselves, and that is a[t] least one reason why they get nowhere. They have the most magnificent cause in the world" (October 9, 1935, *Letters* 286–87). What a tangle of contradictions! The "whole left" is "a mob of wailers" and thus will "get nowhere"; but "they have the most magnificent cause in the world" and "I do very much believe in leftism *in every direction* even in wailing" (emphasis added).

Whatever Stevens could have meant by "leftism in every direction," he was clearly unwilling to choose the communist direction, as he declared in several letters to Latimer; for example: "So that there may be no doubt about it, let me say that I believe in what Mr. Filene calls 'up-to-date capitalism.' I don't believe in Communism" (November 5, 1935, *Letters* 292).[27] Two other statements by Stevens in his letters further clarify his views of Marxism. In a letter to Latimer dated March 17, 1936, he writes:

> For my own part, I believe in social reform and not in social revolution. From the point of view of social revolution, *Ideas of Order* is a book of the most otiose prettiness; and it is probably quite inadequate from any social point of view. However, I am not a propagandist. Conceding that the social situation is the most absorbing thing in the world today, and that those phases of it that you and I regret as merely violent have a strong chance of prevailing in the long run, because what now exists is so depleted, . . . it is not possible for me, honestly, to take the point of view of a poet just out of school. (*Letters* 309)

What immediately prompted this passage—and Stevens's unjustly harsh assessment of *Ideas of Order*—was a stinging review of the book by the English critic Geoffrey Grigson (discussed below). The review's title reflects Grigson's contempt: "A Stuffed Goldfinch."[28] In this letter, Stevens dismissed Grigson as "a propagandist. His group is interested in the social revolution, if a social revolution may be said to be going on."

Four years later, Stevens refined and elaborated his political self-assessment in response to being located "on the right" by Hi Simons (a scholar who had replaced Latimer as Stevens's chief literary correspondent): "Of course, I believe in any number of things that so-called social revolutionists believe in, but I don't believe in calling myself a revolutionist simply because I believe in doing everything practically possible to improve the condition of the workers, and because I believe in education as the source of freedom and power, and because I regret that we have not experimented a little more extensively in public ownership of public utilities." He continues: "What really divides men into political classes in respect to these things is not the degree to which they believe in them but the ways and means of putting their beliefs into effect. There are a lot of things that the workers are doing that I do not believe in, even though, as the same time, I want certainly as ardently as they do to see them able to live decently.... I think this explains my rightism." Acknowledging that "it is nonsense to quibble about" political labels like left and right, he adds: "If right means in common use what I say it means, then the leftism of common use is something that I'm definitely not interested in" (January 12, 1940, *Letters* 350).

Without question, Stevens was somewhat confused by these labels; otherwise, he never would have entertained for an instant Simons's characterization of him as being on the right—or in declaring to Latimer that he hoped he was "headed left."[29] Oddly, he never uses the term that best seems to identify his political views: liberal. But even with this confusion, Stevens had interesting things to say about Marxism. Latimer had asked him "whether I feel there is an essential conflict between Marxism and the sentiment of the marvelous." Stevens replied:

> I think we all feel that there is a conflict between the rise of the lower class, with all its realities, and the indulgences of an upper class.... My conclusion is that, while there is a conflict, it is not an essential conflict.... [It is] temporary. *The only possible order of life is one in which all order is incessantly changing.* Marxism may or may not destroy the existing sentiment of the marvelous; if it does, it will create another. It was a very common fear that Socialism would dirty the world ... [likewise Communism]. I think that this is all nonsense. Of course, that would be the immediate effect, as any upheaval results in disorder. (November 5, 1935, *Letters* 291–92, emphasis added)

This sense of inevitable change and the temporary "dirtiness" of social upheaval directly informs the poem Stevens was working on at the time he wrote Latimer, "Mr. Burnshaw and the Statue." Stanley Burnshaw, literary reviewer for *New Masses,* had provoked this poetic response with his review of *Ideas of Order.* Before we discuss that review, and the others concerning *Ideas,* one other motivation for Stevens's leftward shift should be noted. When Burnshaw's review appeared in *New Masses,* Stevens's response (conveyed to Latimer) was quite temperate—and revealing: "The review in *Masses* was a most interesting review, because it placed me in a new setting" (October 9, 1935, *Letters* 286). Although "new setting" can refer to the social-class perspective Burnshaw applies to Stevens's poetry, it also means simply the *New Masses* itself, the most radical and venerable of the many far-left magazines and, for the political mid-thirties, the tip of the new avant-garde. Despite his denigration of the magazine as "one more wailing place," Stevens liked being associated with it. In the letter describing his pro-Filene views, he adds ambiguously: "It is an extraordinary experience for myself to deal with a thing like Communism." Although his next sentence makes this "dealing" sound like an unpleasant necessity—"Nevertheless, one has to live and think in the actual world" (November 5, 1935, *Letters* 292)—I think "extraordinary experience" also has a positive meaning. A letter to Latimer a few weeks later in almost the same language confirms this surmise. Referring to Latimer's sending *Ideas of Order* to the *New Masses,* Stevens writes: "Merely finding myself in that *milieu* was an extraordinarily stimulating thing" (November 21, 1935, *Letters* 296). Though fully aware of his political differences with the *New Masses,* he enjoyed being connected with this center of the radical movement, just as William Carlos Williams and many other modernists did. If the magazine was condescending to his book (I will argue below that it was not), it was at least paying attention to him. The same frisson could be said for his association with Latimer and Alcestis Press. He certainly knew that the press published politically radical poets; in fact, the fourth (and last) issue of the *Quarterly* was a "Revolutionary Number" comprising "strictly revolutionary" poets selected by Latimer's communist associate Willard Mass. Stevens also received other books published by Alcestis Press, such as Ruth Lechlitner's "unapologetically radical" *Tomorrow's Phoenix,* which he apparently enjoyed (Filreis 126–27, 132–33). For a poet whose audience had previously been a relatively small and self-selected group of aesthetes and fanciers of modernism, this new linkage to the contemporary, radical avant-garde, and to a group of younger poets, must indeed have seemed "extraordinarily stimulating."[30]

REVIEWS OF *IDEAS OF ORDER*

Reviewers disagreed on whether *Ideas of Order* marked a change from Stevens's earlier work and on how much (if at all) Stevens brought the contemporary world into his new work. Leftist reviewers were highly skeptical. Before the book was published, but after several of its prominent poems had appeared in magazines, Edwin Rolfe pronounced a eulogy in *Partisan Review:* "Wallace Stevens is remembered by *Harmonium;* he is no longer a living poet."[31] Babette Deutsch felt that Stevens's world in the new book was still essentially hermetic. Though she concedes, "There are moments when the present intrudes, as in 'Sad Strains of a Gay Waltz.' . . . [o]r again, in 'Mozart, 1935,'" she nonetheless concludes: "Stevens is not concerned with the present. He is too much engrossed with what is present particularly to himself. If one comes to these verses with a raw sense of the times in which we live . . . their delicate aloofness may offend."[32]

Other leftist reviewers echoed Deutsch's complaint about Stevens's self-involvement. Isador Schneider, reviewing the Knopf edition, found that the "ideas" alluded to by the title "are neither clear nor stated with much conviction." Though he admired Stevens's craftsmanship, Schneider found the poetry lacking in "significant content."[33] Theodore Roethke, in a one-paragraph notice in *The New Republic,* noted changes in Stevens's style ("the colors are less exotic, the associations less strange than in *Harmonium*"); but Roethke nonetheless regrets that Stevens's sensibility was still "content with the order of words and music, and [did] not project itself more vigorously upon the present-day world."[34]

By contrast, F. O. Matthiessen and John Holmes credited Stevens with "a mature apprehension of actual society" (Matthiessen) and noted that "recent moods of the real world have affected him" (Holmes). Matthiessen was especially laudatory, calling *Ideas of Order* "the nearest approach to major poetry being made in this country to-day" and recommending the book for a Pulitzer Prize. William Rose Benét, on the other hand, still typed Stevens as "a virtuoso and voluptuary of language."[35] The most ruthless review was Geoffrey Grigson's, which dismissed the book as another *Harmonium* with "less panache, periwinkle, cantilena, fewer melons and peacocks, but still the finicking privateer . . . observing nothing, single artificer of his own world of mannerism. . . . Too much Wallace Stevens, too little everything else" (18).[36]

If Grigson's review mildly irked Stevens (see *Letters* 309), it was Burnshaw's review in *New Masses* that really got to him.[37] That review, Stevens's poetic response to it in *Owl's Clover,* and Burnshaw's 1961 commentary and reprint of his review in the *Sewanee Review* have all been bundled in literary history, and no Stevens biographer or scholar omits this mini-chapter in his career.[38] But the affair is often misrepresented as a hostile action and reaction,[39] when, in fact, it was far less acrimonious than that on both sides. Though he does belittle *Harmonium,* Burnshaw does not attack *Ideas of Order;* rather, he construes it within a theory he was then developing of "middle ground" (i.e., bourgeois) writers anxiously teetering between left and right.[40] In turn, Stevens's "Mr. Burnshaw and the Statue" does not ridicule the critic—it mentions him only once and then quite obliquely—but rather responds, quite abstractly, to the Marxist philosophy Burnshaw represents from a sympathetic, but non-Marxian perspective. As Stevens explained to Latimer after finishing the poem: "You will remember that Mr. Burnshaw applied the point of view of the practical Communist to *Ideas of Order*. I have tried to reverse the process: that is to say, apply the point of view of a poet to Communism" (October 31, 1935, *Letters* 289).

Burnshaw admitted in his 1961 article "Wallace Stevens and the Statue" that when he reviewed Stevens's book he was young and somewhat in awe of the poet, still unsure of many poems in *Harmonium*. Nothing of that awe or uncertainty comes through in his 1935 review, however, for, as he also concedes, "tentativeness and humility were unthinkable [in a *New Masses* review]....A too-temperate stance was simply a foolish timidity."[41] Applying the radical jargon of the day, Burnshaw 1935 calls Stevens's new poetry "confused" but recognizes how much it changed from *Harmonium*. That book was "mainly sense poetry" and "is the kind of verse that people concerned with the murderous world collapse can hardly swallow today except in tiny doses." But Burnshaw accurately observes that "it is verse that Stevens can no longer write. His harmonious cosmos is suddenly screeching with confusion. *Ideas of Order* is the record of a man who, having lost his footing, now scrambles to stand up and keep his balance" (365). Of course, from the Marxist perspective of "'Middle-Ground' Writers" this confusion and scrambling proceeds inevitably from Stevens's socio-economic class: "Acutely conscious members of a class menaced by the clashes between capital and labor, these writers [Stevens and Haniel Long] are in the throes of struggle for philosophical adjustment. And their words have intense value and meaning to the sectors within the class whose confusions they articulate" (366).

Allowing for the clichéd Marxist rhetoric, is this assessment of Stevens really off base? Weren't his latest political interest ("headed left") and his socioeconomic status in conflict? And doesn't his questionable usage of "left" and "right" betray the confusion of someone heading into unfamiliar waters? Finally, don't poems like "Mozart, 1935" express a deeply conflicted attitude toward the poet's role in the present? Given this evidence, Burnshaw's conclusion that Stevens was seeking "philosophical adjustment" was spot-on.

Burnshaw concludes that Stevens's new poems "have intense value and meaning" not just for others of his class, conflicted like himself, but "for us as well"—that is, for radicals or at least for the staff and readers of *New Masses*. Further, for Stevens to "sweep his contradictory notions into a valid Idea of Order" depends on a "full realization of the alternatives" facing him as an artist (366). Though it comes directly from Burnshaw's theory expounded in "'Middle-Ground' Writers," this prediction has validity for Stevens: he was to struggle with his own "alternatives" over the next few years. The "alternatives" Burnshaw alludes to are fascism and communism; Stevens's alternatives approximated whether or not to abandon the concept of pure poetry and change his rhetoric and style to reflect the social shift toward collectivism. Given the acuteness and generally favorable assessment in Burnshaw's review, it is not surprising that Stevens called it "most interesting." What *is* surprising is that it impelled him to write his own complex response in a long poem that subsequently became part of a book of long poems, *Owl's Clover.*

STATUES, MR. BURNSHAW, AND *OWL'S CLOVER*

Stevens was quite clear about his intentions in writing "Mr. Burnshaw and the Statue," the second of the five poems in *Owl's Clover* (*CPP* 570–75). Besides his remark about it presenting "the point of view of a poet to Communism," he also described it to Latimer as "simply a general and rather vaguely poetic justification of leftism" (November 15, 1935, *Letters* 295). But a "justification" on Stevens's terms—he was not about to start writing propaganda or in a proletarian style that abandoned the complexity of his imagery and tone. Quite the contrary, *Owl's Clover* is, arguably, his most opaque collection of poems—clarity of intention did not translate into clarity of argument. (Fortunately, however, Stevens provided detailed explications of it to Latimer and, later, to Hi Simons.) It is also a book that both Stevens and most of his later critics judged a failure. After lopping off large sections of it for its inclusion in *The Man with the Blue Guitar,* Stevens later omitted it entirely from the 1954 *Collected Poems.* But it is an essential work of his political period, and I wish to consider "Mr. Burnshaw" in detail as emblematic of the book's conflicted themes, images, and perspectives.

Stevens began writing "Mr. Burnshaw" in October 1935, immediately after Burnshaw's review appeared in *New Masses* on October 1. He finished it by the end of the month and announced it to Latimer, adding that he wished to "illustrate by a poem which might seem largely gaseous the sort of contact that I make with normal ideas" (October 31, 1935, *Letters* 289). "Normal ideas" in this case are political ideas, specifically Marxian. Yet, he also acknowledges using "a good many stock figures" that make the poem seem "most un-Burnshawesque"—an indirect way of saying that his abstruse rhetoric made no concessions to proletarian style, even if his subject and themes had changed. Symbols—"stock figures"—would carry much of the poem's burden.

The central symbol of "Mr. Burnshaw"—and of *Owl's Clover* as a whole—

is a marble statue of horses seemingly in motion. Stevens was somewhat contradictory, however, about what the statue symbolized. In a letter to Latimer dated November 5, 1935, he stated it was a symbol of "art" (an abstraction he disliked using, he said), but more specifically, "it is a symbol of things as they are" (*Letters* 290). Four years later, after he had drastically cut *Owl's Clover* for *Blue Guitar,* he viewed the symbol even more broadly in an unpublished prefatory note to the Burnshaw poem: "[T]he statue is regarded not as a symbol of art, but as a manifestation of the civilization of which it is a part. It is irrelevant, hence dead, a dead thing in a dead time. It will be replaced, as part of incessant change."[42]

The beginning of "Mr. Burnshaw and the Statue" supports the second explication:

> The thing is dead . . . Everything is dead
> Except the future. . . .
>   except what ought to be,
> All things destroy themselves or are destroyed. (*CPP* 570)

The perspective—more precisely, the voice—here is clearly Marxian, probably Burnshaw's: destroy the corrupt present (capitalism and the decadent art it breeds) in order to remake the future completely. The first section condemns the sculpture as "a thing / Of the dank imagination, much below / Our crusted outlines hot and huge with fact." But here Stevens begins to undercut the voice with irony: "crusted outlines hot and huge with fact" describes Marxian plans for the future in unpleasant images of ponderous materialism. Conversely, the condemned horses "go clattering / Along the thin horizons, nobly more / Than this jotting-down of the sculptor's foppishness"—an image of the fugitive imagination.[43]

Parts II and IV shift the mode to an invocation of "celestial paramours" to chant "requiems for this effigy."[44] As muses, their function is to reconcile us to the new order, to align past ("autumn sheens") and future ("glistening serpentines") in order "to diffuse the new day" (*Letters* 367). Part IV, however, again undercuts that future, as the paramours usher in

>   a place
> Of fear before the disorder of the strange,
> A time in which the poets' politics
> Will rule in a poets' world. Yet that will be
> A world impossible for poets, who

Complain and prophesy, in their complaints,
And are never of the world in which they live. (572)

The self-referential quality of these lines is hard to ignore. The immediate future promises that a poet's politics—obviously Marxian and con-
trolling all aesthetic questions—will dominate. But since poets "are never
of the world in which they live"—as Stevens felt he could not be fully of
the world (at least in the *Harmonium* years)—how can this materialist vision rule? Stevens here cannot quite bring himself to abandon the older,
romantic image of the poet as outsider and visionary (rather than social
propagandist).[45] He reconciles the dilemma rather limply by urging the
"mesdames" (who now morph into poets) to "Disclose the rude and ruddy
at their jobs"—that is, write proletarian poetry—and by suggesting that
the traditional poetic images (peacocks, ploughman, doves) must change,
and that the "vast disorder" these images must now reside in "may, / So
seen, have an order of its own, a peace."
   But as he tells the "mesdames" in part VI, "it is not enough to be rec-
onciled / Before the strange. . . . It is only enough / To live incessantly
in change. . . . So great a change / Is constant. The time you call serene
descends / Through a moving chaos that never ends." And like the poets
who "may" find a new order in the disorder, "change" for the mesdames
"composes, too, and chaos comes / To momentary calm." The speaker here
addresses himself as well as the mesdames:

                    Shall you
      Then, fear a drastic community evolved
      From the whirling, slowly and by trial; or fear
      Men gathering for a mighty flight of men,
      An abysmal migration into a possible blue? (572)

This is a central theme, as Stevens later explained: "What this poem is concerned with is adaptation to change. . . . It is impossible to be truly recon-
ciled, if one romanticizes the past (ploughman, peacocks, doves). Nor is
one a part of the oncoming future, if one enters it with indifference (fa-
talism), traceable to a sense of its impermanence. . . . What is necessary is
to recognize change as constant" (*Letters* 367).
   What will this changing world of "The Mass" look like? In part V
Stevens presents a memorably hideous image to replace the obsolete statue:
a "gigantic solitary urn, / A trash can at the end of the world"[46] where
"buzzards . . . eat the bellies of the rich." But, once again, the speaker of-

fers an ironic hope that, as the world moves "out of the hopeless waste of the past / Into a hopeful waste to come,"

> even
> The colorless light in which this wreckage lies
> Has faint portentous lustres, shades and shapes
> Of rose, or what will once more rise to rose,
> When younger bodies, because they are younger, rise
> And chant the rose-points of their birth, and when
> For a little time, again, rose-breasted birds
> Sing rose beliefs. (573)

Put less poetically, what the masses trash today may arise, phoenix-like, into something beautiful tomorrow, even if it is politically pink and idealistic ("rose beliefs"). This qualified hope provides the poem's only attractive images: "rose-breasted birds / Sing rose beliefs."

The poem concludes with the mesdames dancing (recalling the wild witches' dance concluding Berlioz's *Symphonie fantastique*), while the "vivid . . . statue falls, / The heads are severed." In place of the marble horses, the speaker urges the muses to "Conceive . . . marble men" and

> make real the attitudes
> Appointed for them and that the pediment
> Bears words that are the speech of marble men. (575)

The undercutting irony here of marble shifted from art to statist propaganda (marble men, marble words) is difficult to ignore. And the words etched in the pediment of the new statues—"the speech of marble men"— are appropriately clunky: "*The Mass / Appoints These Marbles Of Itself To Be / Itself*" (Stevens's emphasis). Yet, the closing lines equivocally suggest that only

> when, at last, you are yourselves,
> Speaking and strutting broadly, fair and bloomed,
> No longer of air but of the breathing earth

does the change running all through the poem reach a kind of apotheosis:

> the pale
> Pitched into swelling bodies, upward, drift

In a storm blown into glittering shapes, and flames
Wind-beaten into freshest, brightest fire. (575)

At once, the fire and light images suggest spiritual transfiguration and apoca-
lypse.

In sum, the poem portrays Stevens at his most conflicted: desiring to
change, recognizing that change is incessant and inevitable, but still clearly
uncomfortable with where the change is going and what it will produce.
Between the destruction of the old aesthetics and the chaos and ugliness of
the new, he can posit only the *hope* that disorder will yield a new order and
peace; that the whirling will come to rest at a still point; that the trashcan
ugliness of "The Mass" will one day produce "rose-breasted birds"; that
"abysmal migrations" may become flights into "a possible blue"; that the
"freshest, brightest fire" will "refine them" (in Dante's image), not destroy
them. Pretty thin gruel. Where the poet fits into this new order, besides
simply recognizing and proclaiming that change is inevitable, is extremely
problematic—at least for a poet who refuses to become a propagandist. The
concluding image of marble men frozen above pseudo-profound words on
marble pediments recalls, by contrast, the delightfully irreverent mice running
up and down another statue ("The Founder of the State") in "Dance of
the Macabre Mice," written only a year before "Mr. Burnshaw." Similarly,
the "severed" heads of the obsolete marble horses eerily echo the guillo-
tined heads falling during the Terror of the French Revolution—violence
that so often accompanies a social revolution. It is not that Stevens is writing in bad faith, but rather that he is trying to convince himself of something that, in his heart of hearts, he doesn't really believe. This poem can
be construed as a "justification of leftism" only in Stevens's special sense
of "left"—*his* left—which translates roughly into "accept the necessity of
change—even radically leftist change; adjust yourself to it; live 'incessantly'
in it; and hope for the best."

CRITICAL RESPONSE TO *OWL'S CLOVER*

Leftist critics who reviewed *Owl's Clover* were divided as to whether the
book marked a definite leftward shift in Stevens's aesthetics; they concurred, however, on the difficulty of its rhetoric. Marxist poet and critic
Ruth Lechlitner doubted that Stevens had changed much and felt that the
book continued his belief that imagination "must be considered as an individual as opposed to a mass or collective concept." The former "achieves
the 'order' of solitude: the plural or mass, represents chaos." Observing that

Stevens "shudders at a time when politics will rule a poet's world," Lechlitner concludes with a touch of menace: "By recognizing the importance of political and social change but refusing to admit the desirability of the union of the mass in an 'orderly' life, Stevens is obviously open to attack from the left."[47] When Stevens read this review, he joked to Latimer: "We are all much disturbed about a possible attack from the Left; I expect the house to be burned down almost any moment" (*Letters* 313).

Eda Lou Walton, reviewing in the *New York Times,* was more generous in crediting Stevens's efforts to address social themes: "He is trying to evaluate the position of the artist in a world of struggle, of action. If this means, for a time, that his poetry is less surely perfect, it means also that his later poetry may be more significant than his earlier work." Like Burnshaw, Walton recognizes that "[h]e is, in a way, arguing with himself" and that the results are not easy to follow: "Stevens . . . finds it exceedingly difficult to speak directly." Nonetheless, she declares that "Stevens is undoubtedly one of our best poets."[48]

Ben Belitt, writing in *The Nation,* also recognizes Stevens's shift but is more critical of the results. Noting that *Ideas of Order* begins a new "poetry of statement," he continues: "In 'Mr. Burnshaw and the Statue' where one is compelled to acknowledge a symbolic function, it is only very painfully that the meanings can be narrowed down from vaguely political contexts to an unclear gospel of living 'incessantly in change' in the stream of contemporary experience." Belitt is particularly critical of the book's opaque rhetoric and lack of fluidity: "Doubtless, the same incongruities which induce [Stevens] to address political reflections to imaginary 'Mesdames' in terms of statuary and the pastoral dance recur to clot his rhetoric with gingerbread and stand in the way of a thoughtful wiriness."[49] That Stevens complimented Belitt on this review is an index of the poet's equanimity—or uncertainty:

> Your review indicates that you are a most conscientious person. . . .
>
> The only thing wrong with the review is that it may mean more to me than to any other person. Life cancels poetry with such rapidity that it keeps one rather breathless. What I tried to do in *Owl's Clover* was to dip aspects of the contemporaneous in the poetic. You seem to think that I have produced a lot of Easter eggs, and perhaps I have. . . .
>
> When you pointed out my difficulty in the second sentence of your review,[50] it is a difficulty that I have long been conscious of and

with which I am constantly struggling. Your review helps. (December 12, 1936, *Letters* 314)

More reviews would mention *Owl's Clover* when it was reprinted (in cut version) in *Blue Guitar*. But even then, several leftist reviewers—Stanley Burnshaw, Isador Schneider, Babette Deutsch, Rolfe Humphries—remained silent, perhaps damning Stevens's efforts more effectively than words could have. And once the published reviews are sifted for their particular biases pro or con, they seem to agree that, though well intentioned, *Owl's Clover* is a failure as social poetry and as Stevens's poetry.[51] As he wrote to Ben Belitt, he was aware of the problem of his discourse. Stevens's next major poem would directly address this problem—and clarify his political-artistic philosophy.

"THE MAN WITH THE BLUE GUITAR": "A WRANGLING OF TWO DREAMS"

When *The Man with the Blue Guitar and Other Poems* appeared in October 1937, it contained the following note by the poet on the dust jacket:

> In one group, *Owl's Clover*, while the poems reflect what was then going on in the world, that reflection is merely for the purpose of seizing and stating what makes life intelligible and desirable in the midst of great change and great confusion. The effect of *Owl's Clover* is to emphasize the opposition between things as they are and things imagined; in short, to isolate poetry.
>
> Since this is of significance, if we are entering a period in which poetry may be of first importance to the spirit, I have been making notes on the subject in the form of short poems during the past winter. These short poems, some thirty of them, form the other group, *The Man with the Blue Guitar*, from which the book takes its title. This group deals with the incessant conjunctions between things as they are and things imagined. Although the blue guitar is a symbol of the imagination, it is used most often simply as a reference to the individuality of the poet, meaning by the poet any man of imagination. (*CPP* 998)

In one important respect, I think that Stevens misrepresents "Blue Guitar": even more than does *Owl's Clover*, it *opposes*, rather than conjoins, "things as they are" and "things imagined." Though there are moments of convergence, notably in the concluding section, the poem is mostly a protracted debate between plural "they," demanding that the artist "must" play "things exactly as they are" (part I), and singular "I" or "he," the artist, who questions and resists their demands, defending the supremacy of his creative imagination. Complicating this opposition, the speaker-artist at times appropriates "their" voice, for example, in part VI, debating with himself. That the artist speaks for Stevens is self-evident. But that the poem represents a repudiation of Stevens's efforts to accommodate leftist aesthetics requires support, since this reading contradicts his statement above.

First, the artist is singular, "the man" in part I, while "they" are the collective voice—and pressure—of the times: the critics and writers espousing leftist aesthetics, the masses they presume to represent, "a million people on one string" (IV). The world "they" live in and the art they demand are depicted as unrelentingly ugly, tinny and two-dimensional. Playing "things as they are" means man must be analyzed ruthlessly. The speaker reflects: "To lay his brain upon the board / And pick the acrid colors out, // To nail his thought across the door . . . So that's life, then: things as they are?" (III–IV). This analytical emphasis is precisely what the guitarist finally rejects in the exhortations of XXXII: "Throw away the lights, the definitions, . . . the rotted names." Feelings—what Stevens called "the irrational" in his lecture at Harvard (see below)—trump rationality and analytical thinking for the artist: "The feelings crazily, craftily call, / Like a buzzing of flies in autumn air" (IV).[52]

Their artist must propagandize for the Left (a far cry from presenting things as they are): "Raise reddest columns. Toll a bell / And clap the hollows full of tin" (X). And the columns and bell—like the statue of marble men in "Mr. Burnshaw"—celebrate a false god, "him whom none believes, / Whom all believe that all believe" (X). Whether it is Stalin or Roosevelt does not finally matter; as false messiah, he is the guitarist's "adversary" to be ridiculed with "hoo-ing" trombones.[53]

Even their view of the natural world is flat: "There are no shadows in our sun . . . There are no shadows anywhere. / The earth, for us, is flat and bare. / There are no shadows" (V). In "Sad Strains of a Gay Waltz," Stevens used "shadows" to suggest the artistic dimension and depth that the outmoded waltz now lacked: "the waltz / Is no longer a mode of desire, a mode / Of revealing desire and is empty of shadows." By contrast, the necessary "skeptical music" of the future "Will be motion and full of shadows" (*CPP* 100–101). Now, however, Stevens is less sanguine about collectivistic art possessing depth and dimension. Continuing a central theme of *Owl's Clover,* the images of an outmoded romanticism will no longer serve in the present chaos: "There is no place, / Here, for the lark fixed in the mind, / In the museum of the sky." The new birds "shriek" and "claw sleep" where "Morning is not sun" (XXXI).

Finally, *their* audience, the "men that live in the land" are "Without shadows, without magnificence" (XXI). Their dreams are stunted, mired: "That generation's dream, aviled / In the mud, in Monday's dirty light, // That's it, the only dream they knew" (XXXIII). In "Sad Strains of a Gay Waltz," Stevens looks more carefully at the "sudden mobs of men":

> These voices crying without knowing for what,
> Except to be happy, without knowing how,
> Imposing forms they cannot describe,
> Requiring order beyond their speech.

By contrast, the artist's world is "washed in his imagination" (XXVI) so that "Things as they are / Are *changed* upon the blue guitar" (I, emphasis added). Though he lives in the everyday world and draws his strength from it—"Here I inhale profounder strength / And as I am, I speak and move" (XXVIII)—he is its sole artificer: "The whirling noise // Of a multitude dwindles, all said, / To his breath that lies awake at night" (XII).

Strengthening his imagination, "It is the sun that shares our works" (VII), as it always did for Stevens;[54] likewise, "It is the sea that whitens the roof"—a perfect imagistic fusion of realism (sea salt whitening the roof) and the imagination (XXVII). Harkening back to the Stevens of *Harmonium,* the speaker can delight purely in the senses—

> Tom-tom, c'est moi. The blue guitar
> And I are one (XII)

> To meet that hawk's eye and to flinch

> Not at the eye but at the joy of it.
> I play. But this is what I think. (XXIV)

> Sombre as fir trees, liquid cats
> Moved in the grass without a sound. (XXV)

—pleasures that "they" would find bourgeois extravagance.

The poet's subjectivity is inextricably linked to and strengthens his transformative vision. Stevens called this subjectivity "irrationality" in his Harvard lecture, delivered in December 1936, while he was working on "Blue Guitar":

> In an age as harsh as it is intelligent, phrases about the unknown are quickly dismissed. . . . That the unknown as the source of knowledge, as the object of thought, is part of the dynamics of the known does not permit of denial. It is the unknown that excites the ardor of scholars, who, in the known alone, would shrivel up with boredom. . . . [W]hen so considered, [the unknown] has seductions more powerful and more profound than those of the known.
>
> Just so, there are those who, having never yet been convinced that the rational has quite made us divine, are willing to assume the efficacy of the irrational. . . . [The surrealist poets, for example, have] made it possible for us to read poetry that seems filled with gaiety and youth, just when we were beginning to despair of gaiety and youth. ("The Irrational Element in Poetry," *CPP* 791)[55]

This same "irrationality" appears in the dream imagery of parts XVIII and XXVI:

> A dream (to call it a dream) in which
> I can believe, in the face of the object,
>
> A dream no longer a dream, a thing
> Of things as they are, as the blue guitar. (XVIII)
>
> The world washed in his imagination,
> The world was a shore, whether sound or form
>
> Or light, . . .
>
> To which his imagination returned,
> From which it sped, a bar in space,
>
> Sand heaped in the clouds, giant that fought
> Against the murderous alphabet:
>
> The swarm of thoughts, the swarm of dreams
> Of inaccessible Utopia. (XXVI)

The "giant" of the artist's imagination fights their "inaccessible Utopia" that is fed by "swarms" (hideous word!) of dreams and thoughts, and described by a "murderous" alphabet, whether the Communists' (CPUSA, GPU, PUOM, etc.) or even the New Deal's (NRA, AAA, WPA, etc.). Thus, the "wrangling of two dreams": the Utopian dreams of the Marxists and the dream*ing* so necessary for the guitarist to realize his art (XXXIII).

Precisely their urge to abstract and categorize (men become masses, dreams become Utopia or reduce themselves to systems that acquire a "murderous alphabet")—deviations from presenting "things as they are"—is what the speaker opposes, as he urges "them" in the penultimate stanza to

> Throw away the lights, the definitions
> And say of what you see in the dark . . .
>
> But do not use the rotted names.
>
> How should you walk in that space and know
> Nothing of the madness of space,
>
> Nothing of its jocular procreations?
> Throw the lights away. Nothing must stand
>
> Between you and the shapes you take
> When the crust of shape has been destroyed.

Here, Stevens sounds very much like E. E. Cummings, inveighing against the abstractions of science and "mostpeople." Only once their "crusted" abstractions[56] are shattered can "they" live authentically and spontaneously:

> You as you are? You are yourself.
> The blue guitar surprises you. (XXXII)

"You are yourself" echoes the concluding fiery transformation of "Mr. Burnshaw and the Statue" "when, at last, you are yourselves." But the guitarist is no didact: he expresses self-doubts in several places (e.g., IX and XV). And, as noted above, there are several passages in "Blue Guitar" in which the artist's situation and "theirs" converge. Part V, for example, is spoken in "their" voice ("The earth, for us, is flat and bare. / There are no shadows."), but its concluding images paraphrase "A High-Toned Old Christian Woman" and "Sunday Morning":

> Exceeding music must take the place
> Of empty heaven and its hymns,
>
> Ourselves in poetry must take their place,
> Even in the chattering of *your* guitar. (V, emphasis added)

Both the artist and "they" must inhabit a world that is never at rest. The "demon" of ceaseless change (XXVII), who "cannot be himself" and so is satirized by nature's solidity (the iceberg), can be as much the artist's own as "theirs": the balance he achieves "does not quite rest" (XXIX). An index of this endlessly "shifting scene" is a world now witnessing war in Spain: "alive with creeping men" and tanks—"mechanical beetles" (VII).

The most important convergence occurs in the last section. Immediately following the "wrangling of two dreams," the voice and mode suddenly shift, acquiring the lilt of a priest giving communion:

> Here is the bread of time to come,
>
> Here is its actual stone.

The speaker unifies "they" and "I" into "we" and "our," continuing the priestly prophecy:

> The bread
> Will be our bread, the stone will be
>
> Our bed and we shall sleep by night.
> We shall forget the day

Though he seems to accept the Marxian promise that today's pain ("the stone") will yield tomorrow's bread and that living in the real means becoming oblivious to the actual ("sleep by night / forget by day"), "except" turns the poem's direction, and he concludes by affirming the power of the imagination, *his* value, now transmuted into "we":

> except
>
> The moments when we choose to play
> The imagined pine, the imagined jay. (XXXIII)

As Stevens put it so eloquently a few years later: "I think [the poet's] function is to make his imagination theirs and that he fulfills himself only as
he sees his imagination become the light in the minds of others."[57]

"The Man with the Blue Guitar" thus marks a major shift in Stevens's
work, politically, thematically, and stylistically. Politically, he has pretty
much given up trying to approach the world from a quasi-Marxist perspective: his ringing affirmation of the artist's imagination here has replaced his uneasy acknowledgment in *Owl's Clover* that the old art and
aesthetic attitudes must be destroyed, the new, ugly world of incessant
change welcomed with the hope that it will one day produce a pleasing
order. Thematically, he has located what will prove his major theme for
the rest of his career: the role of the imagination in a world bereft of the
old myths. And his style has undergone a remarkable clarifying, from the
ponderous, semi-opaque symbols and turgid rhetoric of *Owl's Clover* to
the tight stanzas, pungent rhymes, and airy, even playful lucidity of "The
Man with the Blue Guitar."

CRITICAL RESPONSE TO *BLUE GUITAR*

The relatively few reviewers of *The Man with the Blue Guitar* were again divided about that poem, but not about the revised "Owl's Clover." William
Carlos Williams, writing in *The New Republic,* felt that the book did not
justify the rumor that "Stevens has turned of late definitely to the left."
Oddly, Williams made no distinction between "Blue Guitar" and "Owl's
Clover" in this regard. He praised the former for its lyricism, but sharply
criticized "Owl's Clover" for its "turgidity, dullness, and a language . . .
[that is] certainly nothing anybody alive today could ever recognize."[58]

Eda Lou Walton, who always admired Stevens's poetry, felt that "the
collection is a distinct advance in Stevens' work," but based her judgment
on the questionable assumption that "[h]e has forsaken any desire to devote
himself to building beauty apart from life."[59] Ruth Lechlitner, who had
excoriated *Owl's Clover,* was now purring about *Blue Guitar:* "His suave
mutations in component rhythms are a delight to the ear; . . . His satire is
never heavy. . . . There are touches . . . of his earlier happy humor." Praising "Romanesque Affabulation" (in "A Thought Revolved") as "a model
of modern poetic technique," she concludes: "As a master of form Wallace
Stevens . . . should be studied by all aspirants to the art."[60]

Horace Gregory, on the other hand, felt Stevens's work had fallen off as
Stevens became more political (perhaps it would be fairer to say: as *Gregory*

became more political, as a poetry editor of *New Masses*): "Today his vision has the same qualities of sharpness [as in the 1931 *Harmonium*], but is now dimmed by the effort to explain his 'position' in a medium ill-suited to the demands of exposition."[61] Dorothy Van Ghent, writing on several modernist poets in *New Masses,* echoes this view; and like Gregory (in his review of the 1931 *Harmonium*), she tries to turn Stevens into a critic of materialistic accumulation and the decadence of imagination.[62] Selden Rodman was even more absolute in rejecting the book: "[His] best work seems to lie behind him, for *The Man with the Blue Guitar* is pretty thin stuff." Curiously, however, Rodman's rationale is that Stevens is too abstract: "[T]his poet's work would profit from a choice of subject that might force him closer to the good earth."[63]

Samuel French Morse, a non-leftist critic who later became a major Stevens scholar, and edited *Opus Posthumous,* wrote a mixed review in *Twentieth Century Verse,* praising "Blue Guitar" as Stevens returning "to the things he knows best," but criticizing the revised "Owl's Clover" for its "heavy structure," its symbolism, and its rhetoric as "too close to allegory."[64] Other non-leftist critics concurred, at least regarding "Blue Guitar": Julian Symons called it "undoubtedly Stevens' most important work."[65] Delmore Schwartz, writing in *Partisan Review,* found the entire book the best example "of how much there is in his poetry beneath the baroque decoration." Observing how the "derangement" of the times forced Stevens "to consider the nature of poetry in its travail among things as they are," Schwartz continues: "This is the way, then, in which Stevens answers these sudden mobs of men, these sudden clouds of faces and arms: he justifies poetry, he defines its place, its rôle, its priceless value."[66]

EVADING A HIGH-PRESSURE SYSTEM

The resolution Stevens achieved in "The Man with the Blue Guitar" of his aesthetic-political dilemma between engaging leftist realism and maintaining the supremacy of the artist's imagination did not significantly change in the closing years of the 1930s. But the "conjunction" he felt that poem achieved evolved into a renunciation of political aesthetics by April 1941, as evidenced by his lecture at Princeton, "The Noble Rider and the Sound of Words." Of course, the whole leftist literary milieu—and its cachet—was in tatters by then with the signing of the Nazi-Soviet pact and America's ever-closer entry into that war. Stevens's romance with the Left, however, showed signs of cooling long before this.

One index of that disaffection was his oscillating feeling about pure poetry. If we review some of his important statements on it in the crucial years 1935 and 1936, his relative weightings of pure poetry and poetry of "reality" reveal significant shifts in his aesthetic philosophy. Stevens told Latimer on October 31, 1935—just when he finished "Mr. Burnshaw and the Statue"—that he had *once* believed in pure poetry "[w]hen *Harmonium* was in the making." Now, however, "we live in a different time . . . [when] life is the essential part of literature" (*Letters* 288). In retrospect, "Mr. Burnshaw" shows Stevens at the peak of his willingness to engage that "life"—and in particular the Marxist interpretation of it—or at least to depict in this poem a philosophical struggle to do so. Even in this letter, however, his ambivalence comes through in his qualifying sentences: "I still have a distinct liking for that sort of thing [pure poetry]. . . . Moreover, I am not so sure that I don't think exactly the same thing [that literature means more than life] now, but, unquestionably, I think at the same time that life is an essential part of literature" (288). His commitment— "conversion" is far too strong—to a new aesthetic and philosophical direction, while distinct, is thus shaky, uncertain, conflicted. A year later, October 1936, in his statement for the dust jacket of the Knopf edition of *Ideas of Order,* Stevens essentially reversed the qualifiers and assertions: "While it is inevitable that a poet should be concerned with such questions [economic changes, involving political and social changes], this book, although it reflects them, is primarily concerned with ideas of order of a different nature, as, for example, . . . the idea of order arising from the practice of any art. . . . This book is essentially a book of pure poetry" (*CPP* 997). By this time, he had finished *Owl's Clover* (it was published the following month) and was about to begin "The Man with the Blue Guitar" with its quite different attitudes toward the artist's responsibility.

Two months later, December 1936, Stevens elaborated on his current thinking in his lecture "The Irrational Element in Poetry." Significantly, he now construes the present as a menacing "pressure" the poet must somehow deal with:

> The pressure of the contemporaneous from the time of the beginning of the World War to the present time has been constant and extreme. No one can have lived apart in a happy oblivion. . . . We are preoccupied with events, even when we do not observe them closely. We have a sense of upheaval. We feel threatened. . . . The only possible resistance to the pressure of the contemporaneous is . . . the contemporaneous itself. In poetry, to that extent, the subject is not the contemporaneous, . . . but the poetry of the contemporaneous. Re-

sistance to the pressure of ominous and destructive circumstances consists of its conversion, so far as possible, into a different, an explicable, an amenable circumstance. (*CPP* 788–89)

Although Stevens's "solution" is vaguely worded, a few points are clear. He feels that this pressure is "ominous and destructive" and that the poet must resist it by turning it on itself, that is, by taking as his subject poetry subjected to that pressure, thereby subordinating the pressure to the poet's imagination and taming it. In "Mr. Burnshaw and the Statue" this translates into allegorizing the conflict between old art and new hopes, old conceptions of beauty and a new tawdriness that may one day become beautiful, provided one accepts the necessity of constant change. In "The Man with the Blue Guitar," the conflict *opposes* the collective new order demanding a sterile realism and an artist who insists on transforming "things as they are" through his imagination. Both books dramatize conflicts Stevens keenly felt between political aesthetics and the artist's imagination, and both present the former as an intense pressure. But where "Mr. Burnshaw" tentatively offers a hopeful, "pink" outcome to a sterile collectivist future, the artist in "Blue Guitar" resists "their" demands to play the tawdry present.

Stevens's lecture at Princeton in April 1941 addresses the same problem described in "The Irrational Element," using remarkably similar language. But now—more than four years after his Harvard lecture and in the tumult of another world war coming ever closer to the United State—he clarifies just how destructive the "ominous and destructive" pressure of "reality" is: "[T]he idea of nobility exists in art today only in degenerate forms or in a much diminished state . . . this is due to failure in the relation between the imagination and reality . . . [and] this failure is due, in turn, to the pressure of reality" (*CPP* 649–50). More specifically than in his 1936 lecture, he cites "an extraordinary pressure of news"—first news of the "[economic] collapse of our system," then "news of a war" that combine to "suggest an impermanence of the future" (655). This pressure is "great enough and prolonged enough to bring about the end of one era in the history of the imagination and . . . the beginning of another." Alluding covertly to his brief fascination with the Left, Stevens continues: "What happens is that [the imagination] is always attaching itself to a new reality, and adhering to it." Here, however, he adds something quite new: "[T]he pressure of reality is, I think, the determining factor in the artistic character of an era and, as well, the determining factor in the artistic character of an individual. *The resistance to this pressure or its evasion* in the case of individuals of extraordinary imagination cancels the pressure so far as those individuals are concerned" (656, emphasis added). No longer is the focus on converting the pressure into a positive force by making *it* the subject of poetry. Instead, Stevens presents his own mode of resistance and evasion: "[Although the poet] has witnessed, during the long period of his life, a general transition to reality, his own measure as a poet . . . is the measure of his power to abstract himself and to withdraw with him into his abstractions the reality on which lovers of truth insist. He must be able to abstract himself and also to abstract reality, which he does by placing it in his imagination" (657). "Abstract" or "abstraction" occurs four times in five lines. Reality must now be completely transformed in the poet's imagination—a process that could well describe the aesthetic philosophy of *Harmonium,* but surely not of *Owl's Clover.*

Lest his audience miss the political implications of this process, Stevens spells them out bluntly: "I might be expected to speak of the social, that is to say sociological or political obligations of the poet. He has none. That he must be contemporaneous is as old as Longinus and I dare say older. But that he *is* contemporaneous *is* almost inevitable. . . . I do not think that a poet owes any more as a social obligation than he owes as a moral obligation, and if there is anything concerning poetry about which people agree it is that the role of the poet is not to be found in morals" (659–60, Stevens's emphasis).[67] So much for the Left: the romance was over.

What had not ended, however, was Stevens's concern for the larger issue of the poet's role and the importance of the imagination itself in a world burdened by the real and bereft of the old myths that once vivified that imagination. This was the "social obligation" that did not go away, as will be discussed in the conclusion.

3

E. E. Cummings

Prolonged Adolescent or Premature Curmudgeon?

Of the four poets under consideration, E. E. Cummings would seem the least complex in his explicit and complete rejection of leftist criticism, politics, and aesthetics. But how he arrived at this position is less obvious and requires some review. In the late 1910s and through much of the 1920s, he had been the quintessential bad boy of poetry, the nose-thumbing, gleeful rebel against the most cherished beliefs and sacred taboos of the American middle and upper classes:

> next to of course god america i
> love you land of the pilgrims' and so forth[1]
>
> a tear within his stern blue eye,
> upon his firm white lips a smile,
> one thought alone:to do or die
> for God for country and for Yale. . . .
>
> the son of man goes forth to war
> with trumpets clap and syphilis (*CP* 272)
>
> o
> the sweet&aged people
> who rule this world(and me and
> you if we're not very
> careful) (*CP* 248)

Cummings consistently embraced whatever was new, original, and shocking as poet, painter, bohemian, and in his social and political attitudes. He vigorously opposed his father's pressure to turn his talents in writing and art to a self-supporting career, stubbornly defining himself then and ever after as "poet and painter."[2] Identifying himself with the European and

American avant-garde, he rejected naturalistic representation for abstraction in his early oils, which he titled *Sound* or *Noise* and numbered sequentially. In his poetry, Cummings's controversial revisioning of virtually all poetic conventions—from lowly punctuation marks and capitals to the way his poems moved across the page—established his lifelong reputation as the maverick rule-breaker and innovator.[3] "It is a supreme pleasure to have done something FIRST," he wrote his father in 1920.[4] It comes as no surprise, then, that Cummings's political and social views in the twenties were equally rebellious, equally guaranteed to flabbergast the Rotarians—and in particular, his father. What the young artist was rebelling against was not merely nebulous concepts of mainstream America but his personal experience of them in his comfortable, bourgeois upbringing in placid, prewar Cambridge, Massachusetts, and particularly in the strong-willed views of his father, the Reverend Edward Cummings. Cambridge, then, represented the epitome of middle-class respectability and accepted beliefs—

> the Cambridge ladies who live in furnished souls . . .
> believe in Christ and Longfellow,both dead (*CP* 115)

—and Cummings, as a preacher's *and* professor's kid (his father was both minister for Boston's South Congregational Church and Harvard's first professor of sociology), had a double dose of this asphyxiating respectability. Achieving his own identity meant not simply challenging this or that belief but repudiating the entire package and open-mindedly exploring the worlds that Cambridge shunned, for example, the prostitutes and dives of Boston and Somerville. As Cummings recalled in his Harvard *Nonlectures* several decades later: "the more implacably a virtuous Cambridge drew me toward what might have been her bosom, the more sure I felt that *soi-disant* respectability comprised nearly everything which I couldn't respect, and the more eagerly I explored sinful Somerville."[5] His years at Harvard only strengthened this repudiation of the genteel life and provided him good friends with whom to explore Boston's demimonde and modernism in all the arts—both realms disturbing to proper Cantabridgeans. These friends were to prove even more helpful later on.

In a memorable letter to his sister from Paris in 1922, Cummings summarized his belief that "find[ing] out for yourself" meant rejecting what you've been taught. Here are some excerpts:

> Of this i am sure:nothing "occurs" to anyone *as an individual* . . . except:
> the person or mind in question has FIRST OF ALL, FEARLESSLY

wiped out, THOROUGHLY AND UNSENTIMENTALLY defe-
cated WHAT HAS BEEN TAUGHT HIM OR HER....

. . . e.g. I am taught to believe that prostitutes are to be looked
down on. Before believing that, I will, *unless I am afraid to do it,* make
the following experiment: I will talk with, meet on terms of perfect equality, without in the slightest attempting to persuade, a pros-
titute. Through my own eyes and ears a verdict will arrive, which is
the only valid verdict for me in the entire world. (*Selected Letters* 85–
86, Cummings's emphasis)

Many of Cummings's early "Sonnets-Realities" practice what this letter
preached, studying prostitutes from various perspectives, sometimes just
reproducing their speech—

"life?
   Listen"the feline she with radishred
legs said(crossing them slowly) "I'm
asleep.Yep.Youse is asleep kid
and everybody is." (*CP* 226)

—sometimes observing with the cool detachment of a Degas:

"kitty". sixteen,5'1",white,prostitute.

ducking always the touch of must and shall,
whose slippery body is Death's littlest pal,

skilled in quick softness. Unspontaneous. cute. (*CP* 126)

Other poems about prostitutes depict the speaker's antithetical feelings of
lust and disgust in having sex with them:

the dirty colours of her kiss have just
throttled
         my seeing blood,her heart's chatter

riveted a weeping skyscraper

in me (*CP* 205)

These snapshots of the demimonde thus derive from the mixed motives of shocking the Cantabridgeans and paying homage to the most common of common people—a proclivity Cummings showed all his life. Aesthetically, however, they don't differ from the intent of other poems to carefully capture a scene or re-create an experience.

World War I focused Cummings's rebelliousness in several ways and established his lifelong hatred of militarism and war. On the day after the United States declared war on Germany, he volunteered for the Norton-Harjes Ambulance Service, partly from his sympathy for France, partly from not wanting to bear arms and be subjected to army regimentation: "It will mean everything to me as an experience," he wrote his father, "to do something I want to, in a wholly new environment, versus being forced to do something I don't want to & unchanging scene."[6] Ironically, the war forced him to suffer the authoritarianism of two governments: the French, when they imprisoned him for suspected disloyalty,[7] and the American, when they drafted him after his return to the States. His war experience gave Cummings something to hate—not just war itself and the impersonal bureaucracies of governments, but also the mindless chauvinism (hiding as patriotism) of the folks back home that made war possible—and something to celebrate: some of his scruffy fellow prisoners in La Ferté-Macé, who would become the "delectable mountains" of *The Enormous Room*.

Cummings's best World War I poems thus continue his war with Cambridge:

my sweet old etcetera
aunt lucy during the recent

war could and what
is more did tell you just
what everybody was fighting

for, . . .
. . . . my

mother hoped that

i would die etcetera
bravely of course my father used
to become hoarse talking about how it was

a privilege and if only he
could . . . (*CP* 275)

Cummings's father, who had once headed the World Peace Foundation,
changed his tune when the United States entered the war, and he cabled
this ditty on his son's departure for France:

I envy your chance
of breaking a lance
for freedom in France
by driving and mending
an ambulance (Kennedy 137)

Apparently, the family could produce but one poet. Back in America in
1918, when Cummings chose to work at his art and wait to be drafted
rather than enter an officer training camp, his father exploded (according
to a conversation the son later reproduced): "[Y]ou dare to tell me that you
refuse to answer that call, that your business is more important than everybody's business, that you will not give yourself to Save the World, will not
avail yourself of the Greatest Opportunity that the World has ever given a
young man to prove himself worthy of the sacrifices that have been made
for him by his parents?" No doubt, his father became hoarse in this diatribe. Cummings's response to it is revealing of both his current and his
future political views: "My country is inside me" (Kennedy 162–63).
    Other war poems give us the voice and view of a doughboy in the
trenches:

you know what i mean when
the first guy drops you know
everybody feels sick or
when they throw in a few gas
and the oh baby shrapnel
or my feet getting dim freezing

Tellingly, the poem contrasts the soldier who knows what war really is
with people, far from the front lines, who

don't and never
never

will know,
they don't want

to
no (*CP* 271)

And since they choose not to know, they will never say "no" to war.

All of these patterns—the desire to shock the proper middle class, to satirize their most cherished beliefs, particularly their mindless patriotism, and to express a vague kinship with the lowly and despised—continued in Cummings's satires of peacetime America in the twenties. Like most of his contemporaries, however, he took relatively little interest in politics, so early poems that can be labeled explicitly "political" are scarce. One such was probably written just after President Warren G. Harding's death in 1924, but it did not appear until the 1931 *ViVa:*

the first president to be loved by his
bitterest enemies" is dead

the only man woman or child who wrote
a simple declarative sentence with seven grammatical
errors "is dead" (*CP* 337)

The poem's conclusion is as blunt as its opening is satirical: who cares?

America's materialist resurgence after the war—and the advertising slogans to promote it—also becomes a target for Cummings's typewriter:

the season 'tis,my lovely lambs,

of Sumner Volstead Christ and Co. . . .
the age of dollars and no sense. (*CP* 265)

my country,'tis of

you,land of the Cluett
Shirt Boston Garter and Spearmint
Girl With The Wrigley Eyes(of you
land of the Arrow Ide
and Earl &
Wilson

Collars)of you i
sing:land of Abraham Lincoln and Lydia E. Pinkham,
land above all of Just Add Hot Water And Serve—
from every B.V.D.

let freedom ring (*CP* 228)

The first excerpt compresses several topical allusions: to Prohibition (the
Volstead Act), money-making and -spending ("dollars and no sense"), and
Bruce Barton's 1925 depiction of Christ as a super-salesman in *The Man
Nobody Knows.* Here again, as in his antiwar and antipuritanical themes,
Cummings's irreverence aligned neatly with the views of his fellow artists and intellectuals. Malcolm Cowley's *Exile's Return* describes how this
criticism of America as materialist and philistine typified the attitudes of
Cummings's generation, prompting the exodus of intellectuals and artists to Paris. Similarly, the contributors to *Civilization in the United States,*
a collection of thirty-three essays on the arts and political and intellectual life in contemporary America (1922), all arrived at the same conclusion: that the United States achieved material success at the cost of spiritual poverty and puritanical repressiveness.[8]

Finally, one early political poem is especially noteworthy, given Cummings's later attitudes toward communism:

16 heures
l'Etoile

the communists have fine Eyes

some are young some old none
look alike the flics rush
batter the crowd sprawls collapses
singing knocked down trampled the kicked by
flics rush(the

Flics,tidiyum,are
very tidiyum reassuringly similar (*CP* 273)

Drawn from Cummings's firsthand experience of seeing the Parisian police ("flics") charge into a communist May-Day demonstration with clubs
flying, the poem sympathizes entirely with the communists. Significantly,

however, it avoids any ideological content and praises the communists for their individuality—for Cummings, if not for the Party, an absolute good—while it trivializes the police as boringly the same ("tidiyum" puns tedium and te deum with an echo of "Tweedledum and Tweedledee"). A few years earlier, during the Russian civil war, Cummings showed similar sympathies as he teased his father with gleeful accounts of the Red Army's successes against the U.S.-backed Whites in 1919:

> Today(Nov. 7)all N.Y.'s radicals are throwing up their hats in celebration of the anniversary of Sovietism: there are big meetings everywhere—and I expect to enjoy myself hugely. (November 7, 1919, *Selected Letters* 62)

> watch out in the meantime for the Boolsheweekee,who have by today's Tribune,mind you,captured 3 armies,60000men,400guns,1000 mitrailleuses,11000 rifles, 18 armoured trains,200 locomotives,1000 wagons, "and large stores of food and munitions"—. . . !!! (January 10, 1920, *Selected Letters* 68)

The "16 heures" poem and these letters are sometimes taken as evidence of Cummings's Marxist sympathies at the time; but that view requires considerable qualification. Nothing in his essays or voluminous notes from the period suggests that Cummings was ideologically committed to Marxism or that he was even "political" in his interests. Both the letters to his father and his poem derive from his sympathy for underdogs—especially underdogs who were vilified by the American press and repressed by Western governments (recall the Red Scare deportations in 1919–1920)—and from his delight in teasing his father's pro-government values.

Placed in the context of his rebellious generation, and compared to the views of Dos Passos and Hemingway, who had also driven ambulances in World War I, and of H. L. Mencken, that generation's pundit for a time, Cummings's political views were unremarkable in their satirical criticism of mainstream American culture during and after the war. Indeed, just as one can discern in Cummings's Cambridge and antiwar satires rebellion against his overbearing father, the same family rebellion can be observed in Dos Passos's early and intense hostility to everything that later became known as "the establishment" (his father was an influential Wall Street lawyer) and in Hemingway's ruthless desire in his vignettes and stories to strip away genteel reticence (his parents were quintessential Victorians).

But in one important respect, Cummings's rebellion differed from these others: he remained close to his family and continued to depend on his father to support him and bail him out of difficulties. Thus, no matter how sharply he tweaked his father's values—with the political satires, with celebrations of floating turds and delectable misfits in *The Enormous Room,* with "hips pumping pleasure into hips" in his "Sonnets-Realities," and with reminders of Soviet successes—Cummings knew that his rebellion would be tolerated, that his parents would continue to love him *and* financially support him so that he could paint and write. At the same time, he had become the center of a new family of friends and artists who espoused modernism and Menckenism. Dos Passos recalls that within this circle of ex-Harvard artists and writers in New York in the late teens and early twenties, "Cummings was the hub. Cummings and Elaine [Orr Thayer].... Those of us who weren't in love with Cummings were in love with Elaine."[9] Moreover, Cummings's poetry and painting were highly regarded and promoted by this circle.[10] His close friends Scofield Thayer and Sibley Watson had taken over *The Dial* in late 1919, and Cummings enjoyed a privileged position at this premiere modernist magazine. Thayer and Watson not only patronized his art generously but published many of his poems, drawings, and essays. Thus, Cummings's rebellions really had a double safety net: while daring and naughty, they cost him no parental support and gained him status and admiration within a new "family." How could he lose?

CRITICAL RESPONSES IN THE 1920S

Cummings certainly did not lose with the critics when he virtually exploded on the poetic scene in the early and mid-twenties with four books in as many years— *Tulips and Chimneys* (1923),[11] *XLI Poems* (1925), *&* (1925), and *Is 5* (1926). Critical praise of his talent and technique was surprisingly generous, given the radical innovations of his style. Even those who frowned on those typographical disjunctions recognized that here was a fresh, genuinely poetic voice (Wilson, Rosenfeld). Several reviewers mentioned Cummings's exuberance (Monroe, McClure), his "richly sensuous mind" (Van Doren), the "high and concentrated pitch of emotion" in his poems (Gorman).[12] The coldly discerning Edmund Wilson was more qualified in his assessment. Praising Cummings's lyricism and his gift for language, he nonetheless sees Cummings's style as "an eternal adolescent, as fresh and often as winning but as half-baked as boyhood."[13]

Perhaps the best example of the early critical attitudes toward Cummings's poetry—and how they changed—appears in a Gorham Munson's extended and carefully considered analysis in 1923.[14] Going beyond the other early critics, Munson considers the kinesthetic effects, rather than just the novelty, of Cummings's typographical innovations: "Cummings *sees* words. . . . *[He] makes punctuation and typography active instruments for literary expression.* Here, his painter's skill in composition aids him. . . . [Unlike Apollinaire's *Calligrammes,* h]is typographical design in every example reinforces his literary content. He has perceived that the printing press has made poetry something to be seen as well as heard; he has realized that visual notation of auditory rhythms stimulate the ears of silent readers" (10, Munson's emphasis). Another of Munson's comments could serve as a conclusion: "Cummings has probably accomplished more original things in rhythm, metre, and stanza than any three other poets combined. And it is precisely by negation that he has attained originality. He has simply cancelled out his Education (the dignified name for an unquestioning acceptance of custom)" (10).

VIVA

Eight years later, in his review of Cummings's *ViVa,* Munson had cooled considerably toward Cummings the innovator:

> At one time I thought that Mr. Cummings, with his versatility in the graphic and literary arts, . . . would occupy the position in New York which Apollinaire before the war and Cocteau since that catastrophe have held in Paris. A small but excited audience sprang up for his early work; copyists of his mannerisms multiplied; studies of his style, substance and language were composed, beginning with an essay by the present reviewer . . . and closing for the moment with Mr. R. P. Blackmur's analysis in the *Hound and Horn.* . . . But through it all Mr. Cummings has remained. . . . a gifted coterie writer, and *Viva* will make plain that he is writing as he grows older for a diminishing coterie. In the direction in which he is pushing he will eventually write for himself alone. . . .
>
>   . . . [T]he general impression *Viva* gives is of a complicated and refined idiosyncrasy. . . . In general, then, [Cummings] writes for the studio, and ignores the fact that a guessing frame of mind is not suited to the nature and purposes of poetry.[15]

What transpired in those eight years to account for this critical about-face? Several factors combined to separate Cummings not just from Mun-

son but from nearly all of the critics who had once been his supporters—
and from new ones as well. As described in the introduction and chapter 1,
by 1931 leftist sympathies were affecting the reviews of critics like Munson and Horace Gregory; but Cummings's poetry had not changed, except to intensify the disjunctive surfaces of poems and to shed the stilted
romanticism of his earliest poems. Inevitably, these critics grew impatient
with this epitome of 1920s experimentation.

Munson mentions a critical essay by R. P. Blackmur, "Notes on E. E.
Cummings' Language,"[16] that was also influential in changing critical attitudes toward Cummings. In this lengthy essay, Blackmur took Cummings
to task for overusing words (like "skilful" or "accurate") that describe or
allude to precision without themselves being concrete or precise. Regarding the word "flower," which appears, by Blackmur's count, forty-eight
times in *Tulips and Chimneys* and twenty-one times in the briefer *&*, "the
word . . . becomes an idea and is used to represent the most interesting and
most important aspect of his poem. Hence the center of the poem is per-
manently abstract and unknowable for the reader, and remains altogether
without qualifications or concreteness" (55). Blackmur ends his essay by
calling Cummings's diction "a kind of baby-talk" (67).

Moreover, after five years of poetic quiescence,[17] Cummings offered up
a book that took no almost notice of the Depression, composed as it was
of poems written throughout the 1920s, some dating back to the postwar
years ("i sing of Olaf") and 1924 ("the first president [Harding] to be loved
by his"). Its satires were often obscure and aimed at all sorts of targets:
some personal, like his ex-wife, Elaine Orr; some topical, like the recent
dual suicide of Harry Crosby and Josephine Bigelow; others aimed at the
government or at the English; and one at what was to become a nexus of
Cummings's particular whipping boys: progress, science, and humanistic
relativism:

Space being(don't forget to remember)Curved. . . .

an electromagnetic(now I've lost
the)Einstein expanded Newton's law preserved
conTinuum . . .

of Course life being just a Reflex you
know since Everything is Relative or

to sum it All Up god being Dead (*CP* 317)

Several reviewers noticed this lack of focus in the satires. Malcolm Cowley wrote in *The New Republic:* "He is depending more on anger—against politicians, officials, soldiers, against literary fakirs, against humanity in general—as a source of poetry. He is paying more attention to public matters like Einstein's theory and the Russian Revolution, but his reaction to them remains private and unsocial."[18] Cowley recalled, by contrast, Cummings's pro-Communist poem in *Is 5*. Writing a few years later, Babette Deutsch identified the real problem with this scattershot approach: "What he fails to realize is that even the active force of satire loses its efficacy when the satirist behaves like Tweedledum in his famous battle with his brother, hitting everything within reach whether he can see it or not."[19]

Reviewers like Munson were also growing impatient with Cummings's typographical dislocations. Horace Gregory predicted: "Within a very few years his typographical mannerisms will be forgotten or merely taken for granted."[20] While no one claimed Cummings's lyrical gifts had diminished, Cowley wondered whether lyricism itself was becoming irrelevant to the times:

> What chiefly impresses the reader of his best poems is the thought that he is perhaps the end of a great tradition.
>
> There is at present no real doubt that lyric poetry is losing the vitality it once possessed. . . . [T]he malady from which it suffers is lack of conviction on the part of its friends. Somehow the focus of interest has shifted. . . . [E]ither [poets] translate their concerns into regions of high philosophy, like Mr. Eliot, or else they write about more public issues. ("Last of the Lyric Poets" 123)

The feeling running through these reviews, stated or implied, was that the poet was growing stale. Thus, Horace Gregory: "If Cummings seems a bit old-fashioned today, it is because a number of his humorous and satirical poems run parallel to the Dada movement in Paris of ten years ago. . . . He is static, embalmed in the same delicate rococo, adolescent phases of love that he discovered himself eight years ago" ("Adolescent Songster" 22). And Eda Lou Walton: "in *Viva,* his latest collection of poems, Cummings is giving us more of the same roses and locomotives."[21] Even William Carlos Williams weighed in against *ViVa:* "[It] seems definitely an aftermath; not quite in the sense of scholarship but of desire satisfied—not quite real any longer."[22] Accusations of staleness obviously do not require a political motive, but one can easily read in Cowley's disappointment about Cummings's "private and unsocial" reaction to public matters (as well as his musings about the death of the lyric poem), in Gregory's dismissive comparison to "the Dada movement ... of ten years ago," and in Munson's rejection of the "coterie" poet writing for an ever-shrinking elite these critics' new expectations that poets (and writers in general) should address the enormous economic and political issues of their day in comprehensible language, rather than cling to the esoteric aesthetics of an age, only just past, that suddenly seemed quite passé. Whether Cummings fully recognized how much the prevailing critical winds had shifted is moot. For by the time *ViVa* appeared in October 1931, he had already done what many writers and intellectuals on the left talked about doing then, but few actually did: he traveled to Russia and spent several weeks there.

EIMI

Just why Cummings undertook this trip is puzzling, given his long-standing distrust of all governments, especially a police state like Russia, and his uncompromising belief in individual freedom. As Cummings's biographer Richard Kennedy comments, "he must have known he would loathe what he found" (309). But by 1931, Russia's achievements seemed to be on everyone's tongue, and several of his friends and acquaintances had visited the workers' paradise or were planning to: Dos Passos, for example, in 1928, and Morrie Werner (who had invited Cummings to accompany him) in 1930. Moreover, while Cummings was in Paris, his friend Louis Aragon, whose Marxist chant "Red Front" Cummings had translated into English, and Aragon's girlfriend, a Russian-born novelist and "ardent supporter of the Russian revolution," both urged Cummings to go, as did the Russian novelist Ilya Ehrenburg.[23] Finally, Cummings's belief in seeing things firsthand rather than accepting secondhand opinion was a powerful factor. His observations, encoded in Cummingsese, went into a diary that Cummings later expanded into a lengthy prose book. Entitled *Eimi,* Greek for "I am"—itself a slap at collectivism—it was a kind of sequel to his first prose book, *The Enormous Room* (1922), in that each depicted the author's subjective impressions of a largely unpleasant experience; and each was structured as an allegorical journey. The first journey (into and out of a French prison) was at least leavened by several celebratory portraits of fellow prisoners; this one was a journey into a bigger prison, "a more enormous room,"[24] and offered little relief.

The book is unfriendly to the reader on two counts. First, Cummings's style, while comprehensible (especially with the help of his later "Sketch for a Preface" to identify some characters and daily itineraries), is challenging. A sample taken at random:

everywhere a terrific(modeled and remodeled and unmodelled by always drinkbringing Mammy Sunshine)putty of nonproletarian of badly thirsting of nobodies—deeplycynically on whom beams the more and more distingué censor of censors;communists don't drink. Whereas the a little drinking Doctor Chinesey more avoids and more these brightly dressed these screaming flatly these lurching dolls("and nobody GIVES a damn").[25]

Roughly translated: the narrator describes a party where people are getting drunk and dancing (thus changing shape like putty—or appearing to as the narrator gets drunk). They are brought drinks by the hostess ("Mammy Sunshine"). The guests are neither proletarian nor politically important. A distinguished Russian censor looks on cynically (the narrator recalling being told earlier that good communists don't drink), while Dr. Armand Hammer ("Doctor Chinesey"), drink in hand, moves out of the way of the flashy dancers.[26] The final quotation repeats something a member of the British embassy just confided to the narrator about the Russian attitude toward the success of the great Soviet experiment.

Obviously, a little of this style goes a long way, and a 452-page book of it—waxing and waning in decipherable difficulty—places a considerable burden on even the sympathetic reader, who may wonder if the game is worth the candle. Not surprisingly, most reviewers complained of *Eimi*'s difficulty and perhaps secretly agreed with a reviewer for the *Boston Transcript:* "[I]t is to be hoped that somebody will have the courage to make the attempt to read it to the very end."[27] (Clearly, the reviewer was not alone in lacking that courage; *Eimi* remains a book more mentioned than read.)

The narrator's attitude toward Russia is also troubling, not because he finds nearly everything he encounters repugnant, but because his values are so entrenched that he seems to have made up his mind that he would find it so before he starts. Even before he arrives, he acknowledges that "I know nothing about these important matters [economic and sociological problems] and care even less" (15); hence, he has no desire to see factories or evidence of Russia's industrial achievement. Primarily, he meets other Americans living in Russia and Russian writers. Cummings's precise ear and gift for mimicry produce superb portraits of these characters. In fact, the book is largely given to reproducing dialogue and scenes with these few characters. But the world they exist in and in most cases believe in is, for Cummings, a world of "un"—"unmen," "unyouths," "nonmen"— "a joyless experiment in force and fear" (50).[28] The composite picture of the Soviet state is thus unrelievedly grim: dreary, repressive, regimented, soulless, scary.

The narrator's journey is an allegorical descent into and out of hell, complete with a Virgilian guide, a structure Cummings reinforces with imagery of closed (shut, spiritually stifling, claustrophobic—Russia, obviously) and open (breathable, spiritually expanding—France, the narrator's point of return). Thus, the book's very first word, "SHUT," describes the window in the stifling train compartment the narrator rides in, while the very last word—"OPENS"—evokes the action of his spirit on returning to Paris. Such a schema obviously leaves no breathing space in Russia except for a few instances where the narrator meets an individual who has resisted the "un" of nonbeing. In debunking the egalitarian myth of modern Russia, Cummings even goes to the opposite extreme of romanticizing the peasants' life before the revolution:

> I feel that whatever's been hitherto told or sung in song or story concerning Russia's revolution equals bunk. I feel that Russia was not once upon a time . . . any number of cringing peasants ruled by an autocratic puppet—Russia was any number of kings,so perfectly so immanently and naturally royal that(with a single negligible exception or "Czar")they did royally disguise themselves as humblest slaves,lest the light of their royalty dazzle a foolish world. . . . And what has been miscalled the Russian revolution surely is a more foolish than the supposable world's attempt upon natural and upon immanent and upon perfect and upon kinghood;an attempt motivated by baseness and jealousy and by hate and a slave's wish to substitute for the royal incognito of humility the ignoble affectation of equality. (255)

Finally, several motifs appear recycled from Cummings's earlier poems, essays, and notes on aesthetics, for example, his preference of verbs to nouns to convey being and becoming (beginning with the book's title), his belief in feeling over thinking (52), and his distrust of science (34).[29]

Richard Kennedy asserts that Cummings's experience in Russia, and the book depicting it, marked a turning point—(I would call it a point of no return)—in his political philosophy: they confirmed his belief in individualism; they vastly intensified his hatred for and fear of anything that smacked of collectivism, including liberalism and the New Deal; and they cemented these beliefs in an increasingly rigid dogmatism (335). But *Eimi* also signifies Cummings's open hostility to and absolute separation from all writers and critics—including many former friends—who had become supporters of Soviet Russia in their turn to the left. For by the time of its publication, March 1933, Cummings could certainly have guessed how they would respond to his book.[30]

Predictably, the leftist critical response to *Eimi* was scathing. According to Christopher Sawyer-Laucanno, "Edmund Wilson and Malcolm Cowley ... were disturbed by what they perceived as Cummings' right-wing turn. As a result their friendship with him remarkably cooled. Muriel Draper, an ardent leftist [and once Cummings's lover and patron], broke with him altogether" (367). Several critics asserted that the book was much more about Cummings than about Russia: Horace Gregory called it "the completion of a *self*-portrait" by a "provincial, Cambridge-bred *American* poet, attempting to high hat an entire social system."[31] Henry Seidel Canby quotes an unnamed "distinguished American novelist" (might it have been the recent Marxist convert Theodore Dreiser?) who opines that "*Eimi* is the work of a clever man with an intense feeling for his own ego and a weak grasp upon external reality, except in its physical aspects."[32]

Other critics took Cummings to task for not making a deeper investigation of Soviet life. "K. D. C.," writing in the *Harvard Crimson*, observes that "the right or wrong of the Soviet regime, in 1933, is a question somewhat more complex and more exacting" than his technique allows: "Not only does Cummings withhold his sympathy from Russia in the mass, but he is so carried away by his distaste that in *Eimi* he has hardly one memorable portrait of character.... [T]here is a dangerous superficiality to his emotional record, as there is to most art of which the main motive is revulsion or retreat."[33] Nathan Asch, writing in *The New Republic*, concurred, complaining how much of Russia Cummings missed: "[He] did not speak to—not even meet—a single worker or peasant, nor visit a single factory, nor dam, nor workers' quarters, nor workers' clubs, nor a prophylactic station."[34]

Apolitical reviews were mixed. George Jean Nathan, writing in *The American Spectator,* dubbed it "The Worst Book of the Month."[35] On the other hand, praise came from Paul Rosenfeld (Cummings's tireless champion), Ezra Pound, and Marianne Moore.[36]

NO THANKS

With his next book of poems, *No Thanks* (1935), Cummings had declared total war on the Left.[37] Unlike *ViVa, No Thanks* and some uncollected poems of the same period contain stinging political satires aimed at communists, leftist intellectuals, journal editors, and Marxist critics. One of the most succinctly humorous is an epitaph to what Cummings saw as the faddism and conformity of this political shift:

IN)
    all those who got
    athlete's mouth jumping
    on&off bandwagons
              (MEMORIAM
               (*CP* 404)

"Ballad of an Intellectual"—a poem Cummings left out of *No Thanks*—gives the conformist theme a more personal animus. The intellectual (Edmund Wilson?), who is also "a critic of note, / a serious thinker,a lyrical pote," probably comes from Cummings's generation, since he quotes Proust, Joyce, and Pound (to wow dowagers and seduce debutantes). But on discovering that he has nothing further to say,

    he pondered a while and he said,said he
    "It's the social system,it isn't me!
    Not I am a fake,but America's phoney!
    Not I am no artist,but Art's bologney! (*CP* 899–900)

Hence, the intellectual quickly converts to "Karl the Marks." The speaker, conversely, is one who "might irretrievably pause / ere believing that Stalin is Santa Claus." Following a jab at Mike Gold, editor of *New Masses* ("All that Glisters Is Mike Gold"), the speaker concludes:

    (but a rolling snowball gathers no sparks
    —and the same holds true of Karl the Marks).

A companion poem, also uncollected, characterizes the "american critic ad 1935" as a

    faggoty slob with a sob in whose cot
    tony onceaweek whisper winsomely pul

    ling their wool over 120 mil
    lion goats. (*CP* 901)

The critic's culpability in Cummings's eyes is not merely in being a bleeding heart—a "sob" sister who is also an SOB—but in being homosexual. Note how lines 2–3 can be read "in whose cot [T]ony onceaweek whisper[s] winsomely." Garden-variety jealousy emerges here as the poem notes that

"all he's got to do is just men / tion something&it sells ten 000 copies."
This, at a time when Cummings's *No Thanks* could not find a publisher.[38]

The much-anthologized "kumrads die because they're told)" (*CP* 413)
continues the theme of conformity, now to a tune played by the Kremlin:
"moscow pipes good kumrads dance)." The "kumrads" are not only smelly
(a quality that offended the poet's nose in Russia, as well) and going nowhere with their hate-soaked ideology—"(travelling in a futile groove"—
but, more damningly, they are afraid of life and "afraid to love." This poem,
in particular, stuck in the craw of Marxist critics, since nearly all who reviewed *No Thanks* cited it. It is worth noting that Cummings used the
same phonetic spelling, "kumrads," to describe two ex-friends, Lincoln
Kirstein and Muriel Draper, whom he blamed for his failure to get his
ballet scenario, *Tom,* produced in 1935. His letter to Hildegarde Watson
implies that his anti-Marxist stance was the deciding factor: "You might
be amused to learn that Kumrads Kirstein and Draper, Inc are said to be
collectively enceinte re a one-&-only-original & jenyouwine(Avoid All
Substitutes)'Uncle Tom's Cabin':the climax whereof is rumored to reveal
a white & a black chorus unanimously declaiming 'workers of the world
unite.'"[39]

The personal animus in these satires—the feeling that Cummings was
now on the outside, looking in artistically, socially, and politically—also
appears in one of his most devastating satires of a perennial urge among
young intellectuals:

> "let's start a magazine
>
> to hell with literature
> we want something redblooded
>
> lousy with pure
> reeking with stark
> and fearlessly obscene
>
> but really clean
> get what I mean. (*CP* 407)

Sawyer-Lauçanno assumes the magazine in question is *Esquire* (390), but
more likely it is one of the new leftist journals that sprang up in the thirties. In any case, the speaker offers some friendly advice to the would-be
editors on capturing "fearlessly obscene" authenticity: "squeeze your nuts

and open your face." One scarcely need imagine that, unlike *The Dial* and
Broom in the 1920s, few of these magazines welcomed Cummings's poems
or provided a venue for his artwork. In one new magazine, Ronald Lane
Latimer's *Alcestis Quarterly,* which did publish several of his poems (including the notorious "kumrads"), assistant editor Willard Mass, an avowed
communist, advised rejecting one Cummings poem because of its anti-
communist themes. As Alan Filreis recounts: in a letter to Latimer, Mass
"knew that as a radical he must reject a poem submitted by [Cummings]
on the basis of Cummings' 'personal nastiness and Fascist tendencies.' Mass
added: 'I . . . admit that Cumming[s]'s ballade was great poetry, but I'm
agin' it just the same.' "[40]

In sum, the motives impelling Cummings's political satires were as much
personal as philosophical: for refusing to jump on the Marxist bandwagon,
he had cut himself off from commissions, magazines, and publishers (not to
mention old friends and acquaintances) at a time when he was barely scrap-
ing by. *No Thanks* lists in its pseudo-dedication fourteen publishers who
had rejected the manuscript.[41] Cummings's bitterness and ill-disguised
jealousy aim at those, like the "intellectual" in the "Ballad," whose political correctness enabled them to flourish in these difficult times. But I
would argue that the source of his bitterness goes deeper. If in the 1920s
he found himself at the center of a surrogate family of admiring artists
and writers, he now felt abandoned by that family, displaced as the bad-
boy darling of the avant-garde, and (insult of insults) attacked as being
rearguard and passé. Surely, it could not have been pleasant to read Philip
Horton declaring in *Partisan Review:* "The *enfant terrible* of 1923 has become the professional *vieux gaillard* of today [1938]—a poet distinctly *manqué.*"[42] Perhaps the cruelest cut for this masterful parodist was to be parodied in his own style; so Babette Deutsch styled her review of *50 Poems*
(1940) "e e cummingsesq":

          :dearmrcummings it is
          late
          r than you th
          ink ;printersink s
                          print
          ingdownand sp   (o)
                      ill
                ing (
                     ver)
                     the

```
                    page doesnt
  excite or delight us
  the same way anymore
```

The poem concludes:

```
          you must forgive us
  if we sometimes
  y
     aaaw
              n
  ;because it is
  Appallingly
  late.
  . . . . . . . . . . . . . . . . .
                      ;we are not asking you for
  something new ,simply
  few
  and (er
  )or better
  ?poems⁴³
```

Having lost his poetic family, it is perhaps not surprising that Cummings expressed a poetic rapprochement with his biological family in the
thirties, particularly his deceased father, whose values he had so continuously satirized in the twenties. In *ViVa* he memorialized his still-living
mother in the poem "if there are any heavens my mother will(all by herself)have / one" (*CP* 353). By 1940, he would do the same for his father
in "my father moved through dooms of love" (*CP* 520). In *No Thanks* he
even adopts his father's ministerial voice, delivering a jeremiad from the
pulpit:

```
  Jehovah buried,Satan dead,
  do fearers worship Much and Quick;
  badness not being felt as bad,
  itself thinks goodness what is meek;
  obey says toc,submit says tic,
  Eternity's a Five Year Plan:
  if Joy with Pain shall hang in hock
  who dares to call himself a man?
```

King Christ,this world is all aleak;
and lifepreservers there are none;
and waves which only He may walk
Who dares to call Himself a man. (*CP* 438)

In this poem, at least, Christ was no longer "dead" for Cummings.

Just as he required financial support nearly all his life, first from his parents (e.g., his mother put up the money for the publication of *No Thanks*) and then from caring friends and patrons like Sibley and Hildegarde Watson, so too Cummings required the emotional and uncritical esteem of a family, as he revealed in a letter to Hildegarde Watson in 1948: "[H]ow wonderful!You-&-Sibley understand me:understand that I'm perfectly helpless unless I'm loved by people whom I can respect—understand that such people are very much rarer than rarest" (*Selected Letters* 188). The loss of a poetic family to provide this love and support, I believe, left Cummings by the mid-thirties feeling even more isolated and defensive; he responded by becoming more extreme and rigid in defining and asserting his individuality.

REVIEWS OF *NO THANKS*

Unlike his ever-tolerant biological family, leftist critics did not cotton to having Cummings's thumb in their eye and met his scorn with their own for *No Thanks*. Isador Schneider, Marxist critic for the *New Masses,* called the book "a literary act of suicide": "[Its] philosophy [contrasting what's "alive" and dead], such as it is, is passé even in Greenwich Village where it throve years ago. . . . We find in these two poems ["kumrads die" and "IN) . . . (MEMORIAM"] the typical ignorance and malice of the anti-Communist."[44]

Critics disagreed about the efficacy of the political satires. Lionel Abel, reviewing for *The Nation,* felt that "only the satiric poems are up to Cummings' earlier level of performance."[45] But two other leftist critics, Babette Deutsch and Kenneth Burke, disparaged what they saw as capriciousness and whimsicality in these satires.[46] In a far more penetrating review, John Finch agreed that Cummings's satires in *No Thanks* are marred by "a lack of direction, a desire to sweep too wide a field," but he attributes this scatteredness to Cummings's embattled sense of isolation: "[T]he popular and critical reception of his earlier writing has worked subtle changes in this poet. It has blunted his satire and sharpened his didacticism. He sometimes loses his temper in *No Thanks* and writes an uncontrolled invective. . . .

But this and the other occasional weaknesses have a deeper origin in that fundamental act of isolation at the genesis of his poems. Out of this act, too, comes [their] strength." Contrasting Cummings's individualism (and Marianne Moore's) with the collectivism of other writers, Finch concludes that in *No Thanks* Cummings "approaches [the theme of individualism] with more certain power and develops it with a proud dignity. The result is deeper poetry than any he has previously written."[47]

It seems odd that leftist critics recognized Cummings's obvious satirical targeting of the Left but at the same time criticized his satires for being amorphous and scattered. Compared to *ViVa,* the satires in *No Thanks* are far more pointed. Leftist critics also overlooked, both in *No Thanks* and in later books of the 1930s, that Cummings's political poems attack other colors on the political spectrum besides red. In a satire warning about proselytizers for the "rissians," the last stanza tells us to "pity the fool" who spews anti-Semitism:

> god help me it aint no ews
> eye like the staek all ried
> but eye certainly hate the juse (*CP* 405)

As much as he despised communism, Cummings was no lover of faswcism. As this poem and a contemporaneous essay ("Exit the Boob") make clear, he saw both political extremes as two sides of the same coin of "dictatorship"—a view that leftist intellectuals were slower to adopt.[48]

Even capitalism received a lick in the political satires of *No Thanks:* "exit a kind of unkindness exit" (*CP* 389) addresses "little / mr Big / notbusy / Busi / ness notman," informing him: "you // are dead / you captain)." How did Marxist critics overlook this one?

COLLECTED POEMS (1938) AND *50 POEMS* (1940)

As Europe moved inexorably toward war in the late thirties—a reality Cummings could scarcely ignore in his frequent trips there—his damning of all totalitarian extremes grew more forceful, as in this 1940 nursery parody of "peas porridge hot":

> red-rag and pink-flag
> blackshirt and brown
> strut-mince and stink-brag
> have all come to town

some like it shot
and some like it hung
and some like it in the twot
nine months young (*CP* 497)

Marxist magazines like *New Masses* ("red-rag"), "pink" fellow travelers,
Hitler's brownshirts, and Mussolini's strutting blackshirts all dominate center stage now. Possibly, Cummings alludes here to their pacts—the Tri-
partite Pact between Germany, Italy, and Japan, the Munich agreement,
and the Nazi-Soviet pact of August 1939—that consolidated the evil. Nowhere present are the Western democracies, which, to judge from his other
poems, Cummings had no faith in anyway: "uncle shylock" was "not interested," for example, when Russia invaded Finland in 1940 (*CP* 641).[49]
Totalitarian crimes—"shot" and "hung"—even invade what might be considered a refuge of innocence, the womb,[50] perhaps an allusion to Nazi
plans to propagate a new generation of the master race with breeding
homes and Hitler Youth camps.

One of Cummings's chief targets in all his subsequent books emerges
in *No Thanks:* his depiction of an American public that has been brain-
washed en masse to believe in modernity, which for Cummings equaled
science, gadgets, and—compliments of Roosevelt's New Deal—economic
security. He dubbed his abstraction "mostpeople":

most(people

simply

can't)
won't(most
parent people mustn't

shouldn't)most daren't
(sortof people well
youknow kindof)
aint (*CP* 412)

Here, the negatives scream inhibition—almost a thematic throwback to
the Puritan-bashing twenties. Since "mostpeople" have not "ever lived,"
they "always)don't // die." Opposed to "mostpeople" are "you and I,"
who share Cummings's values, an elite twosome that cleverly includes the

reader. In the introduction to *Collected Poems* (1938), the poet spells out in prose these opposed values: "The poems to come are for you and for me and are not for mostpeople—it's no use trying to pretend that mostpeople and ourselves are alike" (*CP* 461). The introduction goes on to stereotype "mostpeople" in a few negative traits: desiring security, being afraid to live in the present moment, subscribing mindlessly to American materialism and technology:

> Mostpeople fancy a guaranteed birthproof safetysuit of nondestructible selflessness. . . .
>   Life,for mostpeople,simply isn't. Take the socalled standardofliving. What do mostpeople mean by "living"? They don't mean living. They mean the latest and closest plural approximation to singular prenatal passivity which science,in its finite but unbounded wisdom,has succeeded in selling their wives. (461)

By contrast, "you and I . . . can never be born enough. We are human beings;for whom birth is a supremely welcome mystery,the mystery of growing:the mystery which happens only and whenever we are faithful to ourselves.You and I wear the dangerous looseness of doom and find it becoming. Life,for eternal us,is now;and now is much too busy being a little more than everything to seem anything,catastrophic included" (461). In this simplistic opposition and scornful reductiveness, Cummings himself is susceptible to the label he attributes to "mostpeople": "snob." Arguably, no other expression of his social views—not even his obtuseness in using "kike" and "nigger" in some poems—has done more to alienate Cummings not merely from critics but also from potentially sympathetic readers.

Collected Poems (which included twenty-two new poems) and *50 Poems* single out one aspect of "mostpeople" for particular contempt: the desire for economic security. By now, Roosevelt's New Deal had established Social Security, and the WPA had successfully put millions back to work in public works projects. Cummings disliked and distrusted Roosevelt, and, like Frost, felt the New Deal (which he called "nude eel") was well along the road to the hateful collectivism he had seen in Russia. Several poems in these books address this theme, including this bagatelle:

> economic secu
> rity" is a cu
> rious excu

se . . .
    for pu

tting the arse
before the torse (*CP* 477)

Playing on the expression "putting the cart before the horse," Cummings
asserts that this economic concern is going "backasswards," and in that position the idea naturally stinks ("pu" is repeated twice more in the elided
lines). Similarly, economic leveling comes in for its share of satire, such as
these lines from his parody of a planned society for "morons," "(of Ever-
Ever Land i speak":

down above all with . . . [that]
    which makes some feel more better
when all ought to feel less worse (*CP* 466)

Two other poems from *Collected Poems* effectively contrast Cummings's
values with those of "mostpeople." In one, he valorizes a destitute individualist—

my specialty is living said
a man(who could not earn his bread
because he would not sell his head)

—while equating material subsistence with mindless conformity and the
loss of integrity:

squads right impatiently replied
two billion pubic lice inside
one pair of trousers(which had died) (*CP* 473)

Some critics assume that Cummings was writing about the Greenwich
Village vagabond Joe Gould, but more likely he was describing himself, since he could not "earn his bread" in this period. To construe his
own situation heroically is understandable, but to suggest that everyone
who *does* earn his bread has sold out and has sunk to very lowest level of
existence—"the sick parts of a sick thing," as he put it in *Santa Claus*[51]—is
shockingly reductive. While the poem echoes Emerson's "Whoso would
be a man must be a non-conformist" and thus evokes the validating ethos

of nineteenth-century New England individualism, its either/or absolut-
ism ignores the way that contemporary economic organization—and especially the breakdown of the system—makes those notions of individualism increasingly problematic.

A much more developed poem, "if i" (*CP* 475) tells us what matters
and what does not:

> if i
>
> or anybody don't
> know where it her his
>
> my next meal's coming from
> i say to hell with that
> that doesn't matter(and if
>
> he she it or everybody gets a
> bellyful without
> lifting my finger i say to hell
> with that i
>
> say that doesn't matter)

Again, how—or even whether—one gets enough to eat is not important
in Cummings's hierarchy of values, though it conceivably might be to
someone who is hungry. What does matter—Cummings's values—is being "beautiful or / deep or generous." Those are the qualities of character
one should "spell . . . out big" because they are "true." While many may
not agree with this weighting, the values at least appear in a well-developed
and entertaining poem in its multiple voices and its satire of popular culture and the media:

>   spell
> that out big(bigger than cosmic
> rays war earthquakes famine or the ex
>
> prince of whoses diving into
> a whatses to rescue miss nobody's
> probably handbag)

Cummings's final book of the decade, *50 Poems,* continues the political themes of the previous two books, but with some refinements. "mostpeople" now acquire such synonyms as "wherelings whenlings" (*CP* 512), shorthand notations for their finite worldview of time and space, while their world becomes "a peopleshaped toomany-ness. . . . a notalive undead toonearishness" (*CP* 528). A more personal attack, "flotsam and jetsam" (*CP* 492), singles out the "thoroughly bretish" writers W. H. Auden and Christopher Isherwood not only for their leftist politics—

vive the millenni
um three cheers for labor
give all things to enni
one bugger they nabor

—but also (as the last line quoted above makes clear) for their homosexuality:

(neck and senecktie
are gentlemen ppoyds
even whose recktie
are covered by lloyd's)

Since Auden and Isherwood had moved to New York in 1939, it is quite possible that Cummings heard them give readings there and was perhaps a bit jealous of the fuss made over them by the literary community.[52]

Opposing these categorical stereotypes are welcome celebrations of individuals, such as the Jewish tailor, Goldberger, expressing his own (obviously Cummings's) values in his own voice:

here is hands machine no

good too quick i know this
suit you pay
a store too
much yes what
too much o much cheap
me i work i know i say i have
not any
never
no vacation here

is hands is work since i am
born is good (*CP* 523)

This poem also stands against the charge, occasioned by the 1944 poem "a
kike is the most dangerous" (*CP* 644), that Cummings was anti-Semitic.
Regrettably, though, these vivid characterizations are not plentiful, and
Cummings's prognosis for the appearance of such distinct individuals is
gloomy:

there are possibly 2½ or impossibly 3
individuals every several fat
thousand years. Expecting more would be
neither fantastic nor pathological but

dumb.

Juxtaposed against these rare individuals are not just "mostpeople" but also
the "civilization" they have created—an observation that brings Cummings very close to the misanthropy of Robinson Jeffers:

and if . . .
than all mankind something more small occurs
or something more distorting than socalled
civilization i'll kiss a stalinist arse

in hitler's window on Wednesday next at 1 (*CP* 514)

And why do you cry my dear, why do you cry?
if England goes down
and Germany up
the stronger dog will still be on top.
If civilization goes down that would be an event to contemplate.
It will not be in our time, alas,
my dear, it will not be in our time. (Jeffers, "May–June 1940")[53]

In both poems, the seemingly unstoppable progress of totalitarian mur-
derers like Hitler and Stalin in 1940, supported by millions of obedient
"citizens," *Landsmen,* and kumrads, casts a dim view of what "civilization" can produce. Instead—and in reaction—Cummings turns more and
more to his beloved, the real "you" of the "you and I" pairing he posits

against the world, in some of his most tender and moving love poems. In sum, then, whether the poems are affirmations of his isolated, embattled individualism and love for his beloved or bitter satires against the world's and "mostpeople's" values, the themes of the later-thirties poetry do not vary. Each poem is a thoroughly original and newly imagined way of saying the same thing.

REVIEWS OF *COLLECTED POEMS* AND *50 POEMS*

Critical response to *Collected Poems* and *50 Poems* did not substantially differ from reviews of *No Thanks,* except in one important regard. Since *Collected Poems* presented an anthology of Cummings's work from *Tulips and Chimneys* (1923) to 1938, critics considered in their reviews his whole career, his contribution to American poetry, and in particular, how or whether his poetry had evolved since the 1920s. As his biographers have noted, the book elicited many favorable reviews, helped establish Cummings's poetry in the canon, and encouraged more scholarly evaluations of his work, such as John Peale Bishop's essay in the *Southern Review.*[54]

For leftist critics, however, *Collected Poems* and *50 Poems* confirmed their judgment that Cummings's poetry had failed to evolve: the "new poems are fixed in rigid attitudes of youth, which now seem to show signs of weariness, caused by the strain of a prolonged defiance" (Gregory); the poetry "shows no technical improvement or intellectual development over a period of fifteen years" (Horton); "Mr. Cummings, it is plain, is a naughty little boy who just never did grow up" (Seaver); the sameness of his subjects (love, spring, death) suggests "a certain lack of sensibility, imagination, and courage" (Mangan).[55] While leftist critics like Horton and Seaver flatly dismissed the poet—"[H]e sold his poetic birthright for a mess of punctuation marks. . . . [which] are his weapons for defense, for walling himself off from his fellow men, for declaring his uniqueness" (Seaver)—others tried to discern the sources of his defiance. For Gregory it stemmed from a complex of fears: "fear of being misunderstood, fear of being less than unique, fear of the many rising against the few, and overall, a . . . fear of loneliness." Rolfe Humphries, writing in *New Masses,* accurately traced the roots of Cummings's politics to his anarchism, which could support communists when they were underdogs, but now opposed them as they appeared successful. For Humphries, this anarchism was timid and "counterrevolutionary. . . . [I]t has no real intention of destroying [institutions]. . . . And since anarchy, in this sense, does inhibit life, it is bound to inhibit poetry."[56]

It is interesting that at least one leftist critic, Horace Gregory, saw Cummings's supposedly frozen adolescence and failure to change with the times as symptomatic of his generation, a view that reiterated the larger war 1930s critics waged against 1920s modernists. That Cummings typified modernists in the 1920s is certainly arguable, but the same cannot be said for his iconoclastic stance in the 1930s: for every Marianne Moore, who forged her own path, there were several Malcolm Cowleys, who changed their themes and styles to reflect their newly acquired leftist politics and aesthetics.

Similarly, critics of all political stripes missed changes in Cummings's poetry in the late thirties that anticipated his later work. The tendency to dichotomize the world into fixed, stereotypical oppositions ("mostpeople" vs. "you and I") became ever more entrenched and rigid in his poetry: the iconoclast was becoming a curmudgeon, ever more isolated from and opposed to the prevailing politics of his times. Yet his style was anything but repetitive. The early thirties witnessed some of his most disjunctive poems, for example, "n(o)w" in *ViVa* and "ondumonde'" in *No Thanks* (*CP* 348, 430), that seem to explode all over the page in baroque exuberance. The first new poem of *Collected Poems,* by contrast, marks a new, classical spareness as the pared lines, often comprising just a letter or two, move straight down, relying heavily on *tmesis,* double entendre, and symmetrical balances within and between the lines:

un
der fog
's
touch

slo

ings
fin
gering
s

wli (*CP* 463)

The second poem of *50 Poems* displays this sparse verticality more severely:

fl

a
tt
ene

dd

reaml
essn
esse (*CP* 488)

Many of Cummings's later poems, including his masterful "1(a" (*CP* 673), display this disciplined verticality, while the explosive all-over-the-page form virtually disappears in the late work.

CONCLUSION

The 1930s thus marked a radical transformation in Cummings's status among avant-garde writers and critics, from the naughty darling of modernism to a pariah seen by leftist critics as frozen in that modernism and now politically reactionary. Cummings, of course, did much to exacerbate this increasingly hostile relationship, not only because of his assertive individualism and hatred of collectivism in all forms, but also because of his increasingly defensive bitterness about losing his favored status and becoming philosophically isolated. His poetic attacks on the Left in the mid-thirties and his growing tendency in the late thirties to dichotomize the world into irreconcilable camps of "you and I" and "mostpeople" only furthered his embattled isolation. At the same time, however, his *Collected Poems* helped establish his poetry in the modern poetic canon. No literature anthology or textbook on twentieth-century American literature thereafter (to the present day) would be complete without a few of his poems (nearly always, alas, the *same* poems). This recognition, combined with prestigious awards like the Bollingen Prize and the slowly growing admiration of critics and reviewers in the forties and fifties, enabled Cummings's poetry to achieve something of a renaissance by the end of the 1940s. But as will be developed in the conclusion, this belated recognition did not mellow Cummings's hostility to what he now saw as mainstream American culture; nor did it ameliorate his growing isolation from it, or soften the stridency of his satirical voice.

   Seen, then, from the perspective of his entire career, the embattled iconoclasm of Cummings's political poetry in the 1930s represents the mid-
stage of his transformation from the playful enfant terrible of the 1920s
to the quirky curmudgeon of the late years. If such thirties poems as
"IN) . . . (MEMORIAM" and "if i" recapture the wit and comic mimicry of his twenties satires, the bitterness of other anti-leftist poems and
the reductiveness of the "mostpeople" satires look ahead to the dismissive sociopolitical poems of the last decades. Perhaps the most remarkable
thing about the political Cummings is that he encompassed both personae
in the thirties: the enfant terrible who never grew up and the curmudgeon who increasingly saw the world through the ever-thickening lens of
his own dogmatic values.

4

Robert Frost

A Lone Striker

In the late 1920s, Robert Frost's poetic status—like his poetry itself—differed significantly from that of the other three poets considered in this book. Where Stevens and Cummings were admired by a small circle of avant-garde critics, and Williams could scarcely even boast that recognition, Frost had achieved widespread popular and critical acclaim beginning with his return to America in 1915 and climbing steadily into the 1920s. His first two books, *A Boy's Will* (1913) and *North of Boston* (1914), published in England, received excellent reviews and sold well in the States, such that when he returned to America he found himself a success, praised by Amy Lowell in *The New Republic* and eagerly courted by the prominent literati of New York and Boston. His next book, *Mountain Interval* (1916), was equally successful—indeed, many of Frost's best-loved poems came from *North of Boston* and *Mountain Interval*. Invitations to lecture poured in, and he accepted the first of many college teaching positions, at Amherst College, that same year. Frost had waited a long time for this recognition—he was forty-one in 1915—and had struggled so much financially that in desperation he had taken his family to England in 1912, hoping for a better response there. But when success did arrive, he never wanted for money or critical praise thereafter. In fact, he became that rarest of poets, one who could support his family by his poetry, supplemented by readings, lectures, and cushy professorial and "poet in residence" appointments. Frost's appeal, unlike that of the other three poets of this study, derived from lyrics that were easy to read and superficially more conventional in using regular rhyme and meter—he followed "the old way to be new," as he put it in 1935.[1] But sophisticated critics quickly recognized the depth, subtlety, and ambiguity in his best poems, a thematic complexity akin to the radically different styles of Eliot, Stevens, and the other modernists. Critical honors were not long in coming: his 1924 *New Hampshire* received the Pulitzer Prize (the first of four Pulitzers his poetry would receive over his career).

Toward the end of the twenties, however, this delirious decade of success seemed to be waning. A trip to England and Europe in 1928 had not gone well; health problems, both physical and mental, began to plague Frost's large family, and he himself fought against periodic bouts of depression. But the most disturbing development for Frost was that his next book of poems, *West-Running Brook* (1928), received several tepid reviews and a few negative ones. The critics who complained said essentially the same thing that was later said about Cummings's *ViVa* and Stevens's *Harmonium* in 1931: that the poet did not seem to be developing. In Frost's case, this yardstick of growth and change was, as Jay Parini observes, quite inappropriate, since his poems often were written many years earlier and then held back:[2] "Frost is not a poet who developed in any obvious ways from book to book, as did Yeats or Eliot or Stevens. Instead, he grew by accretion. His peculiar method of hoarding poems (going back to them, often decades later, to revise) only adds to the difficulty of discerning 'development.' In a sense, Frost achieved his vision early, and he restates, re-creates, refigures this original vision in book after book. There are no great leaps forward, only deepenings, confirmations, and subtle extensions."[3]

Nonetheless, while most critics praised the book, some lavishly, Parini notes that "the suggestion had been put forward that he was an escapist, a poet out of touch with his times" (267). A critic reviewing for *Booklist* wrote: "Mr. Frost is, unlike so many modern poets, undisturbed by the encroachments of a hard, unyielding machine civilization upon his New England quietude."[4] Granville Hicks, writing for the *Springfield Union Republican,* praised Frost's "tough-minded" skepticism but complains that Frost "has created the ordered world in which he lives only by the exclusion of many, many chaotic elements in the real world. Perhaps it is this fact that explains why Frost is, even at his best, a very perfect minor poet, not the major poet for whom America is looking."[5] Other reviews were also mixed. Frederick Pierce wrote in the *Yale Review:* "Our admiration is for the sincerity and delicate insight with which the theme is handled. Our disappointment is because of the smallness, limitation, almost barrenness of the theme itself."[6] Several critics—most notably Mark Van Doren, Theodore Spencer, and Babette Deutsch—complained of the unevenness of the selection, with "trivial" poems alongside important ones.[7] Spencer found the book as a whole "disappointing. . . . [T]here is an impression of thinness . . . which Mr. Frost has not given before. One feels that he has lost or abandoned a view of life which was, in its implications, tragic, and adopted instead an allegorizing method which is far less important" (77). Though he pretended otherwise, Frost was thin-skinned about reviews and "annoyed by the suggestion that he was out of step, or that he was burying his head in the sand" (Parini 267). The reviews of his next book, *Collected Poems,* did not make him feel any better.

That book appeared in November 1930 as the Depression was becoming deeply embedded; but since the collection ended with the poems of *West-Running Brook,* it took no notice. Though in 1930, critics like Granville Hicks and Isador Schneider had not yet moved to the far left, they nonetheless were losing patience with the narrowness of Frost's subjects, despite their respect for his overall achievement. And since this volume presented Frost's collected work to date, they felt at liberty to evaluate his career. Noting "how compact and unified Frost's work is," Hicks writes: "[H]e has occupied himself with a limited body of experiences. He has, in short, found for poetic purposes, a world of his own." But in this world "[w]e find . . . nothing of industrialism, . . . of the disrupting effect that scientific hypotheses have had on modern thought. . . . [and nothing of] Freudianism." As a result, Frost "cannot contribute directly to the unification in imaginative terms of our culture." Frederick Carpenter arrived at essentially the same conclusion: "He has not the cosmic imagination which creates its own world, as Walt Whitman had. . . . [I]n choosing a quiet happiness in preference to a turbulent greatness, Mr. Frost has merely cut himself off from the central American tradition." Isador Schneider (like Hicks, soon to write for *New Masses*) was harsher in faulting Frost's unworldliness, even while lavishly praising his other achievements: "Mr. Frost . . . is singularly out of touch with his own time. . . . We may go therefore to his poetry for diversion and relief from our time, but not for illumination."[8]

On the other hand, Genevieve Taggard, who would soon be writing poems about strikes, cautioned: "Any effort . . . to strip Frost down to singleness of meaning in the interests of propaganda must be opposed. The wisest and most mature poet of our time should not be hacked at and shaved down to suit a pigeonhole." Taggard was referring to the New Humanists, but her caveat applies perfectly to left-wing critics.[9]

Parini plausibly judges that *Collected Poems* "solidified [Frost's] reputation" (267); indeed, the book earned him a second Pulitzer Prize and election to the American Academy of Arts and Letters. But battle lines were being drawn. As left-leaning critics became more ideological as the Depression worsened, their tolerance of Frost's localized world grew ever shorter. Far more important, however, Frost's poetics suddenly and unexpectedly expanded in poems to come, but not in ways leftist critics welcomed. For now the poet was doing precisely what Hicks et al. said he should do, that is, respond to contemporary issues: industrialism, unemployment and destitution, revolution and collectivism, the New Deal, the welfare state, and Franklin Roosevelt. But as he well knew, his attitudes toward these issues would rankle the Left.

FROST'S POLITICS

What precisely were Frost's political views in this period? While writers have summarized them,[10] using Frost's poems of the period as illustration (supplemented by letters, interviews, and essays) provides the best index. These poems went into his next book, *A Further Range* (1936), but they were written between 1931–35 and show Frost indeed ranging further than he had previously. As he said later, the book "has got a good deal more of the times in it than anything I ever wrote before."[11] Indeed, the longest poem in *A Further Range* was one of his first political poems (a term he used himself)[12] of the thirties. "Build Soil," composed in May 1932, is a pastoral dialogue between two farmers, one a farmer-poet (Tityrus), who seems a Frost manqué, the other a failed potato farmer (Meliboeus). Their names come from Virgil's "First Eclogue," but their speech and concerns are thoroughly contemporary. The times "seem revolutionary bad," Meliboeus complains ungrammatically: he is forced to sell his interval farm and buy a run-down place "only fit for sheep" (*CPPP* 289). But the phrase also alludes slyly to the revolutionary talk in the air that spring, 1932, not only from leftist writers (more on this below) but also concerning the Bonus Army's march on Washington that May, which alarmed the Hoover administration.[13] Tityrus wonders if the times have "reached [such] a depth of desperation" that he should stop writing poetry about "love's alternations, joy and grief . . . for the uncertainty of judging who is a contemporary liar" (290)—precisely Frost's self-reflexive situation.

The two go on to discuss solutions, and Meliboeus bluntly asks (twice!): "Is socialism needed, do you think?" The question gives Tityrus-Frost the chance to opine on socialism, first that it is already "An element in any government" but is never found in a pure state, even in "oligarchic" Russia. But then he redefines socialism as social restraints placed on runaway greed, political ambition, and ingenuity, as well as on "exploiting businesses." He concludes: "Bounds should be set / To ingenuity for being so cruel / In bringing change unheralded on the unready."[14] Frost favored this restraining, regulatory function of government, of creating economic boundaries—walls—as he states in a letter to Louis Untermeyer contemporaneous with this poem: "I'm in favor of a skin and fences and tariff walls. I'm in favor of reserves and withholdings" (*RF to LU* 223).[15]

Tityrus goes on to deliver another Frostian opinion:

> We're always too much out or too much in.
> At present from a cosmical dilation
> We're so much out that the odds are against
> Our ever getting inside in again. (293)

Idiosyncratically, "out" means out in society (another kind of "socialized"); "in" means within oneself or introverted. Tityrus's point is that we need to develop fully our character as individuals before mixing in society. He uses the analogy of a painter who keeps colors "unmixed on the palette" versus one who muddies his palette by mixing them, concluding:

> long before I'm interpersonal
> Away 'way down inside I'm personal.
> Just so before we're international
> We're national. (293)[16]

The gist of Frost's argument is that to create individual strength to meet these hard times, we must resist becoming too social (and politically socialized) too quickly—precisely what his contemporaries were doing. Real strength resides in the individual forming and hardening his or her own character—in short, "rugged individualism."

Frost expressed the same view elsewhere, for example, in an interview in 1931: "A person is always being pulled out of himself socially . . . He should know when to say, 'I am too much out of myself—too overt.' . . . You co-operate in order that you may be a better individual. You associate yourself with your fellows in order that you may be stronger yourself. . . . But I am mostly interested in solitude and in the preservation of the individual. . . . Most of oneself should be within oneself."[17]

Finally, Frost brings out the central metaphor that gives the poem its title: Just as one should hold back on socializing until one's character is fully developed, one should "make a late start to market," first building soil by plowing it under:

> Plant, breed, produce,
> But what you raise or grow, why feed it out,

> Eat it or plow it under where it stands
> To build soil. For what is more accursed
> Than an impoverished soil pale and metallic?
> . . . .
>   Turn the farm in upon itself
> Until it can contain itself no more,
> But sweating-full, drips wine and oil a little. (295)

The metaphor expands in several directions. First, Frost gets in a dig at Russia and its American sympathizers among his "friends":

> Friends crowd around me with their five year plans
> That Soviet Russia has made fashionable.
> You come to me and I'll unfold to you
> A five-year plan I call so, not because
> It takes ten years or so to carry out,
> Rather because it took five years at least
> To think it out. Come close, let us conspire
> In self-restraint (295)

Clearly, the advice also describes Frost's method of holding back his poems, often for many years, while they ripened subconsciously in his mind.

    Tityrus's conclusion—and the poem's—now becomes self-evident:

> Keep off each other and keep each other off.
> You see the beauty of my proposal is
> It needn't wait on general revolution.
> I bid you to a one-man revolution—
> The only revolution that is coming.
> . . . .
>   Steal away and stay away.
> Don't join too many gangs. Join few if any.
> Join the United States and join the family—
> But not too much in between unless a college. (296)

Meliboeus conveniently concurs:

> We're too unseparate. And going home
> From company means coming to our senses. (297)

Ironically—or rather, appropriately—this was a public poem, the Phi Beta Kappa poem that Frost gave at Columbia University on May 31, 1932. Unquestionably, its themes, although obliquely couched, ran precisely counter to the prevailing politics on a college campus as liberal-left as Columbia, as well as counter to the rapidly intensifying radicalism of Frost's friends. Choose individualism over joining groups and "gangs"; nationalism must precede internationalism; socialism should equal restraint and boundaries, not the nationalization of the means of production; plus digs at Russia's Five-Year Plan and at the belief (widespread among leftists in 1932) that a social revolution in the United States was imminent. What motivated Frost knowingly to fly in the face of his audience's politics? For that matter, what impelled him to deliver a political poem at all? Two motives suggest themselves, one intrinsic to Frost's character, the other quite of the moment.

Put simply, Frost enjoyed getting under people's skin, being "impish" (Parini's word), "devilish" (Frost's word).[18] Peter Stanlis lists some examples: In 1939, he told an audience at the Bread Loaf School of English, "What some people call 'exploitation,' I call employment." Tongue partly in cheek, he praised poverty, calling himself a "ragged individualist" (this at a time when he owned several homes). Alluding to Eleanor Roosevelt's desire to abolish poverty, Frost said: "When I think of all the good that has come from poverty, I would hesitate to abolish it." And regarding Social Security, he offered this: "to live assertively with courage, men needed some 'social insecurity'" (32).

Frost knew that "Build Soil" would cause a stir; in fact, he called it "the big dislodger" (August 20, 1932, *RF to LU* 226) and boasted to Untermeyer: "[I]t rather stole the occasion for some reason from the great Walter Lippmann. In a way it was a monkey-shine and he needn't have minded poetry's having a little the best of it for once in a political age. But I'm afraid he did mind, whether from wounded vanity or lack of humor; and I'm sorry, for I admire him and should like to count him friend. There is a devil in me that defeats my deliberate intentions" (December 13, 1932, *RF to LU* 231).

Frost describes the immediate impetus for "Build Soil" in a letter he wrote two weeks before the presentation: "The trouble with everybody's mind is everybody is caught out in the big forum.[19] Gee you ought to have seen the document Waldo Frank wanted me to sign. He and [Lewis] Mumford and [Edmund] Wilson got it up. He said follow us and you can be a leader of your generation. They propose to use the class-conscious workers for the time being. I have half a mind to tell the class-conscious workers on them. But always ganging up at Geneva or somewhere else. When all you have to do to be saved is to sneak off to one side and see whether you are any good at anything" (May 13, 1932, *RF to LU* 223). The "document" Frost refers to was a manifesto urging a "temporary dictatorship of the class-conscious workers," signed and circulated by Waldo Frank, Edmund Wilson, Lewis Mumford, Sherwood Anderson, and John Dos Passos in the spring of 1932.[20] Frost must have resented the absurd lure Frank held out of being "a leader of your generation"; indeed, the promise underscored what was already obvious: how out of touch Frost's political and poetic values now were. The poem—and its public provocation, delivered near the very center of the radical movement—was Frost's response.

In this sense, Frost's anti-leftism differed somewhat from Cummings's. At times they sounded identical, as in their disbelief that any collectivity can affect what truly matters.

Cummings: Nor will anything ever persuade me that, by turning Somerville [a working-class town adjoining Cambridge] into Cambridge or Cambridge into Somerville or both into neither, anybody can make an even slightly better world. Betters worlds (I suggest) are born, not made; and their birthdays are the birthdays of individuals.[21]

Frost: "no change of system could possibly make me a bit better or abler, the only two things of any importance to me personally." (September 15, 1934, *RF to LU* 243)

But Cummings's political satires in the mid-thirties were more defensive and reactionary, some aimed directly at the leftist critics who had abandoned modernist aesthetics and abandoned Cummings himself. Frost, by contrast, enjoyed challenging left-wing ideas of his time—socialism, collectivism, later the New Deal's welfare state—while asserting his own values of self-reliance and individualism. As Stanley Burnshaw observes about "Build Soil," "Frost had indeed taken his stand: on the opposite side of the ideological barricades, firing against all Liberal-Radical-Socialist enemies, salvos of his conservatism."[22] Frost, moreover, did not allow political differences to affect his friendships. He maintained a friendly debate with his liberal son-in-law, Willard Fraser, and stayed friends with Burnshaw, the poetry critic and theorist for *New Masses* in the mid-thirties, as well as with Louis Untermeyer, a more moderate leftist. Early in his lifelong friendship with Untermeyer, Frost defined their political differences: "I am interested in what is to stay as it is; you are interested in what is not to stay as it is. We can't split on that difference. We operate in mutually exclusive spheres from which we can only bow across to each other in mutual appreciation" (March 12, 1920, *RF to LU* 97).

The much-discussed question of the day about writing political poetry and, in particular, proletarian poetry, agitated Frost, but he expressed his views in letters, essays, and lectures more than in poems. Fulminating in a letter to Untermeyer about an article by Archibald MacLeish,[23] which he paraphrases as "publishers ought possibly . . . to play up originality in art more than they do because the originality of today in art is the revolution of tomorrow in politics," Frost rejects the linkage and relegates politics to a distinctly lower level than art: "Tell me any poetic or belle lettre originality of any day that became the revolution of any day following. . . . If you want to play with the word revolution, every day and every new poem of a poet is a revolution of the spirit: that is to say it is a freshening. But it leads to nothing on the lower plane of politics. On this lower plane of thought and opinion the poet is a follower" (February 17, 1935, *RF to LU* 255).

When he addressed an audience at the Rocky Mountain Writers Conference a few months later, Frost explicitly rejected the poet's social or class-oriented responsibilities. Lawrance Thompson paraphrases and summarizes: "The true poet should not devote himself to representing or weeping over the unchanging social and industrial evils. . . . As for the present trend of the so-called 'proletarian' writers expressing grievances and insisting on change, Frost bluntly disassociated himself: 'It is not the business of the poet to cry for reform.' So far as he was concerned, the poet should mind his own business, and to illustrate what he meant, he read . . . 'Two Tramps in Mud Time'" (425).

Frost had developed this notion of grievance poetry in his introduction to E. A. Robinson's *King Jasper,* written a few months before the conference. More a statement of his own aesthetics than an appreciation of Robinson, it distinguishes between political poetry—the poetry of grievances—and Frost's own poetry of grief: "The latest proposed experiment of the experimentalists is to use poetry as a vehicle of grievances against the non-Utopian state. . . . The grievances of the great Russians of the last century have given Russia a revolution. The grievances of their great imitators in America may well give us, if not a revolution, at least some palliative pensions. We must suffer them to put life at its ugliest" (*CPPP* 742). Frost then

narrates a scene in which he is challenged by a young enthusiast of proletarian poetry. Though Frost no doubt recasts the encounter to his advan-
tage, it reveals his attitudes:

> I had it from one of the youngest lately: "Whereas we once thought
> literature should be without content, we now know it should be
> charged full of propaganda." Wrong twice, I told him. . . . But he
> returned to his position after a moment out for reassembly: "Surely
> art can be considered good only as it prompts action." How soon, I
> asked him. But there is danger of undue levity in teasing the young.
> The experiment is evidently started. Grievances are certainly a power
> and are going to be turned on. . . . [The grievance poets] may seem
> like picketers or members of the committee on rules for the moment.
> We shan't mind what they seem, if only they produce real poems.
>   But for me, I don't like grievances. I find I gently let them alone
> wherever published. What I like is griefs. (742–43)

Grievances are political, griefs personal: "Beyond participation of politicians and beyond relief of senates lie our sorrows" (February 23, 1932,
RF to LU, 219). The introduction riled at least one leftist critic. Newton
Arvin, reviewing *King Jasper* in *The New Republic,* commented that Frost's
condescension toward younger, leftist poets concerned with grievances,
as well as his complacent view that "life goes so unterribly" in America,
places him at an "astronomical distance from the rest of us." Arvin also
made the valid point that Frost's skepticism and complacency were just as
prone to cant as leftist poetry was.[24]

POLITICAL POEMS IN *A FURTHER RANGE*

Despite Frost's apparent rejection of political poetry—in fact, simultaneous with it—he wrote his own: many poems, in fact, distinguish *A
Further Range* from all his other volumes. Doubtless, the most famous and
most anthologized is "Two Tramps in Mud Time" (*CPPP* 251–52). Its popularity derives from its being dramatic and, like "Stopping by Woods on
a Snowy Evening" and "The Road Not Taken," posing a dilemma. The
drama is edged in uncertainty, even lurking danger. Two "tramps" suddenly appear "Out of the mud," intentionally disturb the speaker ("put
me off my aim") from his wood-chopping, and, by one tramp lingering,
plant the idea firmly in the speaker's mind that "He wanted to take my
job for pay." It is how Frost shades the dilemma that is most revealing. Jay

Parini explains: "These were stressful economic times, and tramps were everywhere—honest men, mostly, in search of a meager living" (288). True, but Frost doesn't call them "honest men"; nor would he dream of calling them "downtrodden workers" or some other proletarian cliché. They are "hulking tramps" and "strangers" with strong connotations of menace and otherness. They are dirty ("sleeping God knows where last night"), limited ("Except as a fellow handled an ax / They had no way of knowing a fool"), and potentially threatening. "Out of the mud"— the very first words—makes them seem scarcely human, almost primeval in their origins.[25]

The weather stanzas that follow, superficially discursive, actually reinforce this tone of menace while providing dramatic time for the speaker to consider his dilemma. The weather is on the cusp of spring, but can go either way: "if you so much as dare to speak / . . . you're two months back in the middle of March." The bird "half knew / Winter was only playing possum. / . . . [and] wouldn't advise a thing to blossom." The water, at night, becomes "lurking frost" with "crystal teeth." All these instances of pathetic fallacy point to unspoken danger: what will the hulking tramps do if the speaker does not offer them his job?

But the speaker, after describing how much he loves his work, shows— or seems to show—his moral sensitivity to the situation:

> I had no right to play
> With what was another man's work for gain.
> My right might be love but theirs was need.
> And where the two exist in twain
> Theirs was the better right—agreed.

Then the poem takes an unexpected turn. Rather than resolving the original dilemma, Frost uses the occasion to present his belief in *not* separating love and need, avocation and vocation:

> But yield who will to their separation,
> My object in living is to unite
> My avocation and my vocation
> . . . .
> Only where love and need are one,
> And the work is play for mortal stakes,
> Is the deed ever really done
> For Heaven and the future's sakes.

All well and good—but what becomes of the tramps? Commentators, frustrated by this teasingly unresolved dilemma, have provided their own resolutions. Malcolm Cowley surmises that "in life the meeting may have had a different sequel" (the poet offers them a different job or even invites them "for a slab of home-baked bread spread thick with apple butter"). But this is like saying Macbeth should not have trusted the witches in act 1. It is out of bounds. Cowley assumes (without support) that the speaker "lets them walk away without a promise or a penny."[26] Parini, by contrast, argues that the speaker's concession ("Theirs was the better right—agreed") is the "final political or moral point" (even though Frost "takes away with one hand what he has given with the other"), and thus "it becomes pointless to worry about what 'did' or 'didn't' happen" (289).

But was this passage the final moral point? Several qualifications intrude. First, Frost labels the "need trumps love" argument as "*their* logic" (emphasis added), implying that it is not the speaker's. Earlier, he offers these unexpected lines:

The blows that a life of self-control
Spares to strike for the common good
That day, giving a loose to my soul,
I spent on the unimportant wood.

One might have expected that self-control spares one's losing one's temper, or striking blows in rage. Why should refusing to "strike [a blow] for the common good" be considered "self-control"? It might better be called indifference.[27] But the passage anticipates the ending. Just as the speaker is no do-gooder, the poet will not provide the expected, even desired proletarian resolution. Just the opposite—he biases the poem against the "tramps" and provides compelling reasons, culminating in his philosophical conclusion, for ignoring their unvoiced request. The poem, in short, is anti-proletarian, Frost's slap at the whole movement. That he read it at the Rocky Mountain Writers Conference to illustrate that "a poet should mind his own business" (see above) suggests that Frost was again baiting his audience as he had done with "Build Soil" in 1932. Thompson surmises that it "may have annoyed some of his listeners" particularly because "Frost's pious way of concluding this poem seemed to sidestep . . . [the unemployment problem it] invoked" (426).

Once Roosevelt's New Deal took hold in 1933, Frost shifted his aim somewhat from radical leftists to the New Deal's policies of social reform. Like Cummings, he parodied the name, calling it in his letters "the New

Deil," Scottish dialect for 'the New Devil" (Untermeyer's note, *RF to LU* 258). As Stanlis explains, "For Frost the New Deal was much too big a step in the direction of the twentieth century ideological totalitarianisms.... Frost believed that the greatest danger to the United States during the 1930's was not its failure to solve the problems of the Depression, nor even the Nazi threat from abroad, but rather F.D.R.'s New Deal program in its movement towards left wing collectivism" (70). What Frost particularly disliked, according to Stanlis, was "its compulsory egalitarianism, its leveling of individual distinctions, its subordination of private freedom, originality, and initiative to mere economic security as the great end of life. Frost believed that ... Roosevelt wished to create 'a homogenized society,' in which the cream of human nature would never be allowed to rise to the top. As Frost perceived it, this was the New Deal Utopian dream for the new masses of the future America.... In a letter to Untermeyer, on March 11, 1937, he ... [wrote]: 'I have so much sympathy with the middle classes in their hour of being wiped out by the New Republic'" (33).

Frost had a chance to see firsthand the New Deal in action—at least an agency of it. Residing in Key West during the winter of 1935, he observed with dismay how the Federal Emergency Relief Administration (FERA) had virtually taken over the indigent town as "a pet rehabilitation project." He writes to Untermeyer:

> The only thing at all socially disturbing is the presence in force of Franklin D. Roosevelt['s] FERA.... There was talk of transporting seventy five percent of the [townspeople]. But nobody could think of anybody who would want them. So the author of a book called Compulsory Spending is here with a staff to put everybody at work on public improvements.... We had to get our rent thru them. They are mildly and beneficently dictatorial. Both the Mayor of the Town and the Governor of the State have abdicated in their favor. Their great object they say is to restore the people to their civic virtue. When in history has any power ever achieved that? (January 10, 1935, *RF to LU* 251)[28]

Frost's poem "A Roadside Stand" (*CPPP* 260–62) in part touches on the same theme of governmental relocation of the indigent (now in New England) and disparages the do-gooders vigorously. The poem first describes a scruffy roadside fruit stand set up by some farmers; then it announces:

It is in the news that all these pitiful kin
Are to be bought out and mercifully gathered in
To live in villages next to the theater and store
Where they won't have to think for themselves any more;
While greedy good-doers, beneficent beasts of prey,
Swarm over their lives, enforcing benefits
That are calculated to soothe them out of their wits,
And by teaching them how to sleep the sleep all day,
Destroy their sleeping at night the ancient way.

Here, Frost sounds exactly like Republican conservatives (most famously Herbert Hoover) who warned that federally administered relief programs would rob the poor of their initiative, their desire to work. Hence, they would "sleep all day," rather than at night from the honest fatigue of a day's work.

This poem, in fact, makes a number of questionable assumptions about the poor, beginning with their identification as such in running a roadside fruit stand. Rather than seeing the operators of this "little new shed" as farm folk running a roadside business to make surplus income, the speaker describes their stand

that too pathetically plead,
It would not be fair to say for a dole of bread,
But for some of the money, the cash whose flow supports
The flower of cities from sinking and withering faint.

If they are not pleading for charity—"a dole of bread"—then why mention it? Of course, mentioning it makes their roadside stand sound even more "pathetic." The proprietors want some of the "city" money going by to

make our being expand
and give us the life of the moving pictures' promise
That the party in power is said to be keeping from us.

The speaker pities their "childish longing," fed on film fantasies, and describes how their stand fails to attract business, only cars stopping for the wrong reasons (directions, gas, etc.). Nowhere in the poem does he mention stopping and talking to the operators; hence, we might conclude that his was one of the passing cars, that his depictions of their motives and pity for their condition are all based on unsupported—and condescending—assumptions.[29] There is also the odd contradiction here that "the party in power," which "is said to be keeping from us [life's promises]," sounds far more like a depiction of the Hoover administration, but the "greedy good-doers" and "beneficent beasts of prey" who talk of relocating the farmers are clearly a parody of New Deal social engineers.[30]

The poem concludes even more strangely—and ominously:

> I can't help owning the great relief it would be
> To put these people at one stroke out of their pain.
> And then next day as I come back to the sane,
> I wonder how I should like you to come to me
> And offer to put me gently out my pain.

The original version of this poem had the subtitle "Euthanasia," which Frost changed in the published version to "On Being Put Out of Our Misery" and then wisely dropped altogether in subsequent collections. Of course, "great relief" is what the "good-doers" of the current "party in power" intend with their social programs. But the final lines (and the deleted subtitle) refer not to amelioration but to mercy killing of the weak and unfit, a Nazi-like horror. The speaker's subsequent rejection of the idea as insane and unfair ("how would I like it done to me?") does not mitigate its shock effect. Like his earlier retraction ("It would not be fair to say for a dole of bread"), the suggestions linger ominously; in both cases, we are intended to see how the speaker thinks. Finally, one wonders who would feel the "relief" in this final solution: the stand's operators who refused to go on relief in the first place, or the speaker himself?

One source of Frost's harsh treatment of what he considered the rural poor in this poem may have been that he felt his own poetry was misunderstood, ironically by "the condescending and welfare-minded" rich, as depicting "a house of the poor." He complained of this to Untermeyer in 1938: "North of Boston is merely a book of people, not of poor people. They happen to be people of simplicity or simple truth miscalled simplicity" (*RF to LU* 305). Toward these socially conscious, misunderstanding rich, he threatens in the same letter: "Before I get through I'm going to drive these social servitors back to the social settlements or to concentration camps where I can starve their sympathies to death."

The apocalyptic death of "social servitors," this time liberal, is precisely the theme of "On Taking from the Top to Broaden the Base" (*CPPP* 271), an aptly titled send-up of economic leveling. Here, the collective speaker challenges a "squat old" pyramidal mountain: "Roll stones down on our head!" He assumes he is safe because he thinks the mountain incapable of further leveling:

> Your top has sunk too low,
> Your base has spread too wide,
> For you to roll one stone
> Down if you tried.

The mountain takes the dare, however, for

> even at the word
> A pebble hit the roof,
> Another shot through glass[31]
> Demanding proof.

The leveling here is no boon to the people, and it produces a mudslide that buries them "in one cold / Unleavened batch." Shifting his voice and perspective rather awkwardly to third person, the speaker narrates the outcome with a mixed tone of godlike detachment (à la Stephen Crane) and Grimm fairy tale:

> And none was left to prate
> Of an old mountain's case
> That still took from its top
> To broaden its base.

Like the speaker's fantasy in "A Roadside Stand," the people are here disposed of in one fell swoop—their just reward for "prating" about leveling, presumably. Even the mud that buries them permits no one to rise, is "unleavened." But this poem offers no teasing retraction and thus becomes an allegory with a clear moral: radically altering the social order can bring on unforeseen disaster that encompasses everyone; level at your own risk. Frost agreed with Lord Balfour "that you can't make people equally rich; you can only make them equally poor." His comments to Untermeyer following this remark—written well after the Depression—are revealing in the way they romanticize poverty: "It isn't merely because poverty can make us equal. It can make us better than that. It can make us purer. It can refine us" (August 9, 1947, *RF to LU* 347).

If these apocalyptic narratives attack New Deal programs, ideology, and beneficiaries in sweeping strokes, one notorious poem, "To a Thinker" (*CPPP* 298), mounts an ad hominem attack on the New Deal's creator, Franklin Roosevelt. Whether Roosevelt is, in fact, the subject is a point of controversy—more accurately, of confusion that Frost intentionally created. When he originally read the poem at the Rocky Mountain Writers Conference in August 1935, its title was "To a Thinker," and Frost told his audience that "he had been forced to suppress [it]. It had been written a year or two earlier, he added, and it might have been publishable as soon as completed. Since then, so many dreadful things had come true, which he had prophesied in this poem, that he now hesitated to print it."[32] He did not hesitate for long, for the *Saturday Review* published it on January 11, 1936, with a significant addition to the title: "To a Thinker in Office," leaving no doubt about the identity of the "thinker." Newspapers got wind of the poem: Mencken's *Baltimore Sun* printed an interview with Frost that reproduced the poem. Though "in Office" is missing from the title (possibly Frost provided an older copy of the poem), the reporter was given to understand that the target was Roosevelt: "[He] asserted he was anti-Roosevelt. . . . He bitterly condemned an alleged Administration policy of regarding farmers as possessors of what he called submarginal minds. And, with something of a flourish, he produced a new poem, 'To a Thinker.' The verse, he indicated, was written about the President."[33]

None of this would matter much if Frost had not later denied the poem was about Roosevelt in a letter to Henry Goddard Leach (March 15, 1936). Now he claimed that he had written the poem three years earlier and aimed it "at the heads of our easy despairers of the republic and of parliamentary forms of government" (*Selected Letters* 427–28). But since the "thinker" in the title and poem is singular throughout, the "despairers" plural, Frost was clearly being disingenuous in this letter to cover his true intent. The inconsistencies about when he wrote the poem and the *Sun* reporter's indirect quotation that he wrote it "about the President" further confirm that Frost was now creating a smoke screen. Finally, when *A Further Range* was in page proofs, he deleted the words "in Office" from the title (*Selected Letters* 428n).

Ironically, the poem that caused this fuss is fairly innocuous. True, it portrays Roosevelt as a shallow opportunist, a wishy-washy "thinker," going "back and forth" in his political views:

> The last step taken found your heft
> Decidedly upon the left.

One more would throw you on the right.
Another still—you can see your plight.
You call this thinking, but it's walking.
Not even that, it's only rocking,
Or weaving like a stabled horse:
. . . .
Just now you're off democracy
(With a polite regret to be),
And leaning on dictatorship

The speaker then predicts that "in less than no time" the president will "be a democrat again." Though "leaning on dictatorship" is rather strong—more justifiable perhaps a year later when Roosevelt tried to pack the Supreme Court—the charge of "flip-flopping" is not unwarranted considering that during the 1932 presidential campaign Roosevelt went back and forth on whether the federal government should fund new relief projects or cut spending. And even one of Roosevelt's most sympathetic biographers acknowledges that FDR was willing to try almost any approach during the worst part of the Depression, even when the experiments contradicted each other.[34]

The poem is not entirely negative, moreover, and offers a backhanded compliment to Roosevelt, calling him "[a] reasoner and good as such" and possessing the "gift" of swaying "with reason"—perhaps an allusion to FDR's persuasive fireside chats. Still, both tone and argument are condescending:

Don't let it bother you too much
If it makes you look helpless please
And a temptation to the tease.
Suppose you've no direction in you,
I don't see but you must continue
To use the gift you do possess

The clause about Roosevelt looking helpless suggests one reason why Frost wanted to conceal his intent. The poem's central conceit of futile motion—walking (back and forth), rocking, looking helpless—is applied to a man who could not use his legs and was confined to a wheelchair. Frost realized his liability here and used it to support his disclaimer to Leach: "I doubt if my native delicacy would have permitted me to use the figure of walking and rocking in connection with a person of the President's per-

sonal infirmities. But I am willing to let it go as aimed at him. He must
deserve it or people wouldn't be so quick to see him in it" (*Selected Letters*
428). The argument sounds persuasive until the final sentence—"he must
deserve it"—challenges Frost's "native delicacy."[35]

Like the retractions in "A Roadside Stand," Frost employs techniques—
in this case, wit and self-deprecating humor—to soften the poem's sting.
Against the president's vacillations, the poet offers his own attitude in this
clever, quotable couplet:

I own I never really warmed
To the reformer or reformed.

And he concludes with a bit of self-spoofing. If Roosevelt must continue
to "repent / From side to side in argument," he should not strain his own
mind, but "trust my instinct—I'm a bard." But also as in "A Roadside
Stand," it is questionable whether these "softeners" really work: the couplet sounds like a Frostian epigram composed at another time and dropped
in, while the final lines seem trite.

"Neither Out Far nor In Deep" (*CPPP* 274) aims its barb not at the
government or at ideological leftists, but at "the people" who depend on
their solutions to the prevailing social and economic problems. The poem
allegorically opposes land and sea, rooted values and the ephemeral, aesthetic variety and dreary sameness of surface, the knowable and the im-
penetrable. In resolutely looking "one way"—out to sea—the people "turn
their back on the land" and the values of self-sufficiency associated with
it. That they can look neither "out far" nor "in deep" does not deter them:
they continue their futile "watch" over the sea's sameness and opacity. The
poem thus depicts them as conformist ("all turn and look one way") and
slightly desperate for a revelation or a panacea—the perfect fodder for a
dictator (whom Frost had already identified in Roosevelt). And the choice
of a "standing gull" as the only other animal along the sand is not accidental: the people, too, are imperceptive gulls—and soon to be gulled—
in keeping their passive vigil instead of acting on their own behalf.

A few critics, beginning with Randall Jarrell, have construed the people's watch as heroic and Frost's attitude toward it as at least partly sympathetic in his "recognition of the essential limitations of man, without
denial or protest or rhetoric or palliation."[36] But others, notably Richard
Poirier, point out "the total *un*reflectiveness of 'the people'": "no detail
of the poem mirrors or reflects anything except inertia and conformity."[37]
Even their plural anonymity as "the people" is no democratic honorific

à la Sandburg, as George Monteiro argues (166); more likely, it satirically echoes the Marxist deification of the collective. Placed in the context of other political poems in *A Further Range*—the "pitiful" "these people" of "A Roadside Stand," the "gangs" one should avoid in "Build Soil," even the troubling twosome in "Two Tramps in Mud Time"—plurality does not bode well in Frost's poems of the thirties.[38] Yet Frost was not as arbitrarily dismissive as Cummings in the latter's straw man, "mostpeople." Frost at least recognized how much the populace was driven by economic circumstance to shift their political values. Responding to Roosevelt's landslide reelection in 1936, Frost writes to Untermeyer: "The national mood is humanitarian. Nobly so—I wouldn't take it away from them." He continues in the same letter: "I don't mean it is humanity [*sic*] not to feel the suffering of others. The last election would confute me if I did" (November 25, 1936, *RF to LU* 284–85).

If the political poems in *A Further Range* express Frost's distrust of leftist ideology, New Deal social tinkering, and even at times "the people," what do they affirm? Such poems as "Provide, Provide," "A Leaf Treader," and "In Time of Cloudburst" provide some definite markers. "Provide, Provide" (*CPPP* 280) shows Frost's darkly humorous side; even the aaa-bbb-ccc rhyme scheme lends itself to humor, which, for William Pritchard, turns the poem into "light verse . . . a neatly-turned piece of entertainment."[39] The title compresses the theme: provide for yourself because you cannot depend on anyone else, and do so when you can because "Too many fall from great and good / For you to doubt the likelihood" that you too will fall. This lighthearted urging of self-reliance, of course, directly challenges the logic of Social Security, in which the federal government now assumed part of the responsibility to save and "provide" for the individual in retirement.[40] But in the speaker's alternatives to the "fate" of eventual destitution there is something troubling:

> Die early and avoid the fate.
> Or if predestined to die late,
> Make up our mind to die in state.

> Make the whole stock exchange your own!
> If need be occupy a throne,
> Where nobody can call *you* crone.

A. E. Housman's bitter reflection in "To an Athlete Dying Young" echoes here, but so does Louis-Philippe's insouciant advice to Frenchmen deprived of the vote to "enrich yourselves" to gain it. How would readers in 1936 respond to "Make the whole stock exchange your own!"? Does its intentional absurdity nullify the poem's theme? The final lines are more disturbing still:

> Better to go down dignified
> With boughten friendship at your side
> Than none at all. Provide, provide!

"Boughten friendship"—gigolos, paid escorts, toadies, and suckups? Jay Parini "cannot imagine a less sentimental, wiser poem" (286); Randall Jarrell deemed it "full of the deepest, and most touching, moral wisdom" (41). Lawrance Thompson described it as "bitterly sarcastic" (437). I would call it humorously but deeply cynical.[41]

The way Frost's speakers characterize and respond to nature in several poems also says something about his values in the mid-thirties. Just as in the earlier "Bereft," nature is often personified as hostile ("A Leaf Treader"), or treacherous (the lurking frost in "Two Tramps"), or at best empty and indifferent ("Desert Places"). To survive and prevail in this climate requires toughness and perseverance. "Leaves Compared with Flowers" (*CPPP* 270), for example, associates flowers and petals with youth ("Petals I may have once pursued"). But now the poet is satisfied with the rougher, darker, but stronger parts of the tree that express analogous qualities in himself:

> But I may be one who does not care
> Ever to have tree bloom or bear.
> Leaves for smooth and bark for rough,
> Leaves and bark may be tree enough.
> . . . .
> Leaves are all my darker mood.

In "A Leaf Treader" (*CPPP* 270–71) the speaker does not hesitate to step on and "mire" fallen leaves until they are "safely trodden underfoot." He seems almost vindictive about the leaves that once were "more lifted up than I. / To come to their final place in earth they had to pass me by." And paranoid too, imagining he "heard them threatening under their breath. / ... to carry me with / them to death." But as the speaker does in "Stopping by Woods," this one stoutly resists their appeal to some death wish in him ("spoke to the fugitive in my heart") and concludes:

But it was no reason I had to go because they had to go.
Now up my knee to keep on top of another year of snow.

In his mind, he has already turned to his next adversary, "another year of snow," using the downtrodden piles of leaves to surmount it, in a kind of Darwinian struggle.

The superb "Desert Places" (*CPPP* 269) brilliantly and subtly merges nature's vacancy with the speaker's loneliness. The tired canard of Frost as a nature poet of the Hallmark greeting card ilk utterly disintegrates with this poem. The fast-falling snow indifferently smothers "All animals . . . in their lairs"; nor does it spare the speaker, who projects his own loneliness into its emptiness:

I am too absent-spirited to count;
The loneliness includes me unawares.

The next stanza repeats "lonely" or "loneliness" three times as the condition expands into the ultimate loneliness of creative silence and death: "A blanker whiteness of benighted snow / With no expression, nothing to express." But here the poem shifts its mode from descriptive to declamatory, its focus from animals to humans, from snowy fields to the stars, and its mood from passive acquiescence and blankness to recognition and defiance:

They cannot scare me with their empty spaces
Between stars—on stars where no human race is.
I have it in me so much nearer home
To scare myself with my own desert places.

"They" ambiguously refers to other people—astronomers, most likely[42]— and imputes to them a malevolence the speaker now resists, but only by acknowledging the same qualities—emptiness, indifference, loneliness— in himself.

One final example, "In Time of Cloudburst" (*CPPP* 259–60), is less confrontational, more philosophical in the way the speaker accepts the consequences of a downpour: "The worst it can do to me / Is carry some garden soil / A little nearer the sea." From this homely example, Frost characteristically expands the meaning to larger destruction, but he seems sanguine about its meaning:

And the harm is none too sure,
For when all that was rotted rich
Shall be in the end scoured poor

The biblical overtones here are unmistakable—the first now will later be
last—and the circular movements of wind, river, and sea in Ecclesiastes can
be heard in "so endless a repetition." Thus, even "When my garden has
gone down ditch," the speaker knows that the soil will settle somewhere
else, where he can start a new garden and "Begin all over to hope." His
concluding plea, then, is that this endless cycle of creation and destruction
"Not make me tired and morose / And resentful of man's condition." He
might have added: "like the poets of grievance."[43]

What these poems underscore is the will to endure and prevail in a difficult, often hostile climate, even as the speaker's stances vary from active
defiance, to philosophical acceptance, to pessimistic identification and self-
recognition. This individual toughness is what Frost would posit against
dependence on the state, whether as Marxian utopia or New Deal panacea. "To bestow . . . bread and butter, yes; but that's not the top thing," he
said in a late interview. "The top thing to bestow is character" (September 1, 1962, *Interviews* 289).

Finally, it must be pointed out that Frost was no apologist for big business. Parini calls him "an agrarian freethinker, a democrat with a small
'd,' with isolationist and libertarian tendencies" (280–81). Much earlier in
his career, as Tyler Hoffman shows (117–22), Frost wrote several poems
depicting the exploitation of millworkers, but never published them. "A
Lone Striker" (*CPPP* 249–50), the first poem in *A Further Range,* shares
some features of these unpublished poems: it sympathetically portrays a
millworker who, because he just missed the closing gate for his shift, is
locked out for a half hour. And like the factory conditions in the earlier
poems, the rules here are harsh, the pay minimal: "His time be lost, his
pittance docked. / He stood rebuked and unemployed." It is generally assumed that Frost based the poem on his own experience in the mills (e.g.,
Untermeyer's note, *RF to LU* 245). But as Hoffman points out, Frost's experience included a job recording absences and tardiness (111)—a perspective more from management than labor. Moreover, the worker responds
to being locked out as an individual, not as a stereotypical member of a
class. Like a schoolboy playing hooky, but without the joy, he wonders if
he is missed, but cannot see in through the blacked-out windows "To see
if some forlorn machine / Was standing idle for his sake. / (He couldn't
hope its heart would break.)" His personifications—"forlorn," "its heart

would break"—suggest a romantic naïveté and certainly no bitterness toward the machines or their owners. But the passage that follows offers one
of the rare glimpses in Frost's published poetry—for that matter in any
modernist's poetry—of a factory's atmosphere:

> And yet he thought he saw the scene:
> The air was full of dust of wool.
> A thousand yarns were under pull,
> But pull so slow with such a twist,
> All day from spool to lesser spool,
> It seldom overtaxed their strength;
> They safely grew in slender length.

Contrasting this nonhuman focus, the next lines praise a single spinner's
skill:

> Her deft hands showed with finger rings
> Among the harp-like spread of strings.
> She caught the pieces end to end
> And, with a touch that never missed,
> Not so much tied as made them blend.

In balancing harsh conditions and human skill and imagination, the poem
resists typecasting. Similarly:

> Man's ingenuity was good.
> He saw it plainly where he stood,
> Yet he found it easy to resist.

"Ingenuity" encompasses the spinner's skillful fingers, but also the whole
system of spools and looms that makes the mill run. But, again, the balance:
"Yet he found it easy to resist"—resist for the poem's contrasting scene
of the woods, where, on a cliff among the tops of trees, "Their breathing
mingled with his breathing." Here, he has time to drink from a spring, to
think about his life and love as he walked.

The concluding section balances the two worlds in his mind:

> The factory was very fine;
> He wished it all the modern speed.
> Yet, after all 'twas not divine,

That is to say, 'twas not a church.
He never would assume that he'd
Be any institution's need.

Now—after his communing with nature—he realizes that he would never
"Be any institution's need." The closing personifications, then, are heavily
ironic: should the industry "pine" (the perfect double entendre!) or even
"die . . . For want of his approval," they should "Come get him" and would
know where to find him. But, of course, the industry will not die for lack
of his love; it does not need him any more than his inactive loom would
feel "forlorn" or stand idle "for his sake." He knows that now, and knows
which world is his real home. The title underscores his singleness and separation: he is "a lone striker"—like Frost himself [44]—unattached to the mill
he sweats in, freest striking out by himself in nature. That singleness directly anticipates the next poem, "Two Tramps in Mud Time," which argues that love and need should be one. Ironically, both poems reside in a
section called "Taken Doubly," which is also apt: the single woodchopper is
literally taken doubly by the two tramps; the balances of "Striker"—harsh
mill conditions versus "man's ingenuity," the mill versus the woods, residing in one versus willingness to work in the other ("come get him")—
are also double.

      Clearly, Frost's stance here is not proletarian: the striker does not hate
the mills: he wishes them "all the modern speed" (another sly Frostian pun).
Though his pay is a "pittance," he does not complain about being exploited. [45]
Yet he knows that his being is sustained in nature, not in the social and industrial world. It is worth observing here that Frost's distrust of industrialism and his rootedness in the rural life share much with the Southern
Agrarians, whose philosophy (stated in *I'll Take My Stand* of 1931) he approved and supported. [46] "We are now at a moment when we are getting
too far out into the social-industrial" he observed in 1930 (*Interviews* 76).
Almost twenty-five years later, he still sounded very much the Southern
Agrarian: "My intolerance has been for the throng today who complain
of the modern pace yet strive to keep it" (*Interviews* 147).

      As Frost could have guessed, one poem mildly critical of industry in *A
Further Range* would not spare him the scorn of leftist critics. Indeed, two
of the book's poems assume a surprisingly defensive (though humorous)
stance of the poet hunkering down against expected attack. The delightful
"A Drumlin Woodchuck" (*CPPP* 257) emphasizes the autobiographical
by its first-person voice; the woodchuck announces: "My own strategic retreat / is where two rocks almost meet." With a back-door escape route,

I can sit forth exposed to attack
As one who shrewdly pretends
That he and the world are friends.

In fact, he prides himself on surviving because,

       though small
As measured against the All,
I have been so instinctively thorough
About my crevice and burrow.

Frost expressed something similar in a letter to Untermeyer that contrasts two philosophical attitudes and metaphors competing in the modern world: "the Darwinian metaphors of . . . survival values and the Devil take the hindmost" and the Marxian "metaphor of the State's being like a family." He continues: "Life is like battle. But so is it also like shelter. Apparently we are now going to die fighting to make it a secure shelter" (November 25, 1936, *RF to LU* 285). Parini describes him once telling an audience: "I keep my head down most of the time like a woodchuck. I keep to my hole. I play it safe" (295). But this was only one persona of Frost; the political poems in *A Further Range* show its aggressive complement.

"Not Quite Social" (*CPPP* 279) is more extreme in its seeming defensiveness than "A Drumlin Woodchuck" and more disturbing in its clash between a grim theme and a humorous, faintly mocking tone. Here the poet, speaking again in first person, expects to be "punished" for something he has done, though "Some of you will be glad I did what I did." His "crime," never specified, involves doing something that, though not expressly forbidden, "wasn't enjoined and wasn't expected clearly." The act could be Frost's vocation of poetry itself; but given the times, it could refer more specifically to his anti-leftist political themes, certainly not "enjoined" in the mid-thirties. The next stanza details a more specific offense: "For merely giving you once more gentle proof / That the city's hold on a man is no more tight / Than when its wall rose higher than any roof." But since Frost's world has nearly always been farm and woods, why confess now? In any case, he reminds the "you" who is to pass sentence on him that he has always been half-kidding and should never be taken for "having rebelled." The last lines show Frost at his "partly mirth[ful]" best. If he is condemned to death, he will "pay a death-tax of fairly polite repentance." It is the smirking "fairly" that gives away the tone of pseudo-contrition. Equally, the title, "Not *Quite* Social" (emphasis added), takes back what it seems to concede. But if this poem features an unrepentant and teasing speaker, it also alludes, albeit playfully, to a world of accusations, crimes, and extreme punishments, a world that would like to execute the speaker.[47]

If Frost, then, is the woodchuck, hunkering down, covering his back, and having an escape exit, he is also the poet unwilling to repent the unfashionable (not quite social) themes in his thirties poetry, themes that can sting, like the white hornet he describes in another poem of *A Further Range,* as well as tease the world that threatens him.

REVIEWS OF *A FURTHER RANGE*

That world was to come down hard on Frost in the leftist reviews of *A Further Range.* As described in chapter 1, 1935–36 marked a high point of writers and critics moving to the left, and Frost's political poems flew directly in the face of this trend. The resulting clash was inevitable. Virtually all critics, political and otherwise, noted Frost's new venture into political poetry, but most found it didactic and weak. Horace Gregory, writing in *The New Republic,* wondered about an apparent contradiction in Frost's persona: "If Mr. Frost sincerely wishes to identify himself with 'A Drumlin Woodchuck' . . . to be 'more secure and snug,' why does he trouble his head about further ranges into politics, where his wisdom may be compared to that of Calvin Coolidge?"[48] Newton Arvin complained the political poems were one-sided, revealing the poet's animus against socialism, but saying nothing about fascism. The apolitical poems he found tired, "pinched and poor in feeling and intellectually commonplace," informed by a homely philosophy "as profitless as a dried-up well."[49] Perhaps the nastiest attack came from Rolfe Humphries, who titled his review in *New Masses* "A Further Shrinking": "There is an aspect of Robert Frost which criticism can dismiss with objugation: when you call him a reactionary ——, or a counter-revolutionary ——, you have, in essence, said it all." Humphries described Frost's political "didacticism" as "unbecoming": "If he fell short as a poet [previously], it was because his quarrel with himself was not sufficiently sharp. He falls short now because his quarrel with others is too much so. . . . Now Frost can be caught in the act of being what he most aims not to be—fuddled, garrulous, deaf, and ordinary."[50]

Apolitical critics, though less pugnacious, were also disenchanted or puzzled by Frost's new range. The critic for the *Christian Science Monitor* perplexes: "[S]trangely enough, the poet who has said 'most propaganda poetry is merely Marxian philosophy, thinly overlaid with verse,' reveals himself, at this point in his career, as a propagandist. . . . [who] translates the philosophy of Frost into poetry." The critic for *News-Week* wrote that the political poems "may well cause readers to wonder whether the author is a poet or a Republican" (apparently, one could not be both). Dudley Fitts, writing in the *New England Quarterly* considered the political poems "ineffectual": "his social attitude suggests. . . . a man who wishes he had never brought up the subject in the first place."[51]

Though there were many laudatory reviews of *A Further Range,* the leftist criticism stunned Frost. He felt especially betrayed by Humphries's blast in *New Masses,* but his explanation to Ted Morrison is both surprising and questionable: "Abuse from The New Masses mass or mess comes particularly hard in that I have twice been approached by them in private to come in and to be their proletarian poet" (February 12, 1938, qtd. in Thompson 490). Was this really true? Frost notes that despite his rural identity, "I would be eligible on the new People's Front theory" (i.e., in the Party's reaching out to middle-class writers). This means that the invitations must have come no earlier than 1935, when Frost's anti-leftist views would surely have been known from his published poems and public readings. Stanley Burnshaw was poetry editor of *New Masses* then, and liked Frost's poetry to boot; yet he knew nothing at the time of any such invitation (Burnshaw 60).[52] It is hard to imagine any leftist editor familiar with Frost's views issuing it. In any case, Humphries's review left no doubt about where Frost stood at *New Masses* in 1936.

Negative criticism usually disturbed Frost, just as complimentary reviews elated him; both were distractions, as he had told Edee Lankes earlier: "I crave whole days weeks months unruffled by thoughts of either praise or blame. I manage to protect myself pretty well. You may ask if freedom from criticism is good for me. It may not be good for my art but it is good for my nature. I know from experience. I believe you need to know less about what the critics think of you than you have known. To Hell with all their unconsidered comment. It is unconsidered and it is not disinterested" (February 8, 1936, qtd. in Thompson 451). Now, Parini describes him as "spiraling downward into depression" and canceling all his commitments, from teaching at Amherst to delivering the Phi Beta Kappa poem at Harvard. And he stopped writing. In a letter to Bernard DeVoto in November 1936, he said he felt ganged up on: "I am stopped in my tracks as if everybody in the opposing eleven had concentrated on me. No, not as bad as that. But I haven't dared look at paper. This is the first letter I have written in four months. . . . I prescribed loafing for myself. I may have been wrong. At any rate herewith, I start again (though in bed again) to quit whining and shirking."[53] Apparently, the woodchuck's burrow had not been deep enough.

COLLECTED POEMS AND A WITNESS TREE

It took Frost nearly a year to recover his equilibrium; several factors collaborated to restore him—temporarily. Sales of *A Further Range* climbed sharply when it was accepted as a Book-of-the-Month Club selection. Also encouraging was a new book of essays in 1937, edited by Frost's publisher at Holt and entitled *Recognition of Robert Frost: Twenty-Fifth Anniversary*. The book was a celebratory collection of critical essays, appreciations, and letters, going back to the earliest years of his career. Contributors included William Dean Howells, Ezra Pound, Amy Lowell, W. H. Auden, C. D. Lewis, and of course Louis Untermeyer. The first essay, by Mark Van Doren, must have been particularly gratifying to Frost. Titled "The Permanence of Robert Frost," it argues for Frost's centrality and universality in modern poetry.[54] The biggest boost to his spirits, however, was winning his third Pulitzer Prize for *A Further Range*. Of course, it didn't hurt to have his close friend Louis Untermeyer on the Pulitzer committee. While there is no evidence that Frost lobbied Untermeyer to receive the award, his letter to Untermeyer following the announcement recognizes (in Frost's typically roundabout way) that Untermeyer's support was decisive: "You don't seriously think it can do any harm for me to have got the Pulitzer a third time? If it does, you can blame yourself more than anybody else" (May 6, 1937, *RF to LU* 292). Noting how Untermeyer had encouraged him in the past, Frost adds: "All of which is to say you are of my party" (292).

Having allies he could rely on to further his reputation mattered increasingly to Frost to offset the leftist critics he had antagonized with his political sallies. A rather unsavory instance of that aid came from a recent friend, Bernard DeVoto, the new editor of the *Saturday Review of Literature*. DeVoto saw Frost as a conservative ally against the leftist onslaught and was eager to help him fight his battles by skewering his critics in a broadside to be titled "The Critics and Robert Frost."[55] Frost secretly instigated the article and carefully monitored its progress. In January 1937 he writes DeVoto: "I am going to have you strike that blow for me now if you still want to and if you can assure your wife and conscience you thought of it first and not I. The Benny-faction must be beyond suspicion of procurement on my part or I will have none of it" (*Selected Letters* 436). After holding DeVoto back a while, he was eager to see the finished piece in print, writing DeVoto in March: "All right, let's hear how good a poet I am. . . . The article as you block it out is too much for me to deny myself" (441). When the article finally appeared in January 1938, Frost wrote DeVoto: "I sat and let Elinor pour it over me. I took the whole thing. I thought it couldnt do me any harm to listen unabashed to my full praise for once in a way" (452). Besides letting Frost bask this way, the article also satisfied the vindictiveness he harbored toward negative critics of *A Further Range.* Indeed, DeVoto's attack on three critics in particular—Horace Gregory, Newton Arvin, and R. P. Blackmur—was so blistering that, as Frost related to DeVoto, another friend of Frost's "didn't see how those three you dealt with *for me* would ever get up from the slaughter house floor."[56] In the broadside, DeVoto goes so far as to claim Frost as "the only pure proletarian poet of our time"—which must have amused the poet.[57] Others were less amused by the article: Lawrance Thompson called it "a typically unrestrained piece of savagery" (*Selected Letters* 452).

The kudos had the desired effect, and by May 1937, Frost sounded again like the old *provocateur* as he joshed Untermeyer:

> I'm your bonfire that you started without a permit . . . and left burning . . . and now look at it: it's got away from you, and if it gets into the woods not even the red-shirted fire fighters of the New Republic will be able to put it out. To be sure I'm not yet a conflagration. . . . But I'm a menace. . . . Some liberals don't think I am anything to worry about. But you know how liberals are. You know how they were about the Russian Revolution and the German Revolution. You can pack the Supreme Court for all of them. Nothing [to them] is crucial. Nothing poetry can do anyway—either in their opinion or as a matter of fact in my own. (*RF to LU* 292)

Frost even playfully imagined forming a group of his adherents to counter the leftists; he tells Untermeyer the following year: "This accidental teamwork [Untermeyer's laudatory essay on Frost and DeVoto's attack on his enemies] suggests what you and he and I could do to these times if we wanted to stage a deliberate putch [*sic*]. But we are reserved for better things than steam-rolling our enemies." In the very next sentence, however, he admits how satisfying he found this steam-rolling: "I confess my imagination is possessed with the magnificence of the forces let loose in action all round us and I am tempted to wish I was one of them instead of what I am" (March 10, 1938, *RF to LU* 304).

Ten days later, Frost's wife died of a heart attack, and these high spirits were utterly vanquished. In 1940, his son Carol committed suicide. Devastated by these losses, Frost managed somehow to keep writing, publishing *A Witness Tree* (1942) six years after *A Further Range*. In between he published another edition of *Collected Poems* (1939), which included *A Further Range*. Reviews of the 1939 *Collected Poems* were fewer and, again, mixed. Louise Bogan wrote a balanced review in the *New Yorker,* praising Frost's lyrics and "good sense [that] has kept him from running any of his tendencies into the ground. That same good sense, on the other hand, has kept him from developing, in any broad way, beyond his first work. . . . In the later Frost, the mold, unbroken, has stiffened a little." Like the critics of *A Further Range,* she did not feel it was "the province of the pastoral poet directly to preach. . . . Frost's later carping and conservatism should never appear in his work at all."[58] Synonyms of this "stiffening" echo in other reviews. The reviewer for *Time,* though praising Frost (in *Time*-ese) as "No. 1 of living American poets," nevertheless complains: "As they wear onward, Frost's *Collected Poems* show an increasing self-complacence of poetic purpose."[59]

It is noteworthy that only one leftist writer, the poet Muriel Rukeyser, bothered to review *Collected Poems*. Apparently, by 1939 leftist critics no longer thought Frost the "menace" he considered himself. Rukeyser's thoughtful review does nothing to change this indifference. She recognizes, as so many other critics have, that he achieved his lyrical brilliance early on and did not essentially change thereafter. Rukeyser considers this stasis a narrowness of spirit: "One thinks of Yeats, his generous full developing mind. Frost stays close, and guards. . . . Early in life, he drew his circle around himself and plainly said, 'I will deal with this.' The attitude does not come through as self-control, but as a rigid preconception of life." She concludes: "Meet him on . . . his own terms, and there is fine work, rewarding place-love, folk-love, solemn or gay recognitions. They are the recognitions of a man desperately determined that this is really all there is, and that this will be enough. It is not all, and it is not enough."[60]

Curiously, none of the critics reviewing *Collected Poems* considered Frost's venture into political poetry as evidence of the poet's growth or development—or at least as an effort to break out of his established genres. They saw it as cranky self-indulgence and inappropriate for this essentially lyrical poet. Rukeyser ignores it altogether. In retrospect, these dual criticisms of Frost—rigidity and the failure of his political poetry—are incompatible and unjust: Even if the poet has failed at a new type of poetry—

and many of Frost's political poems were surely not failures—he cannot fairly be considered static and fearful of growth.

CONCLUSION

Frost's poetry in the 1930s follows a familiar pattern for the four poets of this study in that he felt compelled to respond in poetry to the leftward movement of his times. But even before Marxism and the Depression became central issues for critics, his poetic reputation was being challenged by critics who felt his poetry was too narrowly focused and did not address broader issues of contemporary American culture. As the literary community became increasingly politicized in 1931–32, Frost had even more reason to feel defensive because left-liberalism and collectivism were so contrary to his own values of individualism and separateness. But he did not simply put his head down and continue to till his own garden. He was keenly aware of the ever-increasing din of political discussions, articles, petitions, and forums in the literary world. Indeed he had no choice but to hear it, as leftist friends approached him with petitions and shared their views in letters, while the most radical magazine of the age asked him (he claimed) to be its proletarian "poet in residence." Moreover, Frost taught regularly and guest-lectured on college campuses, where leftist ideas were being fervently discussed by students and sometimes faculty. When he was invited to give six lectures at the New School for Social Research in New York in 1931, for example, he knew he would be around "radicals" and "Jews"; but he gave the lectures anyway.[61]

Frost's response to this literary upheaval was not to retreat into a burrow like his drumlin woodchuck but to join the literary fray, meet politics with politics, and show the world that this bucolic poet packed a hornet's sting. Long before leftist critics attacked his poetry for ideological reasons in 1936, he was delivering anti-collectivist poem-lectures like "Build Soil" and writing anti-proletarian poems like "Two Tramps at Mud Time." His wife, Elinor, urged him not to publish "Build Soil" or the Roosevelt-baiting "To a Thinker," but Frost "wanted to make his position known," as Burnshaw states: "He was quite sure of the rightness of what he declared, as were those who denounced him as wrong" (60, 42). Unlike Cummings's anti-leftist poems, these poems are more assertive than defensive and bitter.[62] They present in various ways Frost's commitment to a locality, not to internationalism; to the need to "build soil" within oneself before expending it in social groups; to rely on oneself rather than on a government or, worse, on a collectivistic ideal to solve one's problems; and to deal with griefs of the heart rather than grievances of a society (except, of course, *his* anti-left grievances).

Nonetheless, several poems in *A Further Range* show a disturbing contempt for the Depression poor, depicting them as almost subhuman in "Two Tramps in Mud Time," revealing (if only for a moment) apocalyptic fantasies of putting them "out of their pain" or burying in a mudslide those who prate about economic leveling. Even Frost's relatively mild satire of Roosevelt depicts bad faith in his later denial of its target and callousness in his choice of metaphors for Roosevelt's political oscillations.

A Further Range, then, signals not just a defensive reaction to the changing political climate (both radical-Marxist and liberal–New Deal) but also an assertive pugnacity: "I could see a good war in letting them have the other sort of thing [a book of political poems] like a bolt from the blues," Frost confided to Untermeyer (January 30, 1935, *RF to LU* 252). He did let them have it—both barrels—and predictably, leftist critics fired back. But not just leftists—critics of all political stripes found the political poems of *A Further Range* less successful than his lyrics, out of place and somehow off-key. For Richard Poirier, it was their self-satisfied tone: "There is a tendency in Frost's more directly political utterances to chuckle . . . over opinions he thinks are outrageous. But even to an admirer—perhaps especially to an admirer—such opinions are the more platitudinous for being simplifications of, say, the poignant and mysterious threats to individualism implicit in 'Stopping By Woods on a Snowy Evening'" (235). There is something to be said for this view. When one compares "Desert Places," from this volume, for example, with its unforgettable opening and its harrowing conclusion, with the fillip of "To a Thinker" ("trust my instinct—I'm a bard"), the slack self-indulgence of the latter becomes obvious. Even a fine poem like "Two Tramps in Mud Time" is arguably maimed by Frost's shift in the conclusion to what Newton Arvin called "oracularity."[63]

Given Frost's assertiveness in these poems and his belligerent mood ("I could see a good war in letting them have [it]"), he might have been thought capable of handling the hostile response and leftist diatribes they aroused. But his public retreat in reaction to these reviews shows that his skin was much thinner than he pretended in his public persona. As Thompson and others have shown, Frost was always extremely solicitous of his own reputation, and the mid-thirties seemed to mark one of its low points.

Or did it? Frost received a Pulitzer for *A Further Range* (his third) and another for *A Witness Tree* (1942). *Recognition of Robert Frost* (1937) provided powerful evidence that his place in modern poetry was secure and would continue so in the canon—he had done far more than "to lodge a few poems where they will be hard to get rid of."[64] His popular appeal, moreover, did not at all diminish in the 1930s—quite the contrary: he continued to pack auditoriums wherever he went in an ever more crowded schedule of lectures; Book-of-the-Month Club took *A Further Range;* and offers of professorial appointments and "poet in residence" positions came from increasingly prestigious universities, such as Harvard. And that final determinant of canonical recognition—the literature anthology— by the 1940s would not be complete without several of his best poems, an achievement that his friend and anthologist, Louis Untermeyer, had something to do with.

In one other way, Frost buoyed up his spirits and his poetic standing in a manner that E. E. Cummings, for example, did not. Frost cultivated allies, like Untermeyer, who lobbied on his behalf, or like DeVoto, who attacked his political enemies, or later Kay Morrison, who served as his secretary and put his affairs in order after the death of his wife. Their assistance provided crucial support to Frost's reputation and state of mind at a time when his problems in the late thirties, literary but especially familial, threatened to overwhelm him. By contrast, Cummings's sense of isolation in the thirties resulted in part from his refusal to cultivate this network of active supporters.

As was noted at the beginning of this chapter, Frost differed from Stevens, Cummings, and Williams in the widespread popularity he enjoyed in the teens and twenties. That popularity, buoyed by Pulitzers and numerous other honors, as well as by his continuous speaking engagements, interviews, and even television appearances in the fifties, also distinguished his career in the years after the 1930s. Indeed, he was virtually America's uncrowned poet laureate, and in that quasi-official status he is often viewed as speaking for the United States during the cold war years, with the unpleasant connotations of being an uncritical supporter of American hegemony. But as will be discussed in the conclusion to this book, Frost was still too independent and unpredictable to become simply a mouthpiece for the United States in these years. More than the other three poets of this study, he continued to write political poems, addressing such paramount issues in the forties and fifties as the arms race and nuclear annihilation. But as with his political poems in the thirties, Frost asserted his distinctive, sometimes curious takes on these issues and, particularly in his many interviews and lectures, continued to enjoy playing the provocateur.

5

William Carlos Williams

Proletarian versus Marxist

Of the four poets considered in this book, William Carlos Williams presents the most paradoxical case in his relations with the Left. Throughout the 1930s he asserted repeatedly his disagreements with the communists and argued that they were thoroughly out of touch with the bedrock American temper. That did not stop him, however, from coediting left-wing magazines like *Contact* and *Blast,* or from joining (and subsequently leaving) several leftist political groups and causes,[1] or from sending his poems and essays to left-wing magazines like *The New Republic, New Masses, Nation,* and *Partisan Review,* or from writing poems, translations, and essays (and organizing medical aid) in support of the Spanish Loyalists once the Spanish Civil War broke out. Though he was hostile to communist ideology, Williams was drawn inexorably to the left by the pressures of the times.

But more than just responding to the powerful pull of literary politics, Williams could be considered a genuinely proletarian writer whose experience with the working class and the poor in the Passaic area came not from theoretical doctrine but from his daily rounds as a doctor, which brought him into continual contact with their struggles to survive the Depression, as well as with their speech and personalities. That experience—tempered by empathy, keen perception, and a poet's ear for diction and rhythms—went into the fiction he wrote in this decade (two novels and two books of short stories) and into a number of excellent poems beginning in the mid-thirties. And it partly explains why Williams kept joining and participating in a panoply of leftist actions, despite frequently embarrassing outcomes and his constant grumbling about them. He came by his radical sympathies naturally, not from a book.

Ironically, but not surprisingly, leftist critics did not recognize his proletarian sympathies or literary skill until well into the 1930s, beginning with the publication of the poetry collection *An Early Martyr* (1935), but taking hold with the novel *White Mule* (1937), the collection of short stories *Life along the Passaic River* (1938), and *The Complete Collected Poems* (1938). Partly, this delay derived from Williams's difficulty in finding publishers for his work—it was not widely accessible until the late thirties. Two small books of the mid-thirties containing some of his best proletarian poems, for example, had a combined run of about 332 copies and were priced far beyond what ordinary readers in the Depression could afford. Another reason for the Left's delay in recognizing him was his refusal to conform his writing—fiction and poetry both—to the proletarian formulas demanded by Mike Gold and company. He was certainly not "proletarian" as far as *New Masses* and *Partisan Review* were concerned. And Williams's brusque honesty in criticizing the strategies of American Communists antagonized major wallahs in the leftist critical establishment; the editors of *Partisan Review,* for instance, roundly condemned and ridiculed him on several occasions. He had a knack, moreover, for stumbling into factional disputes, such as the bitter rivalry between *New Masses* and *Partisan Review,* and for joining leftist groups and signing petitions whose hidden agendas he did not initially grasp. All of this gaucherie also factored into his rocky relations with the Left. Yet, by the end of the decade, even as his own proletarian sympathies were shifting from direct expression to subordination into the epic of *Paterson,* he could claim what Frost, Stevens, and Cummings could not: both general recognition from critics across the political spectrum (with a few exceptions, of course) and the particular approbation of the Left.

WILLIAMS IN THE EARLY 1930S

Both in his medical practice and his poetry, Williams suffered in the worst years of the Depression. His practice declined sharply as the working class of Rutherford had little or no money to spend on doctors. In the winter of 1933, Williams wrote Louis Zukofsky that his practice was "plumb shot to hell," and Williams's biographer Paul Mariani describes that practice a half-year later as "almost at a standstill."[2] That Williams often refused to send bills to hard-up patients and would not raise his fees meant that he had to work longer hours—when work was available (*New World* 297). Because it often was not, he found himself with more free time to write, but with less motivation. Here, too, Williams experienced what so many other poets did in the Depression: the drying up of publishers. Poetry was seldom a profitable venture, but in good times, major publishers were more willing to accept the loss. Not so in the Depression.[3] In Williams's case, this dearth went back to 1923, the last year he found a publisher for the innovative blend of poetry and prose of *Spring and All.* Though he continued writing poems throughout the twenties, including the poetry-journal *The Descent of Winter* (1928), and wrote some excellent ones in 1930 (e.g., "The Wind Increases," "Rain," "Death," and "The Botticellian Trees," the last receiving *Poetry* magazine's Guarantor's Prize for $100), he complained often about lacking a publisher and turned to writing fiction—short stories—that same year. In this medium he was productive, and a book of his stories found a publisher, Angel Flores, fairly quickly. *The Knife of the Times* appeared in March 1932. The few reviews it received were more descriptive than evaluative, however. An anonymous reviewer for the *New York Herald Tribune Books* found that his style carried over the compression of his poetry and used "a contemporary and matter-of-fact vernacular," while Gertrude Diamant, writing in the *New York Post,* found Williams's analysis of characters to be as detached and clinical as a doctor's "stenographic" analysis.[4] At about the same time (1930), Williams returned to a novel, *White Mule,* that he had started earlier and would work on sporadically through the mid-thirties. Meanwhile, the literary scene of the early 1930s seethed with political discussions and symposia, new journals, and an increasingly ideological aesthetics. Williams immersed himself in it.

LITTLE MAGAZINES AND LITERARY POLITICS

Unlike Stevens, Cummings, and Frost, Williams often took on the responsibility of editing little magazines. From Alfred Kreymborg's *Others* in the mid-teens, to *Contact,* his first venture with Robert McAlmon in the early twenties, Williams welcomed the chance to influence literary standards, not only through editorially selecting writing he respected (including his own) but also in the many manifestos, editorials, and articles he wrote for these short-lived ventures. At the end of the twenties, just as *The Dial* was folding, Richard Johns launched a magazine, *Pagany,* named for Williams's novel of the preceding year, *A Voyage to Pagany.* Williams could scarcely turn down Johns's request that he (Williams) help edit the magazine, especially since it committed itself to Williams's long-standing demand for an American literature grounded in the locality.[5] But by the time the first issue appeared in the spring of 1930, the leftward shift of writers and intellectuals had already begun. Thus, Williams was either defiant or oblivious when he declared in the first issue's "Manifesto" that the "word, a meaning hardly distinguishable from that of place," could still "rehabilitate our thoughts and our lives."[6] He was not about to change the aesthetic philosophy he had developed throughout the late teens and twenties. Likewise, the magazine's editorial policy of representing "a diverse and *ungrouped* body of spokesmen, bound geographically [i.e., American]" ignored the growing leftist demand for politically engaged literature of the proletariat.[7] As Mariani observes, "pressures especially from the left would soon make such a laissez-faire position harder than ever to hold on to" (*New World* 300).

Williams found this out soon enough. In September 1931 he was asked to edit another journal, this time by his friend Nathaniel West, who, with Robert McAlmon, would serve as associate editor. The magazine would be published by David Moss and Martin Kamin and titled (once again) *Contact*. Like its 1920s namesake, this one had a short life span, folding after its third issue in November 1932; but the way it folded and Williams's editorial stance expressed in his "Comments" further demonstrate his defiance of leftist aesthetics. Both West and Williams saw the magazine as "a continuation of the little magazines of the 1910s and 20s" (*New World* 320), but now, February 1932, Williams had to face, as he put it in the first issue's "Comment," "the confusion there is [all] about us and the despairing minds" to ask "what in the world is writing good for anyway?"[8] His answer was no different than in his manifestos for *Pagany* and the earlier *Contact:* "[T]he underlying significance of all writing . . . is the writing itself. . . . A writer . . . has use for but one thing, the word that is possessing him at the moment he writes. . . . A magazine without opinions or criteria other than words moulded by the impacts of experience . . . would be timely to a period such as this" (7–9). What *was* different by 1932 was Williams's emphatic repudiation of political aesthetics: "There's no sense in slobbering at the mouth over humanity and writing that way. . . . To plead a social cause, to split a theory, to cry out at the evil which we all partake of—gladly: that's not writing. . . . A writer has no use for theories or propaganda" (8–9).

Though Williams certainly recognized this rapidly intensifying leftist pressure, he was not always clear about communism itself. In his "Comment" to the third issue, he rejects an attitude toward poetry that he attributes to his nemesis, T. S. Eliot: "that poetry increases in virtue as it is removed from contact with the vulgar world."[9] Attacking this easy target, he adds a puzzling comment:

[Rejecting this view] is one of the reasons to welcome communism. Never, may it be said, has there ever been great poetry that was not born out of a communist intelligence. They have all been rebels. . . .

> The unchristian sweep of Shakespeare, the cantless, unsectarian bit-
> terness of Dante against his time, this is what is best in communism.
> The same for the words of St. Francis. The spirit is one. It is also one
> with the imagination. It will not down nor speak its piece to please,
> not even to please "communism."
>
> Nothing is beyond poetry. It is the one solid element on which
> our lives can rely, the "word" of so many disguises. (131)

Whatever Williams may have meant by "communism" in the first half
of the first paragraph above—and he seems to mean a rebellious, non-
sectarian literary spirit that responds to its times—it had nothing to do
with actual communist aesthetics in 1932, as the paragraph's last sentence
seems to recognize in imputing to official "communism" a demand for
conformity. The quotation then resolves into familiar ground: the writer
writes to please no faction; he focuses on the "word." Left unresolved is
the potential conflict between a poetry that must "grasp the full significance of its day" or fail (131), and a pure poetry that concerns itself solely
with the word.

If the editors of *Contact* were in aesthetic agreement, the publishers
were not. Kamin insisted that the third issue feature American communist writers. When Williams demurred, postponing that issue for the indefinite future, relations with Moss and Kamin ruptured and the magazine
was aborted after only three issues. The experience left a bitter taste. Seeing the consequences of defying the leftist juggernaut, Williams vowed to
edit no more magazines. Regrettably, it was a lesson he would keep having to relearn throughout the 1930s.

Despite his forthright defense of "pure poetry" in these years, the powerfully contemporaneous view that poetry must reflect and respond to its
times gradually embedded itself and created increasing dissonance in Williams's aesthetics in the early thirties. Three statements in three different
genres—letter, poem, essay—show how he struggled with these conflicting
positions and gradually altered his. The earliest was a long, manifesto-like
letter he wrote to Kay Boyle in December 1931.[10] In it, Williams em-
phatically rejects the Marxist dictum that literature's most important element is its social content:

> And this should blast the occasional pushing notion that the form
> of poetry (as that of any art) is social in character. Such an opinion
> is purest superficiality. The form of poetry is that of language. It is
> related to all art first, then to certain essential characteristics of lan-

guage, to words. . . . It is not formed "like" the society of any time; it might be formed in a manner opposite to the character of the times, a formal rigidity of line in a period of social looseness. . . .

. . . [P]oetry is related to poetry, not to social statutes. It will, nevertheless, make its form of what it finds. And so does *seem* to be a social eye. It is nothing of the sort. It remains itself . . . related only to poetry. (*Selected Letters* 130–31, Williams's emphasis)

But even as he explicitly rejects political poetry, Williams acknowledges, by the back door as it were, that poetry inevitably reflects its time: "[P]oetry, in its sources, body, spirit, in its form, in short, is related to poetry and not to socialism, communism or anything else that tries to swallow it; [I want] to reconcile this with the equally important fact that it deals with reality, the actuality of every day, by virtue of its use of language. Doing so, naturally it reflects its time, by coincidence" (131).[11]

In October 1933, eight of Williams's poems appeared in *Poetry,* followed by this "Foot-Note":

Walk on the delicate parts
of necessary mechanisms
and you will pretty soon have
neither food, clothing, nor
even Communism itself,
Comrades. Read good poetry![12]

Although he chose a safe venue for this poem in the politically neutral *Poetry* magazine, it was cheeky of Williams to lecture the "Comrades." And though he probably intended "necessary mechanisms" to refer to poetry (see "The New Poetical Economy" below), the unqualified phrase could easily be read as social or economic mechanisms—for example, private ownership, which the "Comrades" certainly intended to walk on. The speaker warns the comrades against treading on poetic mechanisms with the crude aesthetics of proletarian poetry, but the consequences he outlines seem illogically sweeping and apocalyptic: "you will pretty soon have neither food, clothing, nor even Communism itself." How would damaged poetics create all this? Even "good" begs the question, since the criteria for that aesthetic evaluation were now being hotly debated. In brief, a condescending, rather muddled poem intended not merely to instruct but to provoke. Just how did Williams expect the "Comrades" to respond to this mini-lecture?

Seeing the poem as a mechanism was a central tenet of a group of younger poets, the objectivists, who were to enter significantly into Williams's poetic career at this point. He had long been friends with the group's co-founder, Louis Zukofsky, and for years Zukofsky helped edit Williams's manuscripts (*New World* 273, 301). Now, as the group began publishing books of its own poetry, Williams reviewed them, and his review in *Poetry* of George Oppen's *Discrete Series* is particularly important.[13] Williams's title "The New Poetical Economy" would likely have misled readers in 1934, since ideas about a "new economy" were much bandied about. But Williams was interested in words, not dollars, and his "economy of means" pertained to writing good poetry. At first, though, it appears that he has converted to social action poetry: "If the poems in the book constitute necessary corrections of or emendations to human conduct in their day, both as to thought and manner, then they are good. But if these changes originated in the poems, causing thereby a direct liberation of the intelligence, then the book becomes of importance to the highest degree." He quickly adds, however: "But this importance cannot be in what the poem says. . . . The importance lies in what the poem *is*." And that "is" depends profoundly on its technique:

> A poem which does not arouse respect for the technical requirements of its mechanics may have anything you please painted all over it or on it in the way of meaning but it will for all that be as empty as a man made of wax or straw. . . . Without the poem being a workable mechanism in its own right, a mechanism which arises from, while at the same time it constitutes the meaning of, the poem as a whole, it will remain ineffective. And what it says regarding the use or worth of that particular piece of "propaganda" which it is detailing will never be convincing. . . .
>
> Only by being an object sharply defined and without redundancy will its form project whatever meaning is required of it. (221, 223)

That seems to settle the matter. But far more than in his letter to Boyle, Williams concedes that poetry must also reflect its times: "It could well be, at the same time, first and last, *a poem facing as it must the dialectic necessities of its day*. Oppen has carried this social necessity . . . to an extreme" (223–24, emphasis added). The power behind this "social necessity"—the influence of the Left—also appears in Williams's complaint: "[P]eople are beginning to forget that poems are constructions. One no longer hears poems spoken of as good or bad; that is, whether or not they do or do not stand up and hold together. One is likely, rather, to hear of them now as 'proletarian' or 'fascist.' . . . The social school of criticism is getting to be almost as subversive to the intelligence as the religious school nearly succeeded in being in the recent past" (225).

In sum, Williams's beliefs in this review are tangled, if not contradictory. He clearly asserts the objectivist credo of the poem as mechanism and rejects the emphasis of the "social school" on thematic content. Yet his concessions—that poetry might "correct" human conduct and thought, that a poem "must" face the "dialectic necessities of its day" (note the Marxian diction) as a "social necessity"—show how leftist tenets gradually informed his thinking. It was no longer enough in 1934 to call for "pure poetry" or see the poem as a machine made of words. Nor would simply repudiating the categorical labels of the "social school" resolve the contradictions in Williams's thought.

Opposing Marxist aesthetics did not prevent Williams from being, in his own way, a genuinely proletarian writer—not proletarian in coming from the working class, nor proletarian by the rigid standards of the *New Masses* of course, but one who depicted working-class people unscripted and located them in a particular time and place. A perfect example is the 1934 poem "The Sun Bathers" (*CP-WCW* 1:371), sandwiched in among such purely imagistic poems as "Nantucket" and "The Locust Tree in Flower." The first two stanzas read like a more skillful version of the proletarian poems published in *New Masses* or a half-dozen other radical magazines:

> A tramp thawing out
> on a doorstep
> against an east wall
> Nov. 1, 1933:
>
> a young man begrimed
> and in an old
> army coat
> wriggling and scratching

The down-and-out: a tramp sleeps out in the cold; a young man is dirty and miserable in a lice-infested, secondhand coat. Even the date contributes something: 1932–33 was the pit of the Depression—and winter is coming on. But not yet. The title tell us, ironically, that they are sunbathers, though not, of course, of the leisure class on the sands of Miami Beach or

Palm Springs (but, then, the sun "belongs to everyone" as a popular song of the time declares).[14] Indeed, the tramp is "thawing out" after spending a cold night. But where the conventional proletarian poem would now insert its message of outrage or hope in the revolution that would abolish such misery, Williams shifts the poem's mood entirely in the final stanza:

> while a fat negress
> in a yellow-house window
> nearby
> leans out and yawns
>
> into the fine weather

Nothing even remotely oppressive. Rather, pleasant visual and kinesthetic images prevail. The negress's diet may not be good, but she's not starving either. She's not toiling under an overseer's whip or a matron's pitiless demands, but yawning and leaning out of the window to enjoy "the fine weather." The "yellow-house" reflects the unmentioned sunlight—a happy image—it may even be her house. What begins as a stereotypically proletarian poem becomes Williams's own type of proletarian poem: a depiction of a scene and characters that most certainly reflects the time, but refuses to impose on it any sort of social message.

COLLECTED POEMS, 1921–1931

"The Sun Bathers" appeared in *Collected Poems, 1921–1931,* published by Carl Rakosi's Objectivist Press. Williams's first book of poems published in the United States since the 1923 *Spring and All,* it did not appear until January 1934. The collection had been rejected by several New York publishers; and even Angel Flores, who had published *The Knife of the Times,* turned it down, complaining of Williams's "hangdog attitude" (*New World* 325). (Had he also swung to the left?) Williams said he had almost given up writing poems in these years, partly out of discouragement, partly (as he confided to Kay Boyle) because "the form has been lacking" (*Selected Letters* 129). But assembling the manuscript for *Collected Poems* relit the spark (*New World* 328), and when the young objectivists accepted the book he was even more encouraged to be part of a rising group that reflected his aesthetics. With George Oppen providing the funds, the Objectivist Press published several other volumes, including *An "Objectivists" Anthology,* containing seven poems by Williams. Though he had been recently burned by his editorial efforts for *Contact,* he felt very much a part of this group, referring in a letter to "*our* budding press" (qtd. in *New World* 339, emphasis added).

Though nearly all the pieces in *Collected Poems* were written before the Depression,[15] several portray ordinary people—future "proletarians": the fickle crowd at a baseball game (*CP-WCW* 1: 233); a waitress Williams encountered at an Atlantic City convention (279); and, in one of his most anthologized poems, a portrait of the mentally impaired servant girl in the Williams household, "To Elsie" (217–18).[16] Originally published in *Spring and All,* this poem construes her "broken / brain" as expressing "the truth about us": a rapacious America, composed of exploiters and the exploited—

> promiscuity between
>
> devil-may-care men who have taken
> to railroading
> out of sheer lust of adventure—
>
> and young slatterns, bathed
> in filth
> from Monday to Saturday
>
> to be tricked out that night
> with gauds

—an America that lacks the "peasant traditions" to give "character" to its imagination, that lacks visionary leadership or even just intelligent planning: "no one to drive the car."

This last failing made Williams sympathetic to the idea of centralized planning that Russia represented. In the same year it announced its first Five-Year Plan, 1928, Williams wrote a long evocation—or, as the title suggests, an "imagination"—of the new Soviet state from the perspective of a single individual, "A Morning Imagination of Russia" (*CP-WCW* 1: 303–6). In this "red cold world of / dawn," the unnamed observer feels a liberating openness now that bourgeois traditions (symbolized by the city) are destroyed:

> There were no cities
> between him and his desires
> his hatreds and his loves were without walls

The new collective state also intensifies his perceptual powers:

> The very old past was refound
> redirected. It had wandered into himself
> The world was himself, these were
> his own eyes that were seeing, his own mind
> that was straining to comprehend

More predictably, as class barriers fall, he feels rapport with "Two miserable peasants. . . . as he had never / known them formerly." Like them, he decides to go unshaven. Though university-trained, he works in the fields, picking herbs and learning from an old woman how to find wild ginger. Finally, he will listen at the soviet and make up his own mind about the issues. He thus becomes "the scales" who "must weigh for them [the local soviet] out / of himself." The poem concludes with a sense of how shaky the Russian experiment is. Like a patient who might not survive radical surgery,

> We are convalescents. Very
> feeble. Our hands shake. We need a
> transfusion. No one will give it to us,
> they are afraid of infection.

The experiment may fail—the patient may die—because the fearful capitalist powers want it to.

Yet, the final lines assert a new authenticity: "We have paid heavily. But we / have gotten—touch." Here, the speaker's conclusion, abandoning the impersonal "he" for the involving "We," is exactly opposite that of Cummings, who describes his senses shutting in the oppressive Soviet state. But, then, Williams experienced Russia in his imagination; Cummings went there.

REVIEWS OF *COLLECTED POEMS, 1921–1931*

Leftist reviewers of *Collected Poems* frequently cited the visual emphasis of Williams's poems and their abrupt and fragmentary quality. Not surprisingly, the critics were put off by these qualities. Babette Deutsch, for example, observed the poems' "unexampled nakedness. . . . this stark and unashamed simplicity of statement. For this man the object seen, the clear line, the pure color, is enough. . . . Clarity, incisiveness, the swift contrast, the pleasure in the grotesque, these are its distinguishing marks." But "[t]he reliance on the eye, the singling out of the brief moment, however intense, is a limitation upon his work. . . . The narrowness of attention which makes for concentration also may make for a certain meagerness."[17]

Phillip Blair Rice, writing in *The Nation,* concurred: "Dr. Williams has excluded more from his verse than any other important poet of his generation. . . . His search for the immediate presentation, his passion for 'objectivity' . . . has led him to eschew not only a great many useful poetic tools—even, usually, metaphor—but also the 'subjective' facts about human nature. He gives us the interiors of houses, but rarely more than the outsides of people. . . . Cleared ground has a neat beauty of its own, but when every one of the trees has been felled, the landscape tends to have a touch of monotony."[18]

For Charles Henry Newman, reviewing for the far-left *Dynamo,* Williams's "emphasis on the particular" reveals the flaws of objectivism, namely, "the failure . . . to co-ordinate and organize experience." Williams "as a doctor in a small industrial town has had an extensive experience, and is familiar with scenes of poverty and industrial life." But "[h]e lacks the partisanship and sympathy necessary to understand [these scenes] completely. . . . He sees details of poverty but he does not recognize or relate it to its cause."[19] Geoffrey Grigson, displaying the same snide sensibility that led him to title his review of Stevens's *Ideas of Order* "A Stuffed Goldfinch," would not even dignify the work as poetry, calling the poems "anti-poetic pips . . . little knocked off bits of unmade poems" that lack artistic control.[20] Only one leftist reviewer, Raymond Larsson, dissented and felt that Williams was "a moralist, a critic of ferocity and acumen" as well as one who depicts "the purity of the actual world of things."[21]

Apolitical critics observed the same techniques but were less judgmental. Conrad Aiken states in *The New Republic:* "What Williams has been after, in short, is a rapid succession of images (things immediately apprehended by the senses) presented in naked succession and in broken rhythm."[22] And Marianne Moore observes Williams "[d]isliking the tawdriness of unnecessary explanation, the detracting compulsory connective, stock speech of any kind."[23] Several critics took up Wallace Stevens's questionable assertion in his preface to the book that "something of the sentimental is necessary to fecundate the anti-poetic" in Williams's poetry.[24] Thus Newman: "The reaction against the 'poetic' indicates a hidden emotional attitude" (26); and Aiken: "[Williams's] avoidance of *completeness* . . . looks like an inverted sentimentalism" (290, Aiken's emphasis). Stevens's "anti-poetic" tag would linger in criticism for years to come, much to Williams's annoyance.

Reviewers echoed Williams's own uncertainty in these years about his future as a poet. Running through nearly all the leftist reviews was an accurate recognition of his modernist techniques alongside impatience that these techniques had not changed. Assessments were mixed: C. G. Poore, in the *New York Times Book Review,* observed that "the public has never even faintly shown signs of taking him up."[25] But Aiken offered some prescient cheer: "[H]e is still, at age fifty, a promising poet" (291).

WILLIAMS IN THE MID-1930S

By the mid-thirties, several new developments moved Williams further to the left but, at the same time, alienated him from one of its most important magazines, *Partisan Review.* Like Stevens, Williams benefited from the Popular Front's welcome of middle-class liberals, non-communist radicals, and even refurbished modernists; his poems began appearing in *The New Republic, The Nation,* and smaller leftist journals.[26] One new leftist magazine in particular, *Blast,* had already succeed in enlisting him as an advisory editor.[27] Its Marxist coeditors, Fred and Betty Miller, sought proletarian fiction and regularly published Williams's short stories. As Paul Mariani describes them: "They were all stories of working-class families he knew in and around Passaic. . . . And these stories revealed more eloquently than any propaganda could what the economic situation in America had done to thousands of lower-class American families, and how these families had somehow managed to survive—when they were not washed under by death itself—with vestiges and even whole pieces of their humanity intact" (*New World* 345). Williams befriended the impoverished young Millers and even let them use his summer cottage when they could not afford rent in New York. According to Charles Doyle, "[Fred] Miller put Williams in touch with New York leftist activity" (*Critical Heritage* 153). But Williams's attitude toward their radical magazine was ambivalent. In a statement intended for the first issue, he asserted repeatedly that the artist "must not under any circumstances debase his art to any purpose"—such as for communist propaganda.[28] Communism, he continues, "poses . . . a question to art": "Shall we give up the essential individualism of artists to serve a proletarian state . . . or shall we cling to the drastic compulsions of the artists even at the cost of having the new state excommunicate us?" (77). Stevens would struggle with his own ambivalence about this question in *Owl's Clover*. Williams's answer in September 1933 is unequivocal: "We are, first, last, and always artists and can never be compelled by the state. Otherwise we are just liars" (77). Yet he also accepts that the principles of good writing in *this* magazine will be "in the cause" (75); his point is just that good writing furthers that cause more than hack writing does. Significantly, Williams felt that "present-day Communism" was "intellectually inescapable" (78); likewise, that the writer "must . . . realistically look for new forms in a more simple organization of *social* materials" (80, emphasis added), and "that it is possible for writing to gain in integrity with its materials by observation of a similar process [efficient use of materials] in society" (80). Finally, he was willing to lend his name to the editorial page "so long as the magazine deals with writing which is attempting to discover in the communistic onslaught materials which are essential to it" (80). As in "The New Poetical Economy," he demands that artists be independent and that good writing requires an economy of means; but he also acknowledges that in these days good writing must employ *social* materials and serve a political end: for this magazine, Marxism. That he joined the editorial staff of such a magazine indicates how far Williams had come in a very few years.

Still, he was not about to convert to Marxism. As he told Marianne Moore in May 1934, "I won't follow causes. I can't. The reason is that it seems so much more important to me that I *am*" (*Selected Letters* 147). Moreover, "he was afraid thousands would be destroyed in the inevitable bloody aftermath" of a Communist revolution (*New World* 348). The economic cause that did attract Williams in these years was radical but not leftist: Social Credit, embodied in the theories of Major C. H. Douglas and espoused tirelessly by Williams's on-again, off-again friend, Ezra Pound. At this point their friendship was on, and the two corresponded frequently about that economic theory. Williams even made speeches advocating Social Credit and published articles on it in Gorham Munson's like-minded magazine, *New Democracy.* In one article, Williams declared he was all for change but "wanted to come out on the other side of the revolution his own man."[29]

Another major development was the advent of a new publisher in 1934–36, the ubiquitous and elusive Ronald Lane Latimer.[30] In the early 1930s, as a graduate student, Latimer had asked Williams and several other prominent poets for submissions to the *Columbia Review* and its subsequent incarnations. By late 1934 he had founded the Alcestis Press and *Alcestis Quarterly,* and, besides publishing poems by Stevens, Williams, Cummings, and several others in the magazine, he planned to bring out books by Wil-

liams, Stevens, Alan Tate, Elizabeth Bishop, and Robert Penn Warren (to
name only those whose books he actually published). Originally, he proposed publishing Williams's autobiography and complete poems. When
Williams demurred, however, he settled for a book of new poems, which
became *An Early Martyr;* the following year, 1936, Latimer proposed a
second book of poems. As Mariani notes (*New World* 382), Williams had
no new poems left, but the commission inspired him to start writing poetry intensively. As with his short stories for Angel Flores and later for
Fred Miller and his poems for the objectivists, a publishing opportunity
got Williams to writing. And while he had not abandoned his concern
for the word and for an American language, two new aims emerge in his
response to Latimer's proposal for the first book: "I want you to discover
not necessarily in my verse, but mine may do, what the new measures are
to be. I want you to reject the slag of what I write and pull out the NEW,
that which relates to the American language and modern times."[31] Focusing on the word is no longer enough to create an American language;
a "new measure" must convey it—an idea that would profoundly affect all
of Williams's subsequent work. And to be genuinely "NEW," the poem
must relate to "modern times." No longer is contemporaneity—"the dialectic necessities of [the] day"—merely a concession or an afterthought in
the hierarchy of Williams's aesthetics.

While the fruits of Latimer's commissions—*An Early Martyr* and *Adam
& Eve & the City*—will be discussed below, it is worth mentioning here
that one of Latimer's aims was to question his modernist clients not only
about their poetry but also about their political views—and even about
their friends.[32] In the same letter quoted above, Williams responded irri-
tably to what may have been one such question on technique: "It makes
me weary for some instructor at Columbia to come up to me after a reading and ask me why I put a certain verse in the form in which I put it.
How in hell am I going to answer him and why should I if I could? Let
him rather look into my verse to discover where the formal occasion lies—
and find perhaps a lead for his deductions. I know he is important, I know
what my difficulties are—but I'll be damned if I'll have the onus of proof
put on me" (*Selected Letters* 152). Unlike Stevens, who answered in detail
many such questions from Latimer and others, Williams was not a patient
explicator of his own work.

Like so many of his contemporaries, he was also deeply affected by the
outbreak of the Spanish Civil War in June 1936. He supported the Loyalist cause with money, contributing to the survivors of the Abraham Lincoln Brigade; with his time, organizing and chairing the Bergen County

Medical Board to Aid the Spanish Democracy; and with his typewriter, composing several poems about the war, translating Spanish revolutionary ballads in 1937–39, writing an essay on Garcia Lorca and Spanish poetry, and a diatribe against Mussolini for helping Franco. His hatred of Mussolini for intervening, moreover, led him to break once and for all with Pound, Mussolini's staunch supporter, and to call him a horse's ass in several letters. As the Spanish war pushed Loyalist sympathizers and anti-fascists to the left, so it moved Williams leftward. He composed his denunciation of Mussolini for the communist-organized League of American Writers.

Williams attended the first American Writers' Congress in the spring of 1935 as an observer and "was impressed by the prevailing tones of 'plainness,' 'frankness,' and 'good feeling'" (*New World* 376). In a letter to Zukofsky he paraphrases Waldo Frank's keynote speech that "the place of the artist in the revolutionary movement was not in the oversimplification of propaganda, the necessities are far more complex than that, but in conditioning the proletarian mind, making it ready for revolution" (qtd. in *New World* 376). Eventually, he joined the group that emerged from this congress, the League of American Writers.

Still, Williams kept his distance from the Communist Party because (in addition to the reasons mentioned above) he was convinced that their revolutionary approach would never work in the United States. He declared this often—to Gorham Munson in March 1934, to Fred and Betty Miller a few months later, and to Kenneth Burke in May 1935[33]—but when he had the temerity to declare it again in a public forum he suffered immediate repercussions. *Partisan Review and Anvil* held a symposium for its April 1936 issue, inviting ten prominent writers, including Williams, to respond to the question, "What is Americanism: Marxism and the American Tradition." When Zukofsky warned Williams to tread carefully in answering *PR*'s questionnaire, Williams brushed off the warning; apparently he had already sent in his answers, because his response to Zukofsky is couched in the past tense: "I thought the questions were asked in good faith, so I answered them that way. If they don't care to publish my replies it makes no difference to me. Please don't try to protect me."[34] He certainly did not try to protect himself in his responses to *PR,* for he bluntly declared that "the American tradition is completely opposed to Marxism." He continues:

> [America's] deeply embedded feeling for a democracy has defeated the more radical thought of each era, such as that of Tom Paine, Gene Debs, Bill Haywood, making their movements and thought seem foreign to the environment. It is this same democracy of feel-

ing which will defeat Marxism in America and all other attempts
at regimentation of thought and action. It will also defeat fascism—
though it may have to pass through that. . . . Marxism is a static philosophy of a hundred years ago which has not yet kept up—as the
democratic spirit has—through the stresses of an actual trial. Marxism to the American spirit is only another phase of force opposed
to liberalism. . . . My opinion is that our revolutionary literature is
merely tolerated by most Americans, that it is definitely in conflict
with our deep-seated ideals. (*Selected Letters* 157–58)

Of course, as a premiere magazine of the Left, *Partisan Review* expected—
and received—a landslide response that Marxism was thoroughly consistent with the American tradition. The strongest dissent was Williams's.
Williams might have expected as much, but what he did not expect (as
his letter to Zukofsky shows) was that *PR* would print his reply. Predictably, his letter produced a storm of protests, and once again the magazine
surprised him by describing these protests in the next issue: "The letters
[responding to the symposium] reflect a lively interest in the subject, which
accounts, perhaps, for the spirited exceptions taken in most of them to
William Carlos Williams' point of view. His 'uniformed notions of Marxism and Americanism,' to quote from one letter, are roundly condemned
by most of the correspondents."[35] Not content to summarize these slams,
PR printed one letter against Williams, a diatribe that insults not only his
political sophistication but his poetry—and modernism generally: "The
only one [among the respondents] who seems to have set out to make an
ass of himself is William Carlos Williams. Where has the man been living
all these years? . . . He can't see economic facts behind the official myths
of liberalism and democracy. . . . If the American masses have, so far, as he
claims, not taken to revolutionary literature, they are even less aware of
Mr. Williams' particular brand of poetry. In fact, the whole school of modernist writing of which Mr. Williams is such a shining light has made no
dent on the American consciousness." For good measure, the editors added
their own disapproval: "Needless to say, the editorial position of *Partisan
Review* is utterly opposed to the direction of thought shown in Mr. Williams' contribution." What really stands out in this heretic-burning is the
boldface title the editors give to the brouhaha: **"Sanctions Against Williams."** Though "sanctions against" here means "disapproval of," the words
and their prominence seem to call for punishment or retribution[36]—a shocking advocacy for a magazine purporting to stand for open-minded discus-

sion. Even taking the narrower view of the title, one can scarcely ignore that this prominent and highly respected magazine singled out a dissenter for the abuse and ridicule of its editors and readers—and this at a time when Popular Front politics called for the inclusion of diverse positions on the Left. The embarrassment was to prove the opening round of a long-lasting fight between Williams and *Partisan Review.*

AN EARLY MARTYR AND *ADAM & EVE & THE CITY:* "THE REVOLUTION WAS COMING"

The two slender volumes that Ronald Lane Latimer published—"companion pieces," Williams called them[37]—came out in September 1935 and September 1936, respectively. Like all of Latimer's books, both were limited but elegant editions—165 copies of *An Early Martyr and Other Poems* and 167 of *Adam & Eve & The City*—"lavishly printed on rag paper," Williams recalled.[38] But at $7.50 and $5.00, respectively, they were priced ridiculously high for the Depression, far beyond the means of average book buyers, and this bothered Williams: "He told Latimer he felt funny being published in an expensive format which no one ever saw, though he also admired the craftsmanship and design that the small fine press could give a poet's work. . . . But he also felt 'hedged round,' in danger of becoming 'precious.' . . . And yet he had no choice."[39] The small editions did not significantly affect Williams's standing as a poet. Yet they represent an important shift of focus and tone in his poetry, and mark a definite movement leftward in his gradual integration of politics and aesthetics.

To be sure, one can still find in these two books such classically imagistic poems as "Flowers by the Sea" (*CP-WCW* 1: 378–79), "A Chinese Toy" (407), and the second version of "The Locust Tree in Flower" (379–80), ruthlessly stripped to a vertical row of one-word lines. "To a Mexican Pig-Bank" (382–83), moreover, introduces one version of "the new measure" that Williams was experimenting with and wanted Latimer to evaluate. This one alternates short and shorter lines, two in each stanza, the latter indented to create a visual oscillation. The form would eventually evolve into the triadic foot of Williams's late poetry.

But it is the proletarian poems, especially in *An Early Martyr,* that make these volumes something new in Williams's oeuvre. He had written about the working class before—Sacco and Vanzetti in "Impromptu: The Suckers," the mentally impaired servant girl in "To Elsie," Passaic millworkers in "The Men," and Depression victims in "The Sun Bathers"—but sporadically. Now a sheaf of poems, interspersed with imagist descriptions, features a "poor old woman," a tramp couple, a woman beaten by police, the rich and poor in mortal conflict, a kind of Robin Hood, a radical poet, and construction workers. The title poem, "An Early Martyr," and the pen-ultimate "A Poem for Norman Macleod" form thematic bookends that express Williams's unqualified sympathy for younger, radical idealists. John Coffey, the "Early Martyr" of 1920, stole furs from a department store and informed the police of it as a protest against private property and the legal system; he planned to speak for the poor during his trial. The court prevented his speech by remanding him to a mental asylum for life.[40] Released early (because the asylum was overcrowded), he was "close to / The edge." As Williams stated later, "I identified myself in his defense. No one at that time [1920] would have thought of this as communistic—it was simply an unworldly dream and I was sympathetic to the dreamer and the dream" (*IWWP* 56). That sympathy and the poet's contempt for the authorities are straightforward:

> They railroaded him
> to an asylum . . .
> without trial
> . . . .
>   finally they
> had to release him—
> . . . .
> They "cured" him all
> right

The poem might have ended there in bitter irony. But it shifts to an affirmation of Coffey's actions and a stirring call for new Coffeys (now fourteen years later) to continue the fight:

> But the set-up
> he fought against
> Remains—
> and his youthful deed
> Signalizing
> the romantic period
> Of a revolt
> he served well
> Is still good—

Let him be
a factory whistle
That keeps blaring—
Sense, sense, sense!
so long as there's
a mind to remember
and a voice to
carry it on—
Never give up
keep at it! (*CP-WCW* 1: 377–78)

The "set-up" Williams's Coffey fights against is clearly capitalism—thus, the brilliant metaphor of "factory whistle," subverting a tool of company control. Though the poem ends weakly, it is almost unprecedented in Williams's work for its naked plea ("Let him be . . .") and political exhortation: "Never give up / keep at it!"[41]

"A Poem for Norman Macleod" (401) assumes a more relaxed and playful manner:

The revolution
is accomplished
noble has been
changed to no bull

Norman Macleod was a young, radical poet whom Williams admired and whose books he reviewed (*CP-WCW* 1: 542n). Projecting a revolutionary future, the poem sees a time when straightforward honesty between equals ("no bull") has replaced the class structure and its accompanying social values ("noble"). Unlike the anger and political earnestness of "An Early Martyr," this poem inserts a joke-like dialogue between a "constipated / prospector" and "Chief / One Horn." The point is simple enough: the chief solves the prospector's problem with direct action;[42] hence,

You can do lots
if you know
what's around you
No bull

What is unusual in this poem is Williams's optimism about the outcome of a revolution, directly contradicting his earlier statements. According to John Thirlwall, who annotated a copy of *The Collected Earlier Poems* based on Williams's comments to him, Williams said of this poem: "I was very much in sympathy with Norman Macleod and his social attitudes to the poor. I felt that the revolution was coming. I was never in favor of the [Communist] Party, but I did think that some revolution [would come] which would bring down the socialites and give the poor people a chance. This treatment will take the bluff out of 'polite' talk. Norman was not 'polite'" (*CP-WCW* 1: 542n).

Themes of self-help and direct action occur often in *An Early Martyr.* In "Proletarian Portrait" (384–85) a young working woman dares to violate social propriety by taking off her shoe on the street. She is also lacking a hat and wearing an apron, as if she had run outside suddenly from someone's kitchen; but her features—"big young . . . hair slicked back"— suggest a figure in a Soviet propaganda poster, a "proletarian portrait."[43] Her purpose trumps social convention, however: a nail in the shoe "has been hurting her," and rather than suffer in silence, or pay a cobbler she probably cannot afford, she acts for herself:

>   Looking
>   intently into it
>
>   She pulls out the paper insole
>   to find the nail

The title and theme are obviously addressed to other proletarians: go thou and do likewise. As in Clifford Odets's *Waiting for Lefty* of the same year, autonomous action finally trumps dependence on authority: Don't wait for a Lefty to tell you what to do; do it yourself. Similarly, "To Be Hungry Is To Be Great" (400) describes how to cook the ubiquitous yellow grass-onion, so that no one need starve.

Some of the proletarian portraits in *An Early Martyr* lack an explicitly political theme and simply present ordinary people doing ordinary things— with one modification: the people are often poor. Both the old woman in "To a Poor Old Woman" (383) and the couple in "Late for Summer Weather" (384) recall the people in "The Sun Bathers": the poems present them enjoying the sensuous moment. The old woman "munching a plum on / the street" may be poor, but she can still enjoy small pleasures which the poem makes large. It repeats "They taste good to her" three times, each time altering the rhythm and placement, as if to capture the

sensuous pleasure of each individual bite. Connotations expand the range
of these pleasures:

> You can see it by
> the way she gives herself
> to the one half
> sucked out in her hand
>
> Comforted
> a solace of ripe plums
> seeming to fill the air

"she gives herself to" (reinforced by "sucked out") suggests that the pleasure is almost sexual, while "Comforted" and the marvelous "solace" allude
to spiritual comfort.[44] Similarly, the couple in "Late for Summer Weather"
is probably poor, to judge from their old clothes (which in 1935 would not
be appropriate to wear in public), and probably out of work: they are described as "Fat Lost Ambling / nowhere . . . [with] Nothing to do." But
they have a good time as they "kick // their way through / heaps of / fallen
maple leaves." And even the sly simile ("leaves // still green—and / crisp
as dollar bills) ironically alluding to their poverty does not really under-
mine their fun: "Hot cha!" Robert Von Hallberg finds that the sponta-
neous pleasure in these poems *is* their political point: "[They] suggest that
rather than helping to organize and propagandize the economic underdogs, ideologues would do well simply to appreciate the immediate access
the poor have to simple human pleasure."[45]

Williams, then, moved in several directions in these books, trying out
long poems ("The Crimson Cyclamen" and "Perpetuum Mobile: The
City") in *Adam & Eve,* experimenting with meter and stanza in "Perpetuum" and "To a Mexican Pig-Bank," at times recalling purely imagistic
moments ("Nantucket"), at others dabbling in political discourse. "The
Yachts" (388–89), certainly the most anthologized poem of these volumes,
is unusual in abruptly juxtaposing imagistic description and social statement. For eight stanzas, the poem is an aesthetic appreciation of beautifully
made racing yachts, which, like the well-made poems Williams admired,
move with effortless grace and speed through their medium. Though par-
tially protected from the ocean by the "well-guarded arena" of enclosing land, the yachts nonetheless resist the sea's personified malevolence—
"lapping their glossy sides, as if feeling / for some slight flaws but fails

completely." Admiration for these aesthetic objects runs all through these eight stanzas: they are "the best man knows / to pit against [the ocean's] beatings":

> they appear youthful, rare
>
> as the light of a happy eye, live with the grace
> of all that in the mind is fleckless, free and
> naturally to be desired.

Suddenly, with no transition, the ninth stanza shifts perspective and attitude toward the yachts. We now see them from the water, amid a surrealistic "sea of faces . . . an entanglement of watery bodies" struggling "in agony, in despair" to stay afloat:

> Arms with hands grasping seek to clutch at the prows.
> Bodies thrown recklessly in the way are cut aside. . . .
>
> Broken,
>
> beaten, desolate, reaching from the dead to be taken up
> they cry out,

The "skillful" yachts ignore their cries "rising / in waves still" and "pass over" the victims.

Critics have long pointed out that the last three stanzas portray the yachts in a social context (the playthings of the rich), symbolizing the indifference of capitalism to the masses during the Depression. The images in these stanzas, Williams said, "are a very vague imitation of Dante"[46] from canto 7 of the *Inferno*, which describes the wrathful in the river Styx struggling to pull themselves aboard the tiny skiff carrying Virgil and Dante. (When he was in Paris, Williams may also have seen Delacroix's magnificent rendering of this scene in the Louvre.) Alluding to his source, Williams begins the poem in terza rima, but after two stanzas he abandons its intricate rhyme scheme, retaining the stanzaic structure of three long lines.

Less obviously, several features of the first eight stanzas anticipate the shocking last three. The yachts are man-made, but like great machines of a factory, they dwarf the "ant-like" crew, which "crawls [over them] // . . . solicitously grooming them." The yachts are, at once, superhuman in scale, indifferent to their servants, pampered not only by the crew, but by racing in a "well-guarded" arena (guarded not only by the land, but also perhaps by police to keep out the riffraff), and are, like movie stars, "surrounded by / lesser and greater craft which, sycophant, lumbering / and flittering follow them." All of these features make the yachts' indifference to the drowning poor somewhat less shocking.

But only somewhat. The poem's radical change of mode, from a semi-realistic narrative of action in stanzas 1–8 (modified only slightly by per-sonifications) to the surrealistic, horrific scene in the last three; its shift of perspective, from being on a par with the yachts (and beyond the ant-like crew) to being in the water with the drowning; and the speaker's accom-panying shift of tone, from admiring the well-made yachts as art objects to implicitly damning them as the toys of the remote rich, continue to shock readers and daringly unbalance the poem. Interestingly, twenty years later, Williams called the poem's first section "a false situation which the yachts typify with the beauty of their movements" as opposed to "the real situation (of the poor) [which] is desperate while 'the skillful yachts pass over.'"[47] Long after Marxist ideology had self-destructed in the United States and its advocates had either recanted or found other causes, Wil-liams had not shed his essentially proletarian point of view.

REVIEWS OF *AN EARLY MARTYR* AND *ADAM & EVE & THE CITY*

Williams was uneasy about how leftist critics would respond to his new poetry. He wrote Latimer early in 1936 that the communists "are the ones that for the next few years (as for the last few) will soon be the major ob-stacle for excellence to hurdle."[48] He need not have worried: most of the leftist critics who reviewed these books noted their social themes (particu-larly in *An Early Martyr*) and liked the way Williams handled them.[49] T. C. Wilson, editor of the leftist *Westminster Review,* felt that the new poems were "much more authentically 'proletarian' than most of the verse now being printed under that label." Although Williams "does not explicitly commit himself to any definite ethos, his growing social consciousness has given him a firm basis both for the selection and interpretation of his subject matter." As Ruth Lechlitner was to judge a few years later, Wilson considers Williams exemplary: "Our young revolutionary poets, who tend to turn their characters into idealized abstractions, would do well to take Dr. Williams as a model. At his best . . . he provides an example of integ-rity and increasing strength and development that is today unrivalled."[50]

Robert Lann's review in *The New Republic* was less enthusiastic—and more obtuse. Apparently unaware of Williams's many statements and poems to the contrary, Lann writes: "Art, he would say today, should be divorced from experience, concerned with the static and defined moment rather than with the dynamic flux because—baldly—life is unpleasant and futile." *An Early Martyr* shows "a profound pessimism." (Did he read only the first poem?) Lann concludes that Williams's modernism "does not seem to be part of the continuing line of social development."[51] Eda Lou Walton, reviewing *Adam & Eve & The City,* partly agreed with Lann that Williams was essentially still one of the imagists—albeit "the best" of them. She recognized, however, that his "poetic paintings are of a real world" including "the laboring world": "[H]e has learned, as few of the other Imagist poets have, to so widen and develop the description of some actual thing . . . as to indicate a more and more intensive or evolving significance."[52] Robert Fitzgerald, too, recognized Williams's "development": "Many of the poems [in *An Early Martyr*] were strong because their subject matter was deep in social tragedy . . . [his poems] have a formal and human density greater than that of most of his previous work."[53]

Ruth Lechlitner's review of *An Early Martyr* is interesting because it integrates Williams's form and content. The social themes, Lechlitner felt, benefited greatly from his "pared-to-the-bone" technique: "Clear observation and unconfused sympathetic understanding combine with an almost flawless perfection of form." Lechlitner, moreover, felt "Williams has gone too long without honor in critical circles because he has been rebel enough to choose his own subjects and method."[54] She was to rectify that oversight herself a few years later in her comprehensive evaluation of *Complete Collected Poems.*

These positive reviews might well have lifted Williams's status and popularity as a poet had the books received larger print runs and circulation. But how many people actually read these overpriced volumes, with so few copies in circulation? As with Cummings's *Collected Poems,* it would take a major and comprehensive publication of Williams's work to begin establishing him as a major American poet.

WILLIAMS IN THE LATE THIRTIES: POLITICS

Through the late 1930s, Williams essentially continued his political involvements and mishaps of the mid-thirties, but gradually shifted away from the Left in his poetry. While protesting that he was too busy, he kept joining—and resigning from—leftist groups, committees, causes. Although his fiction continued to overshadow his poetry in these years, both in productivity and critical recognition, he published the first comprehensive edition of his poetry, *Complete Collected Poems, 1906–1938,* which garnered many more reviews than did his mid-thirties books under Latimer and did much to solidify his poetic standing. His luck in acquiring new publishers continued to improve as he found his ideal publisher in James Laughlin's New Directions Press. Politically, his sympathies were still leftist, still opposed to communism, but they flirted at times with its chief literary medium, *New Masses.* Aesthetically, while he still believed that poetry must recognize social conditions, he grew more interested in searching for a new measure and for a radically new form to accommodate the large work based on his own region, *Paterson,* which he had been mulling over since the late twenties. "Paterson: Episode 17," written about 1937, became part of book 3, finished a dozen years later.

The aesthetic balance Williams struck in his mid-thirties thinking between pure poetry (concentrating solely on the word) and social perception still obtained, albeit uneasily. In his 1938 review of Sol Funaroff's poetry, for example, Williams seems to retreat to his early-thirties position when he declares unequivocally: "[I]t is words that are [the poet's] materials and *not,* as a poet, states of society. . . . [Y]ou cannot write a poem paying primary heed to social conditions, you cannot write a poem with anything but words." But a few sentences later—as if remembering that he's publishing this review in *New Masses*—he writes: "We cannot allow ourselves to forget the first principle of the Marxian dialectic: to use *poetry,* also, to forward the universal purpose."[55] Of course, there is no real contradiction between these statements. As Williams had said on many occasions, good poetry can further social ends more than bad, propagandistic poetry.

Williams's political relations with the Left in these years were almost comical in his knack for getting into the crossfire of feuding sects and of joining committees whose agendas he only partly understood. But like the Funaroff review, they show his desire to publish in the most radically leftist journals and stay involved with leftist issues. Once again, *Partisan Review* played a Machiavellian role in embarrassing him. Some background is necessary: in early 1936 the communist poet H. H. Lewis submitted to *PR* a laudatory review-essay that Williams had written on Lewis's poetry. Although *Poetry* had published a much-cut version of this essay in January,[56] both Lewis and Williams wanted to see the full essay in print. The editors of *PR* rejected the essay, and in a heated exchange of letters with Lewis, they quoted Williams's symposium response (fresh on their desk) as one justification.[57] Their accompanying comment reflects unvarnished scorn for Williams: "This will show you that Williams has no right to pass judgment on revolutionary poetry because he is opposed to it and doesn't understand it. You know perfectly well that people like yourself have always considered Williams a bourgeois decadent and lo, suddenly he emerges in your eyes as another Plekhanov."[58] According to Reed Whittemore (256), Lewis passed along this letter to Williams (it is in the Williams papers at Yale).

Given *PR*'s abusive treatment and contemptuous attitude toward him, Williams might have been expected to have nothing further to do with this magazine. But when the reconstituted magazine appeared to offer an olive branch by soliciting a poem in the summer of 1937, Williams complied. Why he did so will be considered below. For his efforts *PR* rejected the poem and then had the temerity to reject a substitute, "The Defective Record." Williams then sent an ambiguous postcard: "Your patience will make the flowers bloom," which led the editors to assume he would send yet another poem. In the meantime, *New Masses* had accepted his essay on Lewis—on one condition. Ordinarily, the two events would have no connection, but the Stalinist *New Masses* had declared virtual war on the anti-Stalinist *Partisan Review,* refusing to publish authors who had appeared in the other magazine. Hearing of *PR*'s announcement of a future poem by Williams, *New Masses* inserted the following note in its November 16 issue announcing the forthcoming Williams essay: "[S]ome of our readers may have seen an advance notice of the Trotskyist *Partisan Review,* announcing the anti-Soviet, anti-Communist contents of the first issue. William Carlos Williams is listed as a contributor, but he writes to the *New Masses* that 'the *Partisan Review* has no contribution of mine nor will I send them any'" (2).

Partisan Review immediately demanded an explanation from Williams. This, in itself, showed astonishing chutzpah given how the editors had treated him (including the rejection of the two poems) and that they themselves had rejected his essay on Lewis. Williams certainly did not owe *PR* any explanation, but he responded nonetheless. Typically, he was both candid and blunt:

> You know, of course, that I have no reason for liking the *Partisan Review.* I have, at the same time, no partisan interest in the New Masses. . . . As my contribution to the New Masses was of longer standing and of more importance to me than the other and since I found the New Masses violently opposed to you on political grounds, so much so

that they refused to print me if I remained a contributor to *Partisan Review,* I made my choice in their favor.

    Their quotation from my letter was correct.[59]

By now Williams was wary enough of *PR* to fear being quoted out of context. He insisted, therefore, that if *PR* printed this letter, it should do so in toto. Once again, however, he underestimated the lengths to which *PR* would go to humiliate him. *Partisan Review* not only printed it, it printed Williams's previous correspondence with the journal, even his post card. Under the mocking title "The Temptation of Dr. Williams," the editors sought to make him look like a dupe and a rube, exploited by *New Masses* in its war to suppress *PR:*

> The *New Masses* refused to print him unless he boycotted *Partisan Review*—a condition in itself humiliating enough for a writer of Dr. Williams' standing. . . . We are distressed that Dr. Williams should lend himself to such shenanigans. . . . In its efforts to stifle independent left-wing expression, the *New Masses* has so far been signally unsuccessful. The Williams episode is its first triumph, so far as *Partisan Review* is concerned. But what a victory! Conditions! Threats! Pressures! These are the tactics of the underworld. . . . When the real situation becomes clear to Dr. Williams, as in time it must, we hope he will send us some more poems. ("Ripostes" 62)

Conveniently, the editors exclude all reference to their earlier efforts to humiliate Williams with "Sanctions" and to their previous rejections of the essay on Lewis and of the Williams poems *they* had solicited. Thus, they disingenuously depict themselves as "puzzled when he writes, 'You know, of course that I have no reason for liking the *Partisan Review.*'" They conclude: "All we know is that he thought well enough of our venture to send us two poems and to promise others" (62). Once again, Williams had egg on his face, and this time he seemed almost to be asking for it.

New Masses kept its word and published the essay, "An American Poet," on November 23, 1937 (17–18). It is certainly one of the strangest pieces Williams ever wrote. Its subject, H. H. Lewis, a Missouri dirt farmer turned poet, wrote utterly pedestrian poems lavishly praising Russia and communism—not quite the sort of poetry Williams might be expected to admire. Yet, the essay strains itself to find positive things to say about a poet who Williams concedes has "a total lack of all other excellence" except for "belief" and "fervor": "[Lewis] is convinced of [his subject's] importance to a fanatical degree" (17). Williams dignifies this fervor by identifying it with the patriots of "our revolutionary tradition": "When he speaks of Russia, it is precisely then that he is most American" (17). And, startlingly, Williams derogates from his own aesthetic values in order to praise Lewis's one quality: "The great segment of all poetry is belief, from which springs the rhythmic nature of the created work." He even speculates that "this [fervor] may be the determining factor of the new quarter of the century, and the one after it. [Thus,] Lewis may be the very essence of the innovator" (18). This qualified prediction—or is it really a fear?—sounds similar to Stevens's anticipation (in "Mr. Burnshaw and the Statue") that future poetry in a collectivistic world will necessarily be ugly. In both cases, the poets convey an ill-concealed anxiety that *their* kind of poetry is obsolete and must change.

Inevitably, some of Williams's compliments are backhanded:

Without saying that Lewis is important as a poet, which is a point that will have to be very carefully considered . . . he is tremendously important in the United States as an instigator to thought about what poetry can and cannot do to us today. (17)[60]

His songs are songs, as good as he can make them, of triumph, realization. . . . From the work of the first quarter of the century he has taken one positive thing, his dialect. (18)

The four booklets [of Lewis's poetry] show little or no progress in form that I can discern. (18)

[T]here is no question of high art. Lewis has read from many of the well-known English and American poets and frankly copied their forms, using them as they come readily to his hand. (18)

Whatever motivated Williams to write this thoroughly disingenuous review—(or had he really convinced himself that Lewis was on to something?)—and to conclude that "[t]he influence of Lewis's work on other writers cannot but be good" had much more to do with Williams's own uneasy relationship with the Left than with Lewis's poetry. That motivation may also explain Williams's curiously compliant behavior toward a magazine that consistently abused and humiliated him, *Partisan Review.* When he devotes nearly a quarter of the review, for example, to praising the cheap, paper-bound editions of Lewis's work, he is clearly reflecting a bad conscience about the lavish, expensive editions of his own poems that Latimer published in the previous two years. But more important, Williams wanted to be published in the leading leftist magazines, the ones that garnered the most readers enjoyed the greatest political cachet at that time. As the official literary journal of the CPUSA, *New Masses* would certainly expect high praise for a long-standing contributor and proletarian cheerleader for Russia like Lewis. Was that praise, then, the dues Williams felt he must pay to be published in this shrine of the Stalinist Left, even if it meant bending his aesthetic standards? I prefer to think that, rather than knowingly compromise his aesthetics, Williams had temporarily deluded himself into thinking that Lewis's monothematic fervor represented a likely future for poetry in a political age.[61] In any case, he was certainly not alone in wanting to be part of the leftist avant-garde. Recall that Stevens found it "extraordinarily stimulating" to be part of "that milieu" when his book was reviewed in *New Masses*. And as Stevens's reviewer Stanley Burnshaw observed later, numerous authors were knocking at the *New Masses'* door in the mid- to late thirties, including Hemingway.[62]

Thus, Williams continued to send poems and prose to leftist magazines, reviewing in the *New Republic,* for example, Muriel Rukeyser's *US1,* Walker Evans's photographs, and Wallace Stevens's *The Man with the Blue Guitar.*[63] While he did not consider Stevens's poems evidence of his reputed move to the left (see chapter 2), he admired the revolutionary élan of Rukeyser's work, particularly her incorporation of heterogeneous material ("the language of an x-ray report or a stenographic record of a cross-examination") "with something of the skill employed by Pound in his material for the Cantos" (141). And he advises her to "make the form that will embody her rare gifts of intelligence and passion for a social rebirth" (142). This praise of using heterogeneous material is not surprising from a poet who was already working on drafts of an epic poem that would employ the same technique and who had already experimented with amalgams of poetry and prose. What's most revealing in this review, however, are his last two sentences: "Her passion will not be sacrificed, on the contrary it will be emphasized, by the success of such attention to technical detail. So will the revolution." "*The* revolution" makes it sound like an inevitable event—and Williams as a supporter of that event. And once again, good writing (albeit not the "revolution" sentence) could further a good cause.

There was no shortage of causes in the last years of the 1930s, but Williams seemed befuddled by the continuous sniping and feuding of various factions on the left, as Stalinists and anti-Stalinists, Trotskyites and anti-Trotskyites, Lovestoneites, and radical gadflies of all sorts continuously tangled. For example, Columbia philosophy professor Sidney Hook had shifted from being a powerful voice advocating communism in the early thirties to an anti-Party, anti-Stalinist leftist in the later thirties. When he organized the Committee for Cultural Freedom (CCF) in May 1939 to oppose the totalitarianism of both orthodox communism and fascism, Williams joined. What could be wrong with defending "cultural freedom," after all? Two months later, he wanted out. As he explained to Robert McAlmon: "Some of the boys started a Committee for Cultural Freedom a month or two ago. They asked me to sign up, which I did. Then I found out it was a covert attack on Communism, linking it up with Fascism. Though I'm no Communist, as you know, I couldn't stand for that so I resigned from their God damned committee."[64] Mariani describes Williams as "having discovered the that the committee had been formed by one splinter group of the left to attack other splinter groups of the left" (*New World* 429). Though this may well have been the CCF's aim,[65] Williams does not mention it in his letter to McAlmon. The reason he does provide is curious, since to attack fascist *and* communist totalitarianism was the CCF's stated, not "covert," aim from its inception.[66] For Williams to have discovered this two months later suggests that he signed on without knowing what the group stood for, simply because "they" had asked him to.

Once again, Williams had stepped into the middle of something, because in daring to attack communist totalitarianism, the CCF immediately drew furious counter-attacks from the Far Left. The chief issue was whether cultural freedom could exist without socialism: the CCF said yes; other leftist groups loudly said no. CCF's founding-announcement in *The Nation* (May 27, 1939), with ninety-six signers including Williams, elicited immediate criticism from an editor of *The Nation* in the same issue and from *The New Republic*. Soon, two new groups formed with the aim of attacking the CCF: the Committee of 400 and the League for Cultural Freedom and Socialism (LCFS). Both published letters or petitions, and among the signers of both groups was William Carlos Williams! The Committee of 400, a communist front group, published an "Open Letter" in *The Daily Worker* on August 14, 1939, that condemned as "fascists and reactionaries" those who believed "the fantastic falsehood that the USSR and the totalitarian states are basically alike." The LCFS was founded by none other than the editors of *Partisan Review* (Dwight Macdonald, Williams Phillips, Philip Rahv, and F. W. Dupee) plus a few of their favorite writers, such as James T. Farrell and James Burnham. Its call for supporters, published in the summer 1939 issue of *PR,* declared: "Obviously, we do not subscribe to the currently fashionable catchword 'neither communism nor fascism.' . . . [T]he liberation of culture is inseparable from the liberation of the working classes" (126).

The CCF was not about to take these attacks lying down. And when one of its illustrious supporters—William Carlos Williams—chose to resign from the group, its supporting newspaper, *New Leader,* decided to make an example of him by publishing a statement about his resignation (authored by a Mr. Lundberg), which apparently reviewed his previous battle with *PR* over the Lewis essay. As it was intended to, the statement offended Williams, who states in an angry letter to James Oneal, editor of *New Leader,* that Lundberg was "apparently in a mood to do me an injury . . . which your emphasis adds force to."[67] Williams must have experienced an unpleasant sense of déjà vu: here were the humiliating experiences with *Partisan Review* and *New Masses* trotted out again in a new effort by a leftist publication to embarrass him. His letter to Oneal attempts to clarify his role in the earlier dispute between *New Masses* and *Partisan Review,* which even for him was now "stale history." He concluded: "I personally am not concerned with the political philosophy of any publication as long as its pages are open to creative writing of merit."

Apparently having learned nothing from his experiences with *Partisan Review,* Williams expected fair treatment from *New Leader:* since it had published "a misleading statement regarding my resignation [from the CCF] . . . perhaps you will publish also this letter . . . [and] correct the statement concerning my relations with New Masses and Partisan Review." But Oneal was having none of it and refused to publish his letter. When Williams complained to Hook about the matter, he received no sympathy: Hook dismissed Williams's charges against the CCF as "demonstrably false" (qtd. in Whittemore 257). Then Williams tried to get Babette Deutsch (another CCF signer) to help him publish the letter in another magazine. Deutsch complied, but as Williams confided to Norman Macleod, "I fear me, if I judge my Committee for Cultural Freedom correctly, I will not get fair play. Wait and see."[68] His suspicions were correct: the magazine apparently never printed it. Finally, he sent it to *New Masses* in October (long after the issue was moot). Williams was clearly confused by all this infighting and by his uncanny capacity to antagonize all sides. In the same letter to Macleod (regarding Macleod's disapproval of a different Williams letter) the poet confesses: "I still can't grasp what in hell anybody can have taken exception to in it. It's beyond me. So much hidden bitterness! About what? Damned if I know."

Not knowing, however, did not prevent him from signing still more petitions and letters—and immediately regretting it. To declare his opposition to the CCF, he lent his name to the groups attacking it, whose published declarations proved nothing short of embarrassing. The Committee of 400's letter condemning anyone who equated Russia and Germany appeared just one week before Russia signed the Non-aggression Pact with Nazi Germany. The LCFS's declaration was a more complicated mess. Williams later told Macleod that he "fell again" only because he saw James Laughlin's name on the LCFS letter—strange logic! Joining such luminaries as James T. Farrell, Kay Boyle, Gorham Munson, Delmore Schwartz, and Katherine Anne Porter, he was willing to overlook the fact that this petition was drafted by his nemesis, the editors of *PR* (chiefly Dwight Macdonald)—apparently, they were ineluctable. The problem, again, was timing. The call for signers appeared in the summer of 1939, but the list of signers was not published until *PR*'s fall issue, *after* the Non-aggression Pact and the start of World War II. As described in chapter 1, numerous CPUSA members and sympathizers, disillusioned by the pact, broke with the Party now that the official communist line had done a backflip and demanded not opposition to fascism but non-alignment in an imperialists' war. Moreover, the published declaration in *PR* had changed substantially. The original call emphasized that the LCFS supported "Complete Freedom for Art and Science" and criticized "formerly progressive cultural circles" (i.e., the CCF) that rejected both communism and fascism and supported a "war drive."[69] No other mention was made of the looming war. The petition published in the fall issue, obviously amended after September 1, called for "opposition to this dance of war in which Wall Street joins with the Roosevelt administration" (127)—essentially, the official communist position. Thus, the signers found themselves marching lockstep with the thoroughly discredited CPUSA. Once again, Williams was disgusted. In early November he told Macleod: "I'm signing no more nothins. I quit."[70] This time, he seems to have meant it. As with so many of his contemporaries after the Nazi-Soviet pact, his active participation in the Left—in its causes, petitions, factions, and squabbles—was about extinguished.

FICTION AND NEW DIRECTIONS PRESS

Williams's admiration for Latimer's Alcestis Press did not survive their second book, *Adam & Eve & The City* (1936). As Mariani notes, Williams grew "disappointed with Latimer's workmanship," having found several errors in galleys. Although Latimer corrected the errors at his own expense, Williams stalled him on his proposal to do a *Collected Poems* (*New World* 386–87). As noted above, Latimer's lavish and unaffordable productions went against Williams's commoner values, and the limited print runs made the books hard to find. In December 1937 he told Latimer frankly: "All my life I've been hoping to get a regular publisher who would put my stuff out in a more or less uniform style. Things seem to be shaping up at present in favor of James Laughlin and his New Directions Press."[71]

As an undergraduate, Laughlin had solicited a short piece from Williams for the *Harvard Advocate* in 1934. Two years later, he began his own press, New Directions, and approached Williams about *White Mule,* the novel that Williams had been trying to publish for more than two years. Williams agreed eagerly and even worked on rewriting the ending to make it stronger—yet another instance of a publishing opportunity inspiring him. The book appeared in September 1937 and began a lifelong publishing relationship that included nearly all of Williams's future work. In the remainder of the decade that work included another book of short stories, *Life along the Passaic River* (1938), the novel *In the Money* (a sequel to *White Mule*—1940), and, most important for Williams's career as a poet, the *Complete Collected Poems* (1938).

Although a detailed discussion of *White Mule* and *Life along the Passaic River* goes beyond the limits of this study, a few aspects of their achievement should be noted. In both the novel and the short-story collection, proletarian characters and themes predominate. *White Mule* concerns the struggles of a working-class couple, Joe and Gurlie, while *Life along the Passaic River* contains "stories of the poor, the oppressed, the outcasts, the victims of the times" (*New World* 405). Williams later said that when he wrote the stories in *Life,* "I was still obsessed by the plight of the poor" (*IWWP* 63). But neither book is "proletarian" according to the prescriptions of the Far Left. As Reed Whittemore observes, "the proles were in his fiction but they were in there as people not pawns. . . . [Williams was] trying to catch the talk of the poor, to put glimpses of their lives on the page, . . . but he was avoiding the easy social-political tags and conclusions that the other [proletarian writers] invariably rushed to" (248). Instead, Williams's protagonist in *White Mule* is an *ex*-labor organizer, who now considers unions "a business like any other." His greatest heresy, however, is to become a strikebreaker and run an open shop—a reversal that two Marxist critics took exception to even while praising the novel (see below).

Both books received highly favorable reviews. Leftist critics of *White*

Mule praised Williams's poetic lyricism and precision, his ear for realistic dialogue, and his unsentimental characterization. For Alfred Kazin, reviewing *White Mule* in the *New York Times Book Review,* the novel happily combines "utter realism" and poetic precision. Kazin also notes the book's lack of cant: "[T]here is no declamation; there is only stasis and ebb and flow around it, the particular given to us with so much honesty, so much understanding, that what we hear is the echo of a communal whisper."[72] Sol Funaroff, a Marxist poet, also felt the novel benefited from Williams's poetic precision—an advance over *The Knife of the Times:* "[H]e has in *White Mule* crystallized and developed a fluent diction which captures the bare movements of reality . . . a verbal tool which dissects the object like a surgeon's scalpel."[73]

Some far-left critics were put off by Joe Stecher's open shop in *White Mule* but still affirmed the novel overall. Fred Miller, Williams's communist coeditor and friend from the *Blast* days, felt that "a one-time union organizer gone completely open-shop needs the explaining he doesn't get here." But Miller admired the novel's "lean, straight, fast-stepping American [style]" and Williams's ability "[t]o see a thing, not approximately but as it is; then, with a few punches of the typewriter keys, to conjure up an image of it . . . [that precisely captures] its essential quality."[74] Willard Maas, communist critic and Latimer's assistant at Alcestis Press, observed that Williams's social consciousness "does not prevent him from making Joe Stecher . . . a strike-breaker and a sympathetic character. Williams's ideas are powerful because there is no attitudinizing or false underscoring."[75] Finally, even Williams's old nemesis, Philip Rahv, was fairly sympathetic and saw in Joe Stecher Williams's artistic dilemmas in the thirties in reconciling aesthetics and social concerns.[76] Williams was delighted by all the favorable reviews of *White Mule:* "The New York press was crazy about it," he recalled. "All the reviews were favorable and I thought I was *made*" (*IWWP* 62).

Life along the Passaic River received fewer reviews, but these too were laudatory and praised the same qualities of Williams's writing: pared-down precision, lack of sentimentality and cant, non-ideological empathy for his characters (Walton), growth in his social awareness (Miller, Mass above), a harmonizing of style and realism (Miller).[77] Even the same medical metaphors recur: "realism with the precision of a surgeon" (Walton); "a verbal tool which dissects the object like a surgeon's scalpel" (Funaroff); "realism intensified with a skill as of X-ray in penetration and analysis" (Walton).[78] Miller even hit on one of Williams's special concerns, observing: "He has shown again the more truly localized the art, the more it is universal."

These reviews confirm that the Left was beginning to recognize Williams's capacities not just as social realist (which they had already done in responding to *An Early Martyr*) but as a stylist who demonstrated that modernist aesthetics and social perspective were not incompatible. More important, these critics were taking Williams on his own political terms, applauding the authenticity of his portraiture and praising, rather than criticizing its avoidance of leftist formulas and moralizing. This recognition and flexibility boded well for the reception of his poetry.

COMPLETE COLLECTED POEMS, 1906–1938

Nineteen thirty-eight was a bounteous year for Williams. The same year *Life along the Passaic River* was garnering positive reviews, New Directions published the first full collection of his poems, dating back to 1906. Although it lacked his most experimental book, *Kora in Hell,* it included such other experiments as *Spring and All* and *The Descent of Winter.* Equally important, it provided a much wider audience for Williams's most recent—and most political—poetry: *An Early Martyr, Adam & Eve & The City,* and the poems he had written since. It is from this last category, poems written between 1936 and 1939, that I wish to consider poems with political and social themes as Williams's final engagement with the decade.

Looking over the thirty poems listed in the Litz and MacGowan edition between 1936 and 1939, it becomes clear that Williams's social emphasis has diminished from *An Early Martyr* and *Adam & Eve.* One finds the ubiquitous imagist poem, such as "Between Walls" and "The Young Cat and the Chrysanthemums"; in addition, several poems are either designated or intended as drafts for the future *Paterson;* and one is distinctly autobiographical: "The Last Words of My English Grandmother." Arguably, only two of the late poems, "The Girl (with big breasts)" (*CP-WCW* 1:444) and "The Halfworld" (463), could be called "proletarian" and comparable to "Proletarian Portrait" in *An Early Martyr.* "The Girl" parallels the latter poem in several respects: its short two-line stanzas; its subject: another bareheaded girl on the street who is possibly poor (though in 1939, how many people of any class would pass up a dime on the street?); and its action: she is staring intently at something. But there the resemblance ends: the woman in "Proletarian Portrait" confronts the nail in her shoe with direct action, a political exemplar; this woman, reading a newspaper as she crosses the street, simply looks down at something "*as though /* she had seen a dime." And her depiction is distinctly sexual: identifying her by her "big breasts / *under* a blue sweater" (emphasis added in both quotations), the speaker is verbally undressing her, making her a sex object, not an object lesson.

"The Halfworld" is less ambiguously proletarian, an apostrophe to a "Desperate young man / with haggard face / and flapping pants." The poem mentions his "fatigue / and isolation" but describes his "commonplace" as "beauty." Curiously, however, it contrasts him not with other people or classes but with nature, whose night shadows are "wrapping you about . . . against / the incestuous // and leaning stars—." He thus shares something with the lice-infested young man of "The Sun Bathers" and the happy-go-lucky couple in "Late for Summer Weather," who are also placed in natural—albeit happier—climates.

A much-better-known poem, "Classic Scene" (444–45), also projects a Marxist theme. It takes as its starting point the celebrated 1931 painting *Classic Landscape* by Williams's friend Charles Sheeler; but Williams takes several liberties with the painting. His "power-house" is "red brick," not white; it has two smokestacks, not the one prominent stack in Sheeler's painting.[79] Most important, Williams's stacks are "commanding an area / of squalid shacks" that are nowhere to be seen in Sheeler's purely industrial scene. This last addition gives Williams's poem a distinctly Marxian tinge. The two stacks he personifies as king and queen—two "figures" "which / sit" "side by side" on a throne-like "red brick chair / 90 feet high"—sharply contrast the "squalid shacks" they command. Sheeler's impersonal, geometrical scene thus becomes Williams's juxtaposition of the mighty and the powerless, a conventionally Marxist personification of monarchical feudalism and its successor, capitalism. He misses one bet, however. Sheeler's clouds are the same color as the "buff" smoke, suggesting how thoroughly the smokestacks pollute the air; Williams's sky is "grey."

Several of these late poems treat social themes, but with more subtlety than the typical proletarian or Marxian patterns. "The Defective Record" (455), one of the poems *PR* rejected in the 1937 fracas, describes an all-too-familiar scene: a developer levels a wildlife area with sand for new homes, thus "killing whatever was / there before—including / even the muskrats." The poem's angry query and answer—"Who did it? / There's the guy"—identifies the builder as a culprit who sees the land only as something "to build a house // on to build a / house on to build a house on." The repetition of this phrase indeed sounds like a "defective record," but it not only captures the developer's one-track purpose but also suggests that his "record" as a good citizen is what is really defective. Williams's environmental concern here was well ahead of its time—something that the apartment-dwelling editors of *PR* apparently could not yet envision.

"Porous" (462–63) at first glance appears a typically imagistic poem:

Cattail fluff
blows in
at the bank door,

But what floats *out* of the bank gives the poem its social twist:

and on wings
of chance
the money floats out,

lighter than a dream,
. . . .
and vanishes.

Not the money, but the plans for it—"on wings / of chance," "a dream"—
are as insubstantial as cattail fluff. Clearly, this money is not floating through
the "porous" walls to pay a depositor's rent; "chance" and "dream" suggest an investment, a gamble. Indeed, it was bad investments of their de-
positors' money that caused so many banks to fail in the early Depression;
now, at least, there is money to float out. Some of it went into Williams's
own vanished dream: a failed venture in oil wells.

The poem in this group that best represents the ambivalent relationship
between Williams's aesthetics and leftist ideology has a misleading title:
"The Poor" (452–53). Readers of the *Complete Collected Poems* in 1938
would naturally expect a depiction or, better, indictment of poverty, not
these sprightly opening lines:

It's the anarchy of poverty
delights me

"Delights"?! Was one allowed to be "delighted" by any aspect of poverty
in the 1930s? But the theme emerges nonetheless: "anarchy" here means
visual diversity in an age of increasing sameness. "[A]mong the new brick
tenements"—all drearily alike, no doubt—the poem celebrates "the old /
yellow wooden house" (the same one as in "The Sun Bathers"?) that breaks
up their monotony. The speaker discovers artistry where none is expected:
"a cast-iron balcony / with panels showing oak branches / in full leaf." Variety appears in "the dress of the children // reflecting every stage and /

custom of necessity—" and in the houses of the poor: "Chimneys, roofs, fences of / wood and metal in an unfenced // age and enclosing next to / nothing at all." The people in this poem neither look nor act conventionally poor: they are not down-and-out. The children's motley clothing is not described as ragged or lice-infested; the fenced yards show pride of possession even if they enclose "next to nothing at all"; and "unfenced age" sounds more like a swipe at a Marxist ideal (or was it New Deal leveling?) than a capitalist reality.

Finally, the poem focuses on one old man dressed comfortably—"in a sweater and soft black / hat"—who shows the same pride of place (even if it's a narrow place) by sweeping "his own ten feet" of the sidewalk. That he sweeps it in a wind that is "fitfully / turning his corner" and may therefore negate his efforts is no matter: the wind "has / overwhelmed the entire city." Like the economic disaster of the Depression, no one is spared; so one does the best one can. In retrospect, it is remarkable that *The New Republic* printed this poem in 1938: its anti-proletarian theme makes Williams sound like Frost, while its aesthetic delight in visual diversity links him to Cummings and recalls an earlier deceptive poem, "The Sun Bathers."

Clearly, Williams speaks for himself in "The Poor" ("delights me") and with a forceful clarity that counterbalances the few, conventionally proletarian or Marxian poems of the late-thirties group. These late poems, then, thematically and stylistically mixed as they are, suggest that the poet has pulled back somewhat from the bolder proletarian themes and leftist sympathies of the mid-thirties, just as Stevens did in "The Man with the Blue Guitar," published a year earlier. Though he would never repudiate that political involvement as Stevens did, it is clear that by the end of the thirties, Williams had his mind on other poetic matters, namely *Paterson*.

REVIEWS OF *COMPLETE COLLECTED POEMS*

Publication of the "Complete" or "Collected" poems of a major poet (or of a candidate for that status) is typically an occasion for critics and reviewers to take stock of that poet's achievement and write serious, often lengthy evaluations. So it was for Frost in 1930 and 1939 and for Cummings in 1938. (Stevens's *Collected Poems* would not appear until 1954.) Such books usually attract far more critical attention, therefore, than a book of new poems does, and sometimes they lead to a major reassessment of that poet's standing. Such was the case with Williams's *Complete Collected Poems*: it was widely reviewed and led to a higher critical estimate of Williams as a poet. No longer could he complain about his poetry being over-looked and ignored.

Carrying over their praise of Williams's fiction, leftist critics greeted *CCP* with enthusiasm and, in marked contrast to their reviews of the 1934 *Collected Poems,* praised the new collection for its aesthetic achievements (notably its distinctly American diction and rhythms) as much as for its social themes. Babette Deutsch, for example, had criticized his 1934 collection for its "reliance on the eye" and its "lack of myth-making power." Now, she praised Williams for having been "truest to [the imagists'] principles of being concise and concrete, and his abrupt music is wholly his own"—this, at a time when modernism and imagism were still flailed by leftist critics. Deutsch also lauded his dedication to "perfecting the language so as to make it express a man's own time." Echoing Fred Miller's praise of the "American" English in Williams's fiction, she continues: "The rhythms [of his poetry] are American, the bright staccato of electric signs flashing and winking. The language is a mixture of colloquialism and fine lyric utterance. . . . Its outstanding quality is a vitality that suffuses every part. . . . [His] work is marked by utter candor, delighted irony."[80]

"Vitality" also appears in Horace Gregory's review for the *Herald Tribune.* Like Deutsch, Gregory praises Williams for having captured "the essential idiom of language spoken in the United States. . . . [B]ecause [his poems] seem to be written from the very center of a spoken language, many . . . seem to possess a classic purity of utterance." Praising the poems for achieving "an almost kinesthetic brilliance," Gregory also recognizes Williams's social poems for their "imaginative insight into their time."[81]

Mason Wade, writing in the *New York Times,* also praised Williams as a social poet, distinct from "his poetic confrères of the Left Bank era, who lost touch with the realities of American life and wondered idly why their work was sterile." In Williams's poetry he finds "none of the premature old age,[82] the sense of spiritual drought, the hollowness that plagued many of his fellow-poets of the Twenties." T. S. Eliot's name is written all over this sentence, so Williams would obviously have approved it. But bashing 1920s modernism in order to praise Williams is an odd strategy considering that Williams was one its chief exponents. The *Complete Collected Poems,* Wade argues, "should do more to establish its author as one of the most interesting American poets than any of the books that have previously come from him. . . . This book cannot be ignored by any one concerned with modern American poetry." Wade's conclusion, however, pulls back: "It should assure William Carlos Williams of the place, just below

the first, that is rightly his among the poets of his time."[83] Louis Untermeyer, by contrast, was more forthright and generous, concluding: "This
is undoubtedly one of the most important books of the year; it may well
be ranked as the most notable in scope and manner. It is a plausible con-
tender for the Pulitzer Prize."[84]

One leftist critic would not have ranked Williams "just below the first."
Philip Horton, who had contemptuously dismissed Cummings's *Collected
Poems* the same year, found Williams's tenacity a bit more troubling: "It is
no easy matter to estimate the achievement of William Carlos Williams.
One cannot feel that he is an important poet, and one knows that he is
not an insignificant one." Reiterating Stevens's "anti-poetic" tag, Horton
particularly disliked Williams's "stripped style": "In its extreme form this
style is little more than experimental . . . its poetic achievement is almost
nil. . . . [A]nd it eliminates the humor and pathos that bring his portraits
of the poor so intimately to life." Still, Horton concedes that Williams has
"added a small body of distinguished poetry to our literature." He closes
with this curious prediction: "[Williams's] anti-poetic naturalism, his lo-
calism and his tough-minded humanity may well serve as astringents and
tonics for many of the ailments of contemporary verse."[85] Williams was
not mollified and fired off an intemperate rebuttal to this review, which
New Republic published in its next issue.[86]

The review that probably most influenced Williams's poetic standing
was Ruth Lechlitner's glowing and detailed survey of his work in *Poetry*.[87]
Lechlitner had asserted in her review of *An Early Martyr* that Williams
had been shortchanged by critics; now she rectified that dearth of attention. Her review of *CCP* was, in Charles Doyle's view, "the first comprehensive assessment of Williams' work to appear in over a decade" (*Critical
Heritage* 20), and it praised both Williams's developing technique over the
years and his "deepening social perceptions." The latter, enhanced by Williams's insistence on the individual, was particularly important to this non-
doctrinaire Marxist critic: "[His collected poetry] shows how close and
consistent this poet's contact with the natural, the human, the heterogeneous but strongly individual facets of American life has been." Despite
her emphasis on Williams's social poetry—"An Early Martyr," for example, "should stand as a model to a good many 'social' poets who often
fail to see that the only valid propaganda is not injected into a poem from
the outside, but is inherent in the inseparability of object and comment"—
Lechlitner has a good eye for Williams's dynamic form: "There is no still
life in his imagery: always tension, the pull of mass against mass: action,
struggle, growth—a life that sucks, curls, bulges, rattles, grips, swells, bursts—

always the acid dip of motion. . . . Whatever has the hard, keen, cold edge delights him: . . . a rose not of limpid velvet, but of copper and steel." She concludes by encouraging Williams to continue working toward an epic social poem in the *Paterson* experiments: "Would it not be possible for him to achieve a fusion or cohesion of those factual, disassociated and separately represented facets of the American social scene into something completely observed: an ordered pattern as inevitable in growth, meaning and fulfillment as the cyclamen in flower? There are evidences in parts of the later poems from *Paterson,* a work in progress, of some such intention. The problem is how to say it: 'no ideas but in things.' How to present the human order through one man who is all men, one city that is all cities."[88]

Of the four poets considered in this book, Williams was the only one to have a book of poems receive major recognition and predominantly favorable reviews from leftist critics. Though that esteem first appeared in the fewer reviews of *An Early Martyr,* it was probably the leftists' strongly favorable response to Williams's proletarian fiction in 1937–38 that paved the way. But that social fiction and poetry did nothing to endear Williams to more conservative critics like Yvor Winters and R. P. Blackmur, both of whom wrote fairly negative reviews of the *Complete Collected Poems.* Both favored cerebral poetry (à la T. S. Eliot) and thus despised Williams's dictum of "no ideas but in things." Winters, writing in *Kenyon Review,* asserts: "Dr. Williams distrusts all ideas and seeks value as far as may be in the concrete. . . . And he distrusts the entire range of feelings which is immediately motivated by ideas, for he is in no position to distinguish good ideas from bad." Despite this absurd claim, Winters makes an astonishing prediction: "[T]he end of the present century will see him securely established, along with Stevens, as one of the two best poets of his generation."[89] Bull's-eye!

Blackmur also disliked in Williams's poems "the terrible persistence of the obvious, the unrelenting significance of the banal." Calling his poetry "unexpanded notation," Blackmur continues: "Dr. Williams tries to write as the average man. . . . [But he] has no perception of the normal; no perspective, no finality—for these involve, for imaginative expression, both the intellect which he distrusts and the imposed form which he cannot understand. What he does provide is a constant freshness and purity of language which infects with its own qualities an otherwise gratuitous exhibition . . . of humanity run-down—averaged—without a trace of significance or a vestige of fate in the fresh familiar face."[90] It is interesting that Blackmur published this review in the magazine that had become Williams's bête noir, *Partisan Review.* At least Rahv and Co. did not call for "Sanctions against Blackmur" for writing "humanity run-down—averaged."

CONCLUSION

This chapter began by describing Williams's relationship with the Left—in his poetry and fiction as well as his personal contacts—as "paradoxical" because in many ways he was the skillful proletarian poet and author the Left was looking for but never fully recognized in his work until the late thirties. Williams himself virtually precluded that recognition with his many statements emphasizing the importance of form and "the word" to the detriment of the thematic and propagandistic. His dismissal of communism's appeal to mainstream America and his ridicule of Marxist obtuseness also enraged the comrades, not least because events proved him correct. But as this chapter shows, Williams's bold assertions did not conceal a divided mind: what one side asserted for formalism, the other increasingly undercut in recognizing the "dialectics" of his time.

Paralleling these aesthetic tensions were political and psychological ones: Williams's need to be at the cutting edge in literary happenings, which in the thirties meant editing leftist journals, contributing to leftist magazines, reviewing leftist poets, joining innumerable groups, signing petitions, attending meetings and congresses—all highly social activities—conflicted with his need—really, any writer's need—for intellectual detachment and time to write. That he never hesitated to speak his mind, fire off an intemperate letter, offer a blunt opinion, or write an article reflecting his thoughts of the moment did not make matters easier for him. Indeed, his knack for entangling himself in literary feuds and for alienating one side or another shows as much political naïveté as it does courageous honesty. But, then, in the tortuous, internecine politics of the Left in the 1930s, the word that often recurs in memoirs and descriptions of the times is "confusion."[91] Far more adroit players than Williams got caught up in the labyrinthine corridors and Machiavellian twists of this most political of eras. Then, too, Williams had his share of mishaps that weren't his fault: communist publishers closing down the magazine he edited; disingenuous editors out to ridicule him; presses (like Latimer's) that promised more than they could deliver and ended up isolating his work; duplicitous front groups.

Through it all, one wonders how fully conscious Williams was of his own ambivalence and conflicting ambitions. Though he complained loudly and frequently, he kept joining committees and groups that would eventually (and inevitably) disillusion him; signing petitions that would come to embarrass him; accepting editorships of magazines that he could have predicted would fold after three issues; offering his opinions to magazines that punished him for his candor. Though he never believed in the communists' program, he was pulled to their orbit by his natural proletarian sympathies and by an unacknowledged desire to be at the center of the action, even to the extent of excessively praising a third-rate proletarian poet in *New Masses*. It is almost as if there were two Williams's in this period: the artist, who, though he struggled constantly to reconcile conflicting goals, ultimately knew what he was about; and the political man, who did not.

Williams's poetry in this period reflects his divided purposes: imagist poems, proletarian poems, often both elements in the same poem (imagistic depiction of a social theme; proletarians in an imagist poem); poems that speak confidently about "the revolution"; poems that express "delight" in "the anarchy of poverty"; poems that are fractured between modernist appreciation of a beautiful object and Marxist outrage at its social costs. That he could, at times, powerfully integrate modernist technique and social theme demonstrated that these styles need not be antithetical; such integrations also represent—as they did for Stevens and Frost—an expansion of his poetics and genuine growth in a difficult decade. And for Williams this expansion emerging organically in a kind of dialectical give-and-take with his modernism, was more natural to the man and the poetry than were Stevens's tortuous struggle with "heading left," Cummings's reactive bitterness, Frost's contentious debates. But also like Stevens, this expansion into the political realm ultimately proved ephemeral. Where Williams was most revolutionary was not in his proletarian subjects but in his modernist insistence on seeing the poem as an object, on the supremacy of the word, on the importance of locality and achieving an American idiom, on the continuous search a new metric and form commensurate with a new age. What is particularly remarkable about his achievement in the thirties is that he brought leftist critics to recognize and praise these qualities in his work—in essence, to soften (in his case at least) their hostility to modernism, to modify the doctrinaire in their social demands for poetry.

Williams's involvement with the Left in his politics and poetry, like Stevens's, seemed to peak in the mid-thirties, then gradually diminish by decade's end, though, unlike Stevens, Williams was still signing petitions in 1939. Somehow, though, through all of his political mishaps and publishing difficulties, he landed on his feet and closed out the decade with critical esteem for his fiction and particularly for his poetry, which was now widely read and appreciated as a whole for the first time. The turmoil and vicissitudes of this decade would have exhausted a lesser man as involved in it as Williams was. For Williams, it seems, finally, to have invigorated him and turned him toward the great work of his late years: *Paterson*.

Conclusion

The preceding chapters document how four poets individually struggled with leftist pressures in the 1930s. But what do their stories tell us collectively about the vicissitudes of the modernist poet in the 1930s? The introduction asserts that, despite the obvious individuality of these four, what they experienced in the 1930s and how they responded to the political Left were not idiosyncratic but, when viewed comparatively, reveal patterns common to essentially apolitical poets in a political age. The introduction also raises questions about whether their engagement with leftist politics helped or hindered their poetry and about how their political poetry in the 1930s affected their poetry in the years following. Let us now consider these questions.

PATTERNS AND DISCONTINUITIES

Without question Stevens, Frost, Cummings, and Williams were deeply affected by the migrations of critics and writers to the Left, rather like celestial bodies yanked from their "normal" trajectories by the irresistible gravitational pull of an intrusive star—or a black hole. The disruption began in the early thirties (1930–33), in the enthusiastic first wave of writers, artists, and intellectuals moving leftward. None of the four poets actively joined this movement; in fact, their reactions to it varied considerably: Stevens seemed largely indifferent, while Williams was certainly interested—he even coedited a leftist journal in 1933 but continued to insist on the modernist aesthetics that had guided his poetry previously. Frost and Cummings both expressed deep skepticism of the new politics—Frost in the long pastoral "Build Soil," which he provocatively read at Columbia University in 1932, Cummings in his Russian journal, *Eimi,* published a year later.

These responses, however, did not appear in the poetry collections published by the four in the early thirties: Frost's *Collected Poems* (1930), Stevens's second version of *Harmonium* (1931), Cummings's *ViVa* (1931), and Williams's *Collected Poems, 1921–1931* (1934). Comprised of poems nearly all written in the 1920s and earlier, these volumes appeared indifferent to the Depression and the new politics. But they were reviewed by critics—in particular the leftward-moving Granville Hicks, Isador Schneider, Horace

Gregory, Raymond Larsson, Babette Deutsch, and Eda Lou Walton—who were very much aware of the times and who concluded that these poets were essentially stuck in their 1920s styles and attitudes. It is important to note, however, that none of the leftist critics attacked these collections on explicitly political grounds; words like "bourgeois," "confused," and "counter-revolutionary" had not yet infiltrated poetic criticism. Rather, the critics tended to express their political attitudes as impatience and sometimes irritability that the poetry of these four had not significantly changed from the 1920s. Gregory's critique of Stevens's "highly polished surfaces" is typical, likewise Gorham Munson's disenchantment with what he considered Cummings's elitist obscurity. The leftist reviewers implied that these poets were growing stale and were increasingly irrelevant to the catastrophic times. It should be noted, also, that these negative critiques were intermingled with admiring ones (e.g., the many positive reviews of Frost's *Collected Poems,* and Walton's praise of Stevens's style). Thus, none of the four poets could justifiably complain that the negative reviews were obviously political.

The second, large wave of leftist conversions crested in the mid-1930s. In the milieu of the News Deal's pathbreaking social programs; the Popular Front against fascism and the resulting Communist appeals to bourgeois writers to join the Left (e.g., the communist-organized American Writers' Congress of 1935); the ubiquitous leftist sympathy for Loyalist Spain and the idealistic participation of the Abraham Lincoln Brigade in that civil war, membership in leftist groups like the CPUSA swelled to a high point, while many thousands more chose to became fellow travelers. Writers of any political stripe would thus have found it virtually impossible in this period to ignore the steadily intensifying pressure to go left. Certainly, these four poets by now felt this pressure keenly and responded to it in their mid-thirties books of poetry: Stevens's *Ideas of Order* (1935) and *Owl's Clover* (1936), Cummings's *No Thanks* (1935), Williams's *An Early Martyr* (1935), Frost's *A Further Range* (1936). Their political responses varied, of course, but the prominence of these responses did not. Stevens expressed a complex of attitudes which regretted that "Marx has ruined nature / For the moment" ("Botanist on Alp [No. 1]") and yet recognized that poetry must respond to and change with continually changing and ugly "reality"; in fact, *Owl's Clover* was intended as the poet's response to Marxism, a "poetic justification of leftism."[1] Frost, too, recognized he was writing a kind of poetry uncharacteristic of him, hence his title. But he turned to this new political poetry with a kind of brio, taking an anti-proletarian stance in "Two Tramps in Mud Time," asserting his philosophy of self-reliance forthrightly in poems like "Provide, Provide!" and attacking New Deal collectivism in critiques of its supporters, supposed beneficiaries, and even of Roosevelt himself. Cummings also attacked leftism (e.g., "kumrads die because they're told") and asserted his most cherished value of individualism in such poems as "if i"; but his political poems were tinged with a defensive bitterness not evident in Frost's critiques. Finally, Williams's closer involvement with leftist causes and aesthetics in this period gave his natural empathy for ordinary people a more explicitly proletarian advocacy in such poems as "Proletarian Portrait" and "The Yachts."

The largely negative responses to the Left in *A Further Range,* and *No Thanks,* and the very mixed one in *Ideas of Order,* might lead one to assume that Stevens, Frost, and Cummings were lashing back at explicitly political attacks from leftist critics. But, as noted above, the negative reviews of their collections of the early 1930s were not explicitly political. It seems clear, then, that what compelled these poets to turn their poetry to the political was the increasingly political pressure of their times and literary milieu, and the ways that these pressures impinged on their personal and literary lives. Stevens encountered the Depression's ravages in the daily news and in the failed companies his job took him to, just as he read of the Left's growing sway in the numerous magazines he subscribed to and books he received. Increasingly, he felt a dissonance between these conditions and his comfortable life and socially aloof poetry. Ugly social conditions and radical responses were the order of the day, and, as he recognized, no poet could remain indifferent to them. Yet, he was reluctant to abandon his belief in "pure poetry" and to accept collectivist aesthetics without qualm. Hence, the dilemma and conflictedness he expressed so eloquently in *Ideas of Order,* and enacted so turgidly in *Owl's Clover.* By 1936 Stevens could describe the "pressure of the contemporaneous" as "constant and extreme. No one can have lived apart in a happy oblivion. . . . We are preoccupied with events, even when we do not observe them closely. We have a sense of upheaval. We feel threatened."[2]

Cummings felt that threat quite personally. He believed both himself and his work snubbed by former friends who had become political: His ballet book went unproduced; his book of poems found no commercial publisher. The former bad boy of American modernism now felt himself displaced from the very avant-garde he had once helped lead. Though his poetry had always been socially and aesthetically rebellious, his twenties satires against mainstream America were written within the approving aegis of modernist comrades. Now, doubly alienated from mainstream

American culture and the new political avant-garde, he increasingly assumed the role of an isolated iconoclast, railing against "kumrads" and New Dealian "punks of progress" ("Jehovah buried,Satan dead").[3]

Though he enjoyed far more popular appeal than his contemporaries, Frost also saw his poetic status increasingly challenged, his political views ever more unpopular in the mid-thirties. Repeatedly, he encountered the mounting leftist tide in correspondence with old friends and acquaintances (like Louis Untermeyer); in the appeals of colleagues (such as those who approached him in 1932 to sign a radical petition); and in the increasingly leftist milieu of college campuses and poetry conferences where he taught and lectured. While this recognition did not shake his self-confidence (not until the leftist criticism of *A Further Range,* at least), it certainly made him aware of being an isolated voice—the individualist he always claimed himself to be—and embattled. His responses in *A Further Range,* however, were spirited rejoinders that asserted his own values of self-dependence and separation.

Williams had always felt compelled to involve himself in literary movements and magazines. When those magazines and movements turned left, he was interested. He had seen what the Depression had done to his patients, and his own politics were too radical for liberal solutions. When the CPUSA organized the first American Writers' Congress in 1935, for example, he attended as an observer; when the Spanish Civil War broke out, he organized a physicians relief committee. But he was skeptical about leftist aesthetics and ideology, for, like Stevens, Cummings, and Frost, he was not about to abandon aesthetic ideas and techniques he had developed with great effort over the past fifteen years. More, he voiced his skepticism publicly in editorials and letters to leftist magazines and in leftist symposia. The thanks he received for his candor was official scorn and ridicule; yet, he kept writing letters, kept joining (and disaffiliating from) committees and causes, and showed an uncanny knack for getting between warring factions on the Left. Despite his personal mishaps with the Left, however, he poetry acquired a distinctly proletarian edge in the mid-thirties. Thus, whether these poets found the new political landscape repugnant (as Cummings and Frost did), troubling but compelling (as Stevens did), or engaging if often misguided (as Williams did), they *had* to respond. It was those negative or skeptical responses to the Left (Williams excepted) that elicited the harshest, most ideological reviews from leftist critics, not the other way around. And the leftist reviews matched the relative stridency and extremity of the negative political poems. Leftist responses to Cummings's *No Thanks* and Frost's *A Further Range* were largely dismissive and contemptuous; to Stevens's more complex attitudes in *Ideas of Order* came a more mixed and nuanced response, reflected in Walton's praise and Burnshaw's inadvertently accurate label of "confusion." Moreover, as Stevens strove to address leftist aesthetics in his rather opaque manner in *Owl's Clover*, leftist critics at least recognized that he was attempting something sympathetic (if unsuccessful), just as they began to see Williams as a proletarian sympathizer in *An Early Martyr* and in his thirties fiction.

The poets' responses to the Left in the last years of the 1930s also show comparable patterns. The intensity of leftist pressure diminished in these years primarily because the Left itself fissured over the Stalinist purges and show trials, the fate of Trotsky, and heightening resistance to Party dogma exemplified by the increasingly influential, anti-Stalinist *Partisan Review.* The final straw was Nazi-Soviet Non-aggression Pact in 1939, which threw the Left into total disarray. As leftist politics disintegrated into squabbling factions, all four poets correspondingly diminished their poetic responses in these years, a disengagement modified by degrees of clarity, individual motives, and directions. Stevens marked the sharpest break from his mid-thirties efforts to engage the Left. Beginning with *The Man with the Blue Guitar* (1937), one sees a progressive separation, an implied declaration of artistic independence that becomes explicit in his 1941 lecture-essay "The Noble Rider and the Sound of Words": "I might be expected to speak of the social, that is to say sociological or political obligations of the poet. He has none" (*CPP* 659–60). It is almost as if Stevens said to himself, "Well, I tried, but failed. Now, I can return to what really has concerned me all along." But he did not precisely turn his back on all social concerns as will be discussed below.

For Frost, disengagement was less clear cut. He continued to write the occasional political poem in his later work, and his political position regarding individualism versus collectivism certainly did not change. But he no longer felt the need to assert that position as often and as provocatively as he did in *A Further Range*. Winning the Pulitzer for that book, along with the aggressive support of critics like Bernard DeVoto and the laudatory *Recognition of Robert Frost: Twenty-Fifth Anniversary,* did much to buoy Frost's confidence, temporarily shaken by leftist catcalls at *A Further Range*. The Left could not gainsay that he was more than ever the un-crowned poet laureate of American poetry. At about the same time, however, he experienced family catastrophes—his wife's sudden death most notably—that must have made leftist attacks seem quite trivial indeed.

In the late thirties, Cummings shifted the focus of his satires from political to social, from Russia to America, from Marxist to mainstream, from the ephemeral to what he feared was becoming permanent. His target was now the benighted "mostpeople," his hero, as always, the nonconformist, small-"i" individual (but now often "we," the speaker and his beloved) who opposes the values of "mostpeople." In poems like "my specialty is living" and the later "when serpents bargain for the right to squirm," and especially in the introduction to his 1938 *Collected Poems,* he excoriates "mostpeople" for their conformity and cowardly striving for security and material prosperity provided by applied science. As the mid-thirties witnessed Cummings's increasing isolation and iconoclasm, now his satirical voice became increasingly cantankerous, his poetry dichotomizing between tender and quite memorable love poems and scathing satires, between the few remaining heroic individuals and nearly everyone else.

Finally, Williams put most of his political energy in the late thirties into literary politics and fiction rather than his poetry. His embarrassing entanglements with *Partisan Review* and *New Leader* and his mishaps with newly spawned political committees and petitions finally soured him on active political involvement. While his novels and short stories in these years continued to focus on the working class, they did so from non-ideological perspectives, for example, Joe Stecher's open-shop advocacy in *White Mule.* Williams's political poems in the late 1930s, likewise, were fewer and more idiosyncratic: the aesthetic pleasure expressed in "The Poor," for example, would doubtless have given a party-line Marxist apoplexy. Despite his political independence, however, leftist critics by the end of the thirties came to recognize the long-standing sympathy in his fiction and poetry for ordinary but often impoverished members of the working class and even applauded (many of them) his modernist aesthetics. Diverse as the political diminutions were for these four poets, these responses again share a common source: What had seemed such a juggernaut in the mid-thirties dwindled into increasingly fragmented and bickering voices. As the Left's compelling presence diminished, so did the compulsion of these four poets to respond to it.

LEFTIST ENGAGEMENT IN RETROSPECT: HARMFUL OR BENEFICIAL?

Hercules, bitten
by a crab loyal to the hydra,
was hindered to succeed

—Marianne Moore, "The Paper Nautilus"

From the perspective of their entire careers, the political poetry that Stevens, Cummings, and Frost wrote in the 1930s may well seem minor, and it would be easy to conclude that their leftist encounters did not advance their work. Stevens thought so little of the poems in *Owl's Clover* that he deleted them, and the book itself, from his 1954 *Collected Poems*. Both Frost and Cummings wrote some inferior political poems in the thirties, Cummings's poems marred by ad hominem vitriol and reductive narrowness, Frost's by occasional smugness and a strange propensity to attack the Depression's victims. Only Williams—typically, the odd man out—escapes this generalization, since his proletarian poems of the mid-thirties were certainly no worse than his earlier and later poems about working-class people, and many were first-rate. But, once again, the issue is not clear cut, not only because the poetic results of these four are uneven but also because leftist pressure arguably produced some unexpected benefits.

The mixed success of the political poems of these four poets has been discussed in the preceding chapters and needs only brief mention here. All four produced some excellent poems with political themes. Stevens may have branded his engagement with Marxism in *Owl's Clover* a failure, but he retained (and rightly so) his earlier, conflicted responses to leftism in *Ideas of Order* and his later, more decisive stand on leftist aesthetics in "The Man with the Blue Guitar." Frost was especially good at creating playful personae to belie serious aspects of his political philosophy: the woodchopper-poet for whom "work is play for mortal stakes"; the clever and prudent woodchuck who knows when to lie low in his burrow. Even poems in which the political theme seems reductive—for example, "Neither Out Far nor In Deep" and "Provide, Provide!"—still retain the concision, wit, and memorable phrase of Frost's best poems. Cummings, too, could transcend his bitterness in poems that wittily affirm his individualistic philosophy rather than attack easy targets. "if i" is a superb example (*CP* 475).

As the preceding chapters demonstrate, all four poets felt compelled by leftist pressure to define their political, philosophical, and aesthetic positions in the 1930s. Even if these redefinitions were contradictory and ambivalent, as many of Stevens's responses to the Left were in *Ideas of Order,* one could argue that the *experience* of self-examination and declaration was salutary. Moreover, if leftist critics in the early thirties had a point in implying that Cummings, Frost, and Stevens were getting stale—and there is a strong case to be made for this view—then the poets' engagement with new issues, in a new type of poetry, might in and of itself have been beneficial—vivifying, invigorating—even if it did not always produce good poems. Frost's title for his mid-thirties book, *A Further Range,* suggests this creative stretching. And Stevens was clearly excited to be involved with the Left, at least in 1935–36. In Williams's case, the issue was not creative expansion so much as direction: his engagement with the Left provided an ideological structure for his natural and lifelong empathy for ordinary individuals, a structure (but not a straitjacket) that Williams could variously apply (as in "Proletarian Portrait") or ignore (e.g., "The Poor"). For Cummings, the benefit is less clear: leftist encounters, such as his trip to Russia in 1931, certainly clarified his hatred of all forms of collectivism versus individualism; but whether that clarification was rejuvenating to either his poetry or social philosophy is highly questionable.

REDIRECTIONS: AFTER THE POLITICAL THIRTIES

If these ventures into a new poetic realm were, so to speak, therapeutic, why did the four poets abandon their political engagement so easily at the end of the 1930s? Of course, this question begs another: *Did* they really abandon their political poetics? A few pages above I argued that the explicitly political poems of all four poets markedly diminished at the end of the thirties, a diminution that appears to have responded directly to a lessening of leftist pressure at that time. One could almost imagine the poets expressing a collective sigh of relief as the divisive and contentious leftist hubbub of the late thirties faded. But in only one case—Stevens's— did an emphatic renunciation of political poetry accompany this reduction; and even here the renunciation is not so clear cut as it might seem. It might be more useful, therefore, to consider not that the four poets turned their backs on political poetry in the 1940s and thereafter, but rather how they may have redirected social and political concerns aroused in the thirties to social themes and issues that they found more compelling or central to their later poetics and political philosophy. To end this study, I shall consider these redirections, recognizing that a brief sketch is no substitute for a full portrait.

STEVENS

Stevens's declaration in his 1941 lecture-essay "The Noble Rider and the Sound of Words" that the poet has no social or political obligation and must resist the "pressure of reality" appears definitive—a total repudiation of his 1930s involvement with the Left (*CPP* 659). But in this same essay he eloquently discusses the poet's "function" after he has eliminated that social role and "is left facing life without any categorical obligations": "Certainly [the poet's function] is not to lead people out of the confusion in which they find themselves. Nor is it, I think, to comfort them while they follow their leaders to and fro. I think that his function is to make his imagination theirs and that he fulfills himself only as he sees his imagination become the light in the minds of others. His role, in short, is to help people to live their lives" (660–61). He continues: "[W]hat makes the poet the potent figure that he is, or was, or ought to be, is that he creates the world to which we turn incessantly and without knowing it and that he gives to life the supreme fictions without which we are unable to conceive of it" (662). Thus, rather than return to the private world of *Harmonium* and to the notion of pure poetry, Stevens asserts the poet's social role. Would he have done so without having undergone his remarkable political awakening in the mid-1930s?

It is, of course, impossible to do justice in a few pages to the complexity and subtlety of Stevens's ideas about the "supreme fictions" the poet must provide, when scholars have devoted whole books to the subject.[4] I wish here only to sketch out how Stevens conceived it in some essays and later poems.[5]

The fictions that the poet provides ultimately address cosmological and theological needs. Stevens clarifies these dimensions in a lecture he gave in 1951 at Mount Holyoke College, "Two or Three Ideas":

> In an age of disbelief, or what is the same thing, in a time that is largely humanistic, . . . it is for the poet to supply the satisfactions of belief, in his measure and in his style. (*CPP* 841)

> To see the gods dispelled in mid-air and dissolve like clouds is one of the great human experiences. . . . [T]heir annihilations . . . left us feeling dispossessed and alone in a solitude, like children without parents, in a home that seemed deserted. (842)

> [I]n an age of disbelief, when the gods have come to an end . . . men turn to a fundamental glory of their own. . . . in a new reality. (844)

Stevens here seeks "to elevate the poem to the level of one of the major significances of life and to equate it . . . with gods and men . . . [as] the central interest, the fresh and foremost object" (845).

Of the many later Stevens poems that address aspects of this supreme fiction, two in particular stand out in the way they articulate its context and nature. Part 8 of "Esthétique du Mal" (1944) dramatizes "the gods dispelled in mid-air" but, unlike their depiction in "Two or Three Ideas," extends them to include Christianity:

> The death of Satan was a tragedy
> For the imagination. A capital
> Negation destroyed him in his tenement
> And, with him, many blue phenomena.
> . . . .
> He was denied.
> Phantoms, what have you left? What underground?
> What place in which to be is not enough
> To be? You go, poor phantoms, without place
> . . . .
> How cold the vacancy
> When the phantoms are gone and the shaken realist
> First sees reality. The mortal no
> Has its emptiness and tragic expirations. (*CPP* 281–82)

Of course, Christianity's "vacancy" was nothing new in Stevens's cosmology: it appears as "haunted heaven" in "A High-Toned Old Christian Woman" (*CPP* 47), a poem that also asserts: "Poetry is the supreme fiction, madame." But where this early poem playfully contrasts the Christian woman's defunct heaven with the speaker's vibrant hedonism and aestheticism, the tone in "Esthétique" is more serious, the consequences of disbelief more social and somber. Now, it is not merely prim old ladies who are the losers; it is the imagination itself that once thrived on—indeed, enabled—the Christian mythos as it had earlier the now-supplanted pagan world. Bereft of the imaginative power that has been eviscerated by disbelief, the modern person is, like the doomed gods, a "phantom" and disturbed ("the shaken realist").[6]

Significantly, however, this section does not end in the nihilism and despair of "the mortal no":

> The tragedy, however, may have begun,
> Again, in the imagination's new beginning,
> In the yes of the realist spoken because he must
> Say yes, spoken because under every no
> Lay a passion for yes that had never been broken. (282)

"The imagination's new beginning"—now enabled by the poet, that "shaken realist"—makes high art—tragedy—possible again, and complementarily, the poet's art becomes the collective imagination: "his imagination become the light in the minds of others."

"Of Modern Poetry" (*CPP* 218–19) describes the poet's new role more specifically in a world where "the theatre was changed / To something else. Its past was a souvenir":

> The poem of the mind in the act of finding
> What will suffice.
> . . . .
>   It has
> To construct a new stage. It has to be on that stage
> And, like an insatiable actor, slowly and
> With meditation, speak words that in the ear,
> In the delicatest ear of the mind, repeat
> Exactly, that which it wants to hear, at the sound
> Of which, an invisible audience listens,
> Not to the play, but to itself, expressed
> In an emotion.

In finding "what will suffice"—how modestly Stevens couches the aim!—the poet is not speaking only to himself (cf. "I was the world in which I walked"), as he was not in Stevens's political poetry. Then, however, Stevens recognized that it would take a "harmonious skeptic" singing in a "skeptical music" to unite the needy "figures of men and their shape" ("Sad Strains of a Gay Waltz," *CPP* 101). Now, the audience's need is just as intense ("that which it wants to hear"), but the poet has become "the metaphysician in the dark" addressing a need that is philosophical and imaginative, not merely political.

"Metaphysician in the dark" does not, however, equal priest: "[T]he truth about the poet in a time of disbelief is not that he must turn evangelist. After all, he shares the disbelief of his time. . . . He turns to himself" ("Two or Three Ideas," *CPP* 847). Still, Stevens devises a number of names for him that all suggest the poet's superior status, a kind of *Übermensch* that Nietzsche describes in *Also sprach Zarathustra*. In "Notes toward a Supreme Fiction," he is "the giant," "the major man . . . the MacCullough," the thinker of the first idea." His poem "refreshes life so that we share, / For a moment, the first idea . . . It satisfies / Belief in an immaculate beginning" (*CPP* 333–34, 330). In "Asides on the Oboe" (*CPP*

226–27), he is, variously, "the impossible possible philosophers' man," "the glass man," and "the central man"

> Who in a million diamonds sums us up.

> He is the transparence of the place in which
> He is and in his poems we find peace.

Within his imagination, even during war,

>   We found,
> If we found the central evil, the central good.
> We buried the fallen without jasmine crowns.
> There was nothing he did not suffer, no; nor we.

Though the old gods are gone—the Judeo-Christian gods in the metonymy of the Jordan River ("That obsolete fiction of the wide river in / An empty land") and the pagan gods "that Boucher killed" in his insipid paintings—"The philosophers' man alone still walks in dew."

Stevens may have misjudged the still-active religious belief of the American public in the forties and fifties and projected onto it his own spiritual skepticism and artistic vision. But there can be little doubt that his meditations in poems and essays about how poetry can provide ordinary people not just temporary diversion and aesthetic pleasure, but a vital renewal of the imagination in a secular age, represent not only a resolution of his own dilemmas about his poetic purpose, but a serious and sustained contemplation of the social function of poetry in the modern world. By the end of the thirties, he had rejected political, and specifically Marxist, conceptions of poetry. But his social concern about people's need for an imaginative mythos and poetry's responsibility to provide it did not fade; in fact, it expanded to become a central theme of his late work. These two realms of his interest—political and social—were not separate, and I would argue that Stevens's social interest matured during his intense political engagement in the 1930s.

CUMMINGS

As leftist political pressures faded at the end of the thirties, Cummings's urge to critique his world through satire had not diminished. Indeed, stinging satires were *always* central to his poetry and poetic identity; what changed in the 1930s was their target and tone. In the twenties his satires were lighter, more playful, and his chief target was the hypocritical respectability of middle-class America: variants of the Cambridge ladies. In the mid-thirties, following the desultory satires of *ViVa,* his target shifted to Marxism and its converts, and his tone grew more strident. By the end of the thirties, and thereafter, he again refocused his target (though not his contemptuous tone) against the conformity of "mostpeople," a conformity dependent on technological materialism, New Deal "security," and egalitarianism. "when serpents bargain for the right to squirm" (*CP* 620), from the 1950 *Xaipe,* is one of the wittiest displays of these targets:

> when serpents bargain for the right to squirm
> and the sun strikes to gain a living wage—
> when thorns regard their roses with alarm
> and rainbows are insured against old age
>
> . . . .
>
> then we'll believe in that incredible
> unanimal mankind(and not until)

The language of labor—"bargain," "strikes," "living wage"—is cheerfully misapplied to nature, as are allusions to New Deal social security and the social leveling: "valleys accuse their / mountains of having altitude." With superior detachment, the speaker and his beloved—"we"[7]—will continue not to believe in "mankind" so long as it continues to maintain its unnatural ("unanimal") social values.

Like Frost, Cummings remained true to his bedrock political theme of celebrating individualism and opposing all collectivities. But while his target in the late thirties and thereafter returned to mindless American conformity—in a sense it had never left this subject; only the types of conformity changed—he did not hesitate (unlike the other three poets) to include the government in his attacks. One of these, "F is for foetus(a" (*CP* 635) was an ad hominem rant against Roosevelt, far nastier than Frost's "To a Thinker." The poem calls Roosevelt "a // punkslapping / mobsucking / gravypissing poppa . . . the // great pink / supreme / diocri / ty of // a hyperhypocritical D // mocra / c." The beneficiary of Roosevelt's largesse is the "crowd" that wants only "freedom from freedom," that is, security.[8] More typically, Cummings attacked government policies and the collective attitudes they fostered. Thus, in 1944, at the height of popular support for the war effort in World War II, he dared to challenge conventional concepts of heroism (memorialized by a statue of a soldier) by declaring that "a hero equals any jerk / who was afraid to dare to answer 'no'" ("why must itself up every of a park" [*CP* 636]). The poem also rails against the declaration by "generalissimo e[isenhower]" that military necessity now supersedes all moral considerations in fighting the war. For all his defiance, however, Cummings never deeply considered the moral dilemma of having to use ugly means for a morally worthy end (stopping Nazism). His other World War II poems simply lambaste American patriotic excess, much as his World War I satires did, but without their humor. In "ygUDuh" (*CP* 547), an inarticulate hater describes how "weer goin / duhSIVILEYEz" "dem / gud / am // lidl yelluh bas / tuds." The pun on "EYE" (for an eye) is made explicit in a passage from "F is for foetus(a":

> (sing
> down with the fascist beast
> boom
>
> boom)two eyes
> for an eye four
> teeth for a tooth (*CP* 635)

In these harangues against war-inspired hatred, unthinking conformity, and vindictive brutality, the poems risk falling into the very conditions they condemn, of hating the haters, belittling others ("a hero equals any jerk") as others belittle the enemy. When compared to such deeply felt meditations on the war of Marianne Moore's "In Defense of Merits" or Williams's "Burning the Christmas Greens," which balance the sickening awareness of mass killing with the hope—demand!—for a better world emerging from the maelstrom, Cummings's antiwar poems appear reductive and absolutist.[9]

Even the consistency of his pacifism faltered when visceral hatred of Russian aggression took precedence. Thus, when Russia invaded Finland in 1940, Cummings implies that "uncle shylock" ought to have intervened instead of being "not interested" (*CP* 641). And when Russia sent tanks into Hungary in 1956, while the United States stood by after encouraging Hungary's rebellion, Cummings's response was the excoriating "THANKSGIVING (1956)" (*CP* 711), which he read at the Boston Arts Festival, much to the embarrassment of its organizers:

uncle sam shrugs his pretty
pink shoulders you know how
and he twitches a liberal titty
and lisps "i'm busy right now"

so rah-rah-rah democracy
let's all be thankful as hell
and bury the statue of liberty
(because it begins to smell)

As in "why must itself," Cummings ignores the larger, more complex issue—here, the risk of a third world war if the United States intervened.
His political opinions were subjective and visceral, not reasoned. Thus,
he depicts American duplicity over Hungary as being leftist ("pink") and
"liberal" (as well as effeminate), even though a Republican administration had just been reelected and the country had just undergone the far-
right depredations of McCarthyism. His arbitrariness here squares with his
feelings in the early fifties about Harvard, where he gave his *non-lectures:*
"Have yet to encounter anybody in any manner concerned with Harvard
who isn't primevally pink" (qtd. in Kennedy 443). Inconsistency appears
again in Cummings's support of McCarthyism in these years without his
considering its chilling effect on one of his most cherished values: non-
conformist self-expression.

Cummings's political views and poems after the thirties thus pushed
the trajectories formed in that decade to increasingly dogmatic extremes.
The 1930s feeling of embattled defensiveness intensified into an increasingly isolated subjectivity, an arbitrary crankiness, a curmudgeonly abso-
lutism. His misjudgment about the offensiveness of such poems as "a kike
is the most dangerous" and "one day a nigger" (*CP* 644, 622) derives from
that isolation.[10] Perhaps what changed most—and most damagingly—in
Cummings's political poems over the years was their loss of playfulness,
of the unpredictability of his wit, of the open-mindedness of his inquiry.
Far more than for the other three poets considered in this study, Cummings's later political sensibility never really recovered from his 1930s experience.

Fortunately, the other side of Cummings's Manichaean worldview—
his love poems and spiritual affirmations—also intensified in these years;
in fact, these poems occupy a far more prominent place in his late work
than do the political satires. And these lyrical masterpieces rightly account

for the best of Cummings's later reputation. Both sides of his poetic sensibility, though—the affirmative and the damning—point in the same direction: to a consciousness retreating into a world of two, to a poetic voice that, even as it brayed harshly against a world of "mostpeople," had not—miraculously—lost the suppleness to sing sweetly to one person.

FROST

As he put the personal tragedies of the late thirties behind him, Frost continued to write political poems in his late work, but changed his focus. Anti-leftist and anti-collectivist poems are far fewer after the 1930s, not only because he no longer felt challenged by radicalism (now dead) and the New Deal (already a fait accompli), but also because the political landscape following World War II had changed so profoundly with the advent of the cold war and the nuclear age. On these issues he spoke out forthrightly in poems, lectures, and interviews.

A Witness Tree (1942) and *Steeple Bush* (1947) contain a few anti-leftist poems, or sometimes just interjected passages or asides. In "A Considerable Speck," the speaker interrupts his narrative of "a living mite" to explain:

> I have none of the tenderer-than-thou
> Collectivistic regimenting love
> With which the modern world is being swept.[11]

Similarly, "The Planners" (*CPPP* 361) gets in a jab at liberal social planners who object that nuclear annihilation will deny them "one more chance to change our manners."

"The Lost Follower" (*CPPP* 325), on the other hand, sympathetically portrays a Utopian idealist who abandons poetry for "the golden light divine" and chooses to live "ungolden with the poor." The speaker recognizes that, even as a friend, it is "dangerous" for him to suggest to the idealist that "the millennium to which you bend / In longing is not a progress-end." As the speaker well knows, however, the idealist will not abandon his "kingdom in the sky / (As yet unbrought to earth)." Though the speaker treats him gently, in fact refers to "my love" for the idealist, the title is harsher in depicting him as both lost and a quasi-religious follower of some pie-in-the-sky utopia. As Frost elaborated in a July 1954 interview, "The opposite of civilization is not barbarism but Utopia. Utopia can let no man be his own worst enemy, take the risk of going uninsured, gamble on the horses, or on his own future, go to hell in his own way. . . . It has to know where everyone is; it has to bunch us up to keep track of us. It can't protect us unless it directs us."[12]

Frost did not see himself as a reactionary, however. In fact, he presents himself in one poem in *A Witness Tree* as advocating "a semi-revolution" because "total revolution . . . brings the same class up on top" (*CPPP* 330). When asked if he was a conservative, Frost replied: "No, I'm not. I'm more radical than they [the social thinkers] think."[13] In fact, in the poem preceding "A Semi-Revolution" he describes with apparent approval an economist's advocacy of occasional economic leveling:

> And when we get too far apart in wealth,
> 'Twas his ideas that for the public health,
> So that the poor won't have to steal by stealth,
> We now and then should take an equalizer. ("An Equalizer," *CPPP* 330)

Much earlier (1920), he had described himself to Untermeyer as "neither a conservative nor a radical and I refuse henceforth to be called either." "Rebel" suited his self-concept much better: "being rebels doesn't mean being radical," he told Untermeyer in 1916; "it means being reckless. . . . It means busting something just when everybody begins to think it so sacred it's safe."[14] While time muted the recklessness, Frost continued to delight in kicking over sacred idols, especially those cherished by the Left.

Rebel or even "semi-revolutionary," Frost had no use for the kind of revolutionary he characterizes in "Harrison" in a poem entitled "A Case for Jefferson" (*CPPP* 357):

> Harrison loves my country, too,
> But wants it all made over new.
> . . . .
> With him love of country means
> Blowing it all to smithereens
> And having it all made over new.

Harrison apparently likes all revolutionary theories—"He's Freudian Viennese by night. / By day he's Marxian Muscovite"—an indiscriminateness that leads the speaker to conclude: "his mind is hardly out of his teens." Appearing in the 1947 *Steeple Bush,* this portrait of the revolutionary is almost quaint (unless Frost had written it much earlier and held it back):[15] the Far Left in the United States was in full retreat by then, suffering HUAC investigating committees and blacklists for its 1930s idealism.

These sparse instances of anti-leftism, however, in no way suggest that Frost had muted his political voice; quite the contrary. Far more than Stevens, Williams, and even Cummings, Frost not only felt compelled to speak out on political issues but was encouraged to do so by his special status as America's most popular living poet and goodwill ambassador.[16] Where the wind had been in his face in the 1930s, it now seemed comfortably at his back. But Frost was scarcely just a cheerleader for the United States; his political poems and opinions in the post–World War II period shared the complexity and doubleness of his best poetry, expressing a skeptical dark side quite out of keeping with the sanguine outlook expected of a poet laureate, and sometimes a quirkiness that ultimately prompted the Kennedy administration (following the Frost-Khrushchev encounter) to avoid him as unreliable.

One important target of Frost's skepticism was scientific technology and how the cold war had turned it to military ends, most notably the atomic bomb and the resulting threat of world annihilation. Yet he could treat this grim prospect with unsettling playfulness. "Bursting Rapture" (CPPP 362), for example, begins humorously with the speaker complaining to his doctor that modern farming had now become so scientifically complex that he "couldn't stand the strain." The doctor then reassures him that his condition is not unusual; indeed, it is shared by nations burdened by technology:

> Their effort is a mounting ecstasy
> That when it gets too exquisite to bear
> Will find relief in one burst. You shall see.
> That's what a certain bomb was sent to be.

The sexualized diction here and in the title intensifies the paradox: what in other contexts would be pleasurable—an ecstatic sexual orgasm—or at least a release of tension, here translates into mass destruction: the bomb is literally the climax of scientific technology.[17] Frost's humor has never been darker.

The arms race in these years got Frost thinking about the biblical injunction to convert swords into plowshares (Isaiah 2:4), only Frost—as usual—saw the matter both ways. When asked to write a poem about an abstract sculpture in the Meditation Room of the United Nations—

a block of iron whose fate symbolized the choice of weapon or tool—
Frost responded with an oblique couplet he titled "From Iron" and sub-
titled "Tools and Weapons" (*CPPP* 476):

> Nature within her inmost self divides
> To trouble men with having to take sides.

"Taking sides" is the microcosmic prelude to war, here a biological inevi-
tability beginning—ending?—with split atoms. If war, then weapons. The
United Nations' undersecretary in charge of public relations, to whom
the poem was dedicated, was not pleased. Frost was not apologetic. He
told an audience at Berkeley in 1958: "It's come up lately, the saying . . .
that weapons should be turned into tools. Right up here in the [Lawrence
Livermore] cyclotron. It never happens. Men never discover anything of
the weapon nature . . . but that they wish it could be made useful to do-
mesticate science. . . . Always the same talk." Frost then recounted his UN
commission, read the poem, and concluded: "And some of you are on the
side of weapons and some of you are on the side of tools. And I'm on both
sides at once, I guess" (Seale 111). On both sides, also, in the humorous
poem, "The Objection to Being Stepped On," from Frost's last book, *In
the Clearing* (*CPPP* 460). The speaker has stepped on an "unemployed"
hoe and gotten smacked "In the seat of my sense." As so often, Frost uses
the incident emblematically to ask:

> But *was* there a rule
> The weapon should be
> Turned into a tool?
> And what do we see?
> The first tool I step on
> Turned into a weapon.

Reciprocity: if weapons *should* be turned into tools (Frost's italicized "was"
skeptically undercuts the ideal), tools *are* turned into weapons. Such paradoxical musings and thematic doubleness, playfully dark humor on grim
themes, all challenge the image of Frost as comforting bard of middle
America in the cold war.

Even the image of Frost as quasi-official spokesman of America requires
qualifying. It is true that in the 1950s he became virtually a national institution: interviewed on television; invited to the White House several times;
traveling to Brazil, England, Greece, and Israel as "goodwill ambassador"

sponsored by the State Department; recipient of innumerable awards, gold medals, and honors by the armload; and of course enjoying the supreme honor of reading a poem at President Kennedy's inaugural. But Frost was too independent—and, as it proved, too quirky—to be simply a mouthpiece of cold war America. Consider his attitude toward the USSR in the Khrushchev-Kennedy years. One might have expected a clear-cut vilification of Russia, but in Frost's curious construction, both countries were democracies in expressing "a more earnest desire than the world has ever had to take care of everybody" (*Interviews* 240, 289). Moreover, he saw U.S.-Soviet competition not as a conflict between good and evil but as "a conflict of good and good" (qtd. in Seale 113), almost a sporting competition. He recalls telling this to Russian acquaintances and following it with a quip almost too chilling to evoke a smile: "Let's shake hands on it before we kill each other" (113). And in his meeting with Premier Khrushchev barely a month before the Cuban Missile Crisis, Frost spoke of "a noble rivalry" between the two superpowers. "God wants us to contend," he explained to Khrushchev—which must have struck the premier of an officially atheistic country as a slightly odd justification.[18] But Frost envisioned the competition as a gentleman's game: "no blackguarding, no dirty play. That's what I came to say" (*Interviews* 289). In the same interview, Frost claimed that "he and Mr. Khrushchev agreed on this. 'I knew he was that way—a real sport'" (289). Even odder was Frost's prediction: "I told Mr. Khrushchev the future of the world for the next hundred years or so lies between the United States and Russia" (289). From prophesying and claiming divine knowledge to projecting Etonian rules on nuclear powers engaged in deadly realpolitik, Frost's views were simply too idiosyncratic and unpredictable to serve as proxies for the State Department. Though well intentioned, he was, as Mark Richardson called him, a loose cannon (65).

The culmination of Frost's unreliability, however, came with his statement to reporters at Idlewild Airport about his discussion with Khrushchev: "Khrushchev said he feared for us modern liberals. He said we were too liberal to fight. I suppose he thought we'd stand there for the next hundred years saying, 'on the one hand—but on the other hand'" (*Interviews* 291). There were two problems with Frost's statement: it was intensely provocative, and it was not true. The following month, during the Cuban Missile Crisis, Frost admitted at the National Poetry Festival in Washington, D.C., that Khrushchev had never said those words (Thompson and Winnick 328). The damage, however, was already done, both in its small contribution to deteriorating U.S.-Soviet relations—which, anyhow, could not have gotten much worse at the time—and in destroying Frost's standing as a cultural goodwill ambassador for the United States. Early and late, Frost spoke only for himself.

Williams has always been the odd man out in this study: involved in political issues and sympathetic to the Left, when the other three poets initially were not; a joiner of groups and forums, when the others remained private. Unlike them, therefore, he was not pulled out of his natural orbit by the surge of leftism in the 1930s. And though his involvement in leftist broils and controversies in the thirties cost him time and energy, and often embarrassed him, it did not alter his political sympathies thereafter or his willingness at times to declare them, even during the cold war.

Evidence of Williams's postwar political views appears particularly in two poems, "Russia" (in *The Clouds* of 1948) and "Choral: The Pink Church" (in the 1949 book *The Pink Church*), as well as more generally in his epic *Paterson*. Still earlier, his superb "Burning the Christmas Greens" of 1944 expressed his profound hope that out of the present conflagration of the war (perfectly imaged by the burning greens roaring in the fireplace) will be born "an infant landscape" transforming the world and those who, like Williams (paralleling those at the Nativity), bore witness.[19]

"Russia" and "Choral: The Pink Church" continue this hopefulness, but now applied to Russia—or, more precisely, what Russia could have become—and now juxtaposed to Williams's contempt for Stalinism and distrust of "church" ideologies, of which orthodox communism was one. "Russia" (*CP-WCW* 2: 144–47), the more focused of the two, is a Whitmanesque plea to Russia to "come with me into / my dream"—a dream in which aesthetics and artists (Mayakovsky, da Vinci, and of course Williams himself) prevail, not politicians, parties, and governments. At the same time, the speaker realizes that, as Auden wrote so despairingly, "poetry makes nothing happen"; that he, Williams, is "uninfluential"; and thus that his dream is unworldly "folly." Thus, Russia will continue to be "idiot of the world," and the speaker's dream will serve only as a "background" while Russia builds its empire. The last lines, however, are regrettably ambiguous:

> These [dreams]
> I dedicate now to you, . . .
>   I lay
> my spirit at your feet . . .
>   I do not

resist you. Among many others, undistinguished,
of no moment—I am the background
upon which you will build your empire.

Williams appears to say here that his dreams for Russia provide the support "upon which" Russia will build its empire, when the logic of the whole poem argues the reverse: that his "background" will be ignored. Likely, he meant that the background will be like the millions of corpses—Stalin's victims—"upon which" Russia built its totalitarian state. But the ending left Williams open to the charge that he supported Russian cold war expansionism. It is a brutal irony that, quite in contrast to his assumption that "this paper [will be] forgotten," the poem was cited years later as proof that Williams was a fellow traveler and unworthy of being appointed "Consultant in Poetry" to the Library of Congress.[20]

Religious references in "Russia"—the physical description of the Zionist Church and Leonardo's *The Last Supper*—receive far more development in "Choral: The Pink Church" (*CP-WCW* 2: 177–80). In "Russia" the references are dismissive: the church is jerry-built from ad hoc materials, in contrast (one assumes) to the spirit of the black parishioners within. And the speaker finds the Leonardo painting admirable for its structural composition, "the simplicity and severity of the background," not for its subject. "The Pink Church," however, contrasts several meanings or applications of "church": as housing conventional Christian belief, as a metaphor for any sort of orthodoxy, including Marxist, and as an aesthetic setting (like Leonardo's *Last Supper*) through which choral music soars and pink light sensually vivifies all it illuminates. It is the last of these meanings—the choral singing and pink as a rejuvenating, erotic light—that stands against the church's repressive function:

> Now,
>   the Pink Church
>   trembles
> to the light (of dawn) again,
> . . . .
> singing!
> . . . .
> transparent to the light
>   through which the light
> shines, through the stone,
>   until

the stone-light glows,
  pink jade
. . . .
and is a church.

"The light / shines, through the stone" suggests that the spirit supersedes the material and the institutional (Saint Peter as the rock on which the Catholic Church is built). And Williams certainly rejects the Church's dogma of original sin, asserting: "Man is not sinful . . . unless / he sin!"[21] But pink is also distinctly sexual and erotic: "the Pink Church: / the nipples of / a woman who never / bore a / child" and "perfect as the pink and / rounded breasts of a virgin!" And Williams's "saints"—Poe, Whitman, Baudelaire—were all considered sensualists. This sensuous and aesthetic pleasure is the source of "Joy! Joy!" and Williams's mention of "Elysium" makes this "Choral" his "Ode to Joy," companion to Beethoven's choral movement of the Ninth Symphony.[22] Complementing this praise of Eros is a rather surprising (for Williams) celebration of pragmatic philosophers— Dewey, William James, and Whitehead (versus a more familiar target: the conventional thinking of philosophy departments: "wondering at the nature / of the stuff / poured into / the urinals / of custom").

 Where, then, does leftist politics come in? Of course, pink was the symbolic color of communist sympathizers—"pinko" was a ubiquitous slur in these years, leveled freely by anti-communists. Significantly, Williams identified himself this way in a letter to Babette Deutsch about this poem: "I AM a pink, plainly and finally. I am *not* a red. I sympathize strongly with the blood, the thing that makes a communist whatever good he is capable of being. The 'pink' of life, of a pink cheek. . . . I won't be put down because I sympathize with the life that at best the Reds symbolize" (*CP-WCW* 2: 477n). Curiously, however, the poem mentions communists only once, although prominently as the last word:

Milton, the unrhymer,
    singing among
      the rest . . .
like a Communist.

Here, Milton's political daring in supporting and working for the revolutionary Cromwell parallels what Williams sees as his aesthetic daring in writing blank verse in "Samson Agonistes" (and indeed in *Paradise Lost*). "Communist," then, has the positive connotations of rebel and innovator.

But the poem also alludes to "The Internationale," the communist anthem, in these lines:

> Come all ye aberrant,
>   drunks, prostitutes,
>   Surrealists—

To these Williams later adds: "the fool / the mentally deranged / the suicide . . . the slaughtered, the famished / and the lonely." Compare:

> Arise, you prisoners of starvation!
> Arise, you wretched of the earth!
> For justice thunders condemnation:
> A better world's in birth!

What makes Williams's allusion brilliant is that it doubles as the beginning of a stirring Christmas carol: "O come, all ye faithful." The pink church, then, symbolizes two opposing—but for Williams, parallel—belief systems—Christianity and communism—both of which began by offering hope to the lowliest; both of which were founded on social egalitarianism; and both (for Williams) hardened into repressive institutions.[23]

Clearly, Williams by the late 1940s was not a communist—he never had been—but a sympathizer with the communist *ideal* of egalitarianism, and with the hopefulness and rejuvenation that the revolution had once meant to its supporters. That he declared himself such during the growing fear and hatred of Russia in the cold war was certainly courageous, but it also smacked of the same naïveté that had gotten him into continuous scrapes with leftist groups during the later 1930s—and this time it cost him a distinguished and plummy position with the Library of Congress.[24] Where Williams had always been most "left" was in his natural identification with and sympathy for ordinary, working-class people—the world of his patients—and in a deep understanding of their locality and his: industrial New Jersey.

These predilections directly shaped the characters and locale of his epic poem, *Paterson,* beginning of course with its gritty, workaday setting: the eighteenth-century Paterson that promised industrial development for Hamilton (literally and symbolically in power of the falls); the industrial exploitation, pollution, and squalor of the nineteenth and twentieth centuries; the modern compensations in Sunday park outings. Appropriately, many of the contemporary characters, notably Dr. Paterson's patients, are working class, as are those caught up in the sensational distractions described in the nineteenth-century news stories. Williams, however, did not intend simply a proletarian history. The poem's mythic level (conveyed by the sleeping giants embodying Paterson and by the river's symbolic force and movement) and its aesthetic themes (e.g., Dr. Paterson's correspondence with would-be poets, the symbolic harnessing ["combing"] of the river's power into poetic language) move beyond its geocultural and social bases and give the poem epic breadth.

Whether he was describing a WPA worker "pissing" into a sluiceway of the river (*CP-WCW* 2: 9–10) or an old man sweeping his own ten feet of sidewalk, the bareheaded woman in public examining her shoe for a nail or the broken-brained Elsie, an old lady munching plums or Breughel's peasants, a red dawn in Russia or the pink light in a church near Rutherford, Williams's affinity with—and unsentimental portraits of—ordinary people was a bedrock of his poetry, a constant that grounded it before, during, and after the 1930s.

I have observed above that Cummings never really recovered from his experience of leftist pressures in the 1930s. But in a larger sense, all of these poets were profoundly affected and in particular ways carried their thirties encounters into their later years. Indeed, how could they not, since all four were virtually forced in the thirties to contemplate a political realm they found intrusive and provocative. Their active responses to the leftist thirties, finally, were too strong simply to put behind them as if they had never happened.

The experiences of Stevens, Cummings, Frost, and Williams in the thirties, moreover, though they seem particular to an intensely political age, really apply to poets in any period. The pressures of the world—expressed as political events, social turmoil, economic booms and busts, and wars—wax and wane in their intensity. But poets are always a part of that world, whether they want to be or not, and feel those pressures, however faintly. At times, as Stevens observed, the "pushing" of those pressures seems overwhelming and virtually demands a response. One thinks of the Vietnam War, for example, and how many poets, who otherwise might have considered their politics a private matter unrelated to their verse, felt compelled to address the war in their poetry, to take a stand. More recently, the catastrophic events of 9/11 have surely embedded themselves in the sensibility of American writers, whether or not those events appear directly in their work. T. S. Eliot once famously described a poet's imagination as constantly amalgamating disparate sensory data: the typewriter clacking, the smell of cooking, and so forth.[25] Surely, the political tides and social sweep of events, measured, reported, and debated endlessly in media old and new, add to that amalgamation and sometimes come to dominate it in the poet's mind. Thus, the myth of the ivory tower—even for 1920s modernists who scorned political and social events of mainstream America (or thought they did)—is just that: a myth. Willy-nilly, the world's pressures seep into the work of even the most apolitical, and however much poets may wish to be, they are never truly alone.

Notes

INTRODUCTION

Epigraphs: Wallace Stevens, "The Irrational Element in Poetry," lecture at Harvard University, December 1936, rpt. in *Wallace Stevens: Collected Poetry and Prose*, ed. Frank Kermode and Joan Richardson (New York: Library of America, 1997) 788 [hereafter cited as *CPP*]; William Phillips and Phillip Rahv, "Literature in a Political Decade," *New Letters in America* 1 (1937): 170.

1. Though Frost is not typically considered a modernist poet stylistically—he followed "the old way of being new," as he put it—the thematic complexity of his best poems and their formal compression—their avoidance of easy discursiveness—arguably justify his designation as a modernist.

2. I use "leftism" here to encompass the range of political positions on the Left from *New Masses* to New Deal. In the chapters that follow, leftist orientations will be identified more precisely.

3. Pound, of course was intensely political, but his pro-fascist support of Mussolini, and Eliot's rightist monarchism for that matter, were not just reactions to 1930s leftism. The rightist views of both poets had deeper and older roots in their personal philosophies. The one poet who might well have been included in this study is Archibald MacLeish. He was excluded primarily for length considerations.

4. Among the scholarly works examining these poets in the literary-political contexts of the 1930s are the following:

For Wallace Stevens, Jacqueline Brogan, *The Violence Within, the Violence Without: Wallace Stevens and the Emergence of a Revolutionary Poetics* (Athens: U of Georgia P, 2003); Angus Cleghorn, *Wallace Stevens' Poetics: The Neglected Rhetoric* (New York: Palgrave, 2000); Alan Filreis, *Modernism from Right to Left: Wallace Stevens, the Thirties and Literary Radicalism* (New York: Cambridge UP, 1994); Alan Filreis, *Wallace Stevens and the Actual World* (Princeton: Princeton UP, 1991); James Longenbach, *Wallace Stevens: The Plain Sense of Things* (New York: Oxford UP, 1991); *The Wallace Stevens Journal* 13.2 (1989); Milton J. Bates, *Wallace Stevens: A Mythology of Self* (Berkeley: U of California P, 1985); Joseph Riddel, *The Clairvoyant Eye: The Poetry and Poetics of Wallace Stevens* (Baton Rouge: Louisiana State UP, 1965); Joseph Riddel, "Poet's Politics—Wallace Stevens' *Owl's Clover*," *Modern Philology* 56.2 (1958): 118–32.

For E. E. Cummings, Milton A. Cohen, "From Bad Boy to Curmudgeon: Cummings' Political Evolution," in *Words into Pictures: E. E. Cummings' Art Across Borders,* ed. Jiri Flajsar and Zeno Vernyik (Cambridge: Cambridge Scholars Press, 2007);

Milton A. Cohen, "The Political Cummings: Iconoclast or Solipsist?" *SPRING: The Journal of the E. E. Cummings Society* ns 6 (October 1997): 70–80; Michael Webster, "'hatred bounces': Satire and Prejudice in the Poetry of E. E. Cummings," *SPRING* 7 (1998): 23–38; Michael Webster, "Cummings' Sinister Dexterity: Exercises in Meaning and Unmeaning," *SPRING* 13 (2004): 90–103.

For Robert Frost, Peter J. Stanlis, *Robert Frost: The Individual and Society* (Rockford College, 1973); Tyler Hoffman, "Robert Frost and the Politics of Labor," *Modern Language Studies* 29.2 (1999): 109–35; Tyler Hoffman, *Robert Frost and the Politics of Poetry* (Hanover: Middlebury College P, 2001).

For William Carlos Williams, Robert Von Hallberg, "The Politics of Description: W. C. Williams in the 'Thirties," *ELH* 45.1 (1978): 131–51; Bob Johnson, "'A Whole Synthesis of His Time': Political Ideology and Cultural Politics in the Writings of William Carlos Williams, 1929–1939," *American Quarterly* 54.2 (2002): 178–215; David Frail, *The Early Politics and Poetry of William Carlos Williams* (Ann Arbor: UMI P, 1987); John Beck, *Writing the Radical Center: William Carlos Williams, John Dewey, and American Cultural Politics* (Albany: SUNY P, 2001).

5. Stevens, Frost, and Williams did write some political poems before the 1930s, e.g., Stevens's "Death of a Soldier," Frost's fairly obscure depictions of factory life, and Williams's evocation of Soviet Russia and his "Elsie" poem (all of which will be discussed in their respective chapters). But political poems were not typical for these poets before the 1930s.

6. Based on membership in the CPUSA (Communist Party of the USA), subscriptions to far-left magazines like *New Masses,* the popular appeal of the Party-organized American Writers Congress of 1935, and the formation of the Abraham Lincoln Brigade to fight in Spain under communist leadership.

7. Cary Nelson, *Repression and Recovery: Modern American Poetry and the Politics of Cultural Memory, 1910–1945* (Madison: U of Wisconsin P, 1989); Cary Nelson, "Poetry Chorus: Dialogic Politics in 1930s Poetry," in *Radical Revisions: Rereading 1930s Culture,* ed. Bill Mullen and Sherry Lee Linkon (Urbana: U of Illinois P, 1996) 29–59; Alan Wald, *The New York Intellectuals: The Rise and Decline of the Anti-Stalinist Left from the 1930s to the 1980s* (Chapel Hill: U of North Carolina P, 1987); Walter Kalaidjian, *American Culture between the Wars: Revisionary Modernism and Postmodern Critique* (New York: Columbia UP, 1993); Michael Thurston, *Making Something Happen: American Political Poetry between the World Wars* (Chapel Hill: U of North Carolina P, 2001); Rachel Blau Duplessis, *Genders, Races, and Religious Cultures in Modern American Poetry, 1908–1934* (Cambridge: Cambridge UP, 2001); Constance Coiner, *Better Red: The Radical Writing of Tillie Olsen and Meridel LeSueur* (New York: Oxford UP, 1995); Paula Rabinowitz and Charlotte Nekola, eds., *Writing Red: An Anthology of American Women Writers, 1930–1940* (New York: Feminist P, 1987); James D. Bloom, *Left Letters: The Culture Wars of Mike Gold and Joseph Freeman* (New York: Columbia UP, 1992).

8. Nelson defines the "dialogic" in 1930s political poetry: "[T]he term points to an additive or echolalic quality in a certain discursive formation—a formation

to which many writers contributed—and to multiple effects and meanings embedded in individual words that are part of a social conversation taking place in poetry." Nelson demonstrates this "choral" effect by forming a collective poem drawn from "echoing" lines of numerous leftist poems ("Poetry Chorus" 56n2, 46–51).

9. Williams, "The New Poetical Economy," *Poetry* 44.4 (1934): 223–24.

10. "Tea at the Palaz of Hoon," *CPP* 51.

CHAPTER 1

Epigraphs: V. F. Calverton, "Leftward Ho!" *Modern Quarterly* 6 (Summer 1932): 26; Frank Chapman, "New Writing," *The Criterion* 16 (October 1936): 164.

1. Malcolm Cowley's thesis in *Exile's Return: A Literary Odyssey of the 1920s,* ed. with introduction by Donald Faulkner (New York: Penguin, 1994) chapters 6–7.

2. William Phillips and Phillip Rahv, "Literature in a Political Decade," *New Letters in America* 1 (1937): 170.

3. Edmund Wilson, "An Appeal to Progressives," *New Republic* January 14, 1931: 234–38, rpt. in *The Shores of Light: A Literary Chronicle of the Twenties and Thirties* (New York: Farrar, 1952) 528, 530.

4. The essay's headnote asserts that it was "the outcome of conversations among the editors, which have been occurring for several months" (518). Yet it is written in Wilson's voice and uses "I" and "me" throughout.

5. John Dos Passos proposed something very similar in the summer of 1932 in response to the survey question "Can a proletarian literature develop in America?" Dos Passos replied: "It seems to me that Marxians who attempt to junk the American tradition, that I admit is full of dry-rot as well as sap, like any tradition, are just cutting themselves off from the continent. Somebody's got to have the size to Marxianize the American tradition before you can sell the American worker on the social revolution. Or else Americanize Marx" ("Whither the American Writer?" *Modern Quarterly* 6 [Summer 1932]: 12).

6. In the survey, cited in note 5, seventeen writers (including Dos Passos, Sherwood Anderson, Malcolm Cowley, Floyd Dell, Edwin Seaver, Henry Seidel Canby, Newton Arvin, Granville Hicks, and Clifton Fadiman) responded to the following question: "Do you believe that American capitalism is doomed to inevitable failure and collapse. . . . in the next decade?" Only one respondent answered no, and one hedged ("in danger rather than doomed"). Several, however, doubted whether capitalism's failure would occur within the decade: "give the old horse more than ten years," wrote Clifton Fadiman.

7. Malcolm Cowley, *The Dream of the Golden Mountains: Remembering the 1930s* (New York: Penguin, 1981) 25; Granville Hicks, *I Like America* 97–98, qtd. in Daniel Aaron, *Writers on the Left* (New York: Avon, 1965) 191.

8. Joseph Freeman, "Social Trends in American Literature," *Communist* July 1930: 651, qtd. in Harvey Klehr, *The Heyday of American Communism: The Depression Decade* (New York: Basic Books, 1984) 72.

9. V. F. Calverton "Left!" *The Left: A Quarterly Review of Radical & Experimental Art* 1.1 (1931): 3.

10. Lillian Symes, "Our Liberal Weeklies," *Modern Monthly* October 1936: 8. Symes identifies 1932 as the year of "the great Leftward Ho migration" (8).

11. Alfred Kazin, *Starting Out in the Thirties* (Boston: Little, Brown, 1965) 12, 79.

12. The phrase "revolution of the word" is associated with the avant-garde late-twenties magazine *transition,* but it continued into the 1930s in William Carlos Williams's frequent statements (discussed in chapter 5) and in the publications of New Directions Press, such as *New Directions in Prose and Poetry* (1937; see Willard Mass's negative review, declaring that "the revolution of the word" is passé, *New York Herald Tribune Books* February 7, 1937: 14). Cowley's depiction of the 1920s "religion of art" appears in *Exile's Return,* particularly in the original conclusion, "Art Tomorrow," republished first in *New Republic* May 23, 1934: 34–36, and later in *Think Back on Us: A Contemporary Chronicle of the 1930s* (Carbondale: Southern Illinois UP, 1967) 56–62.

13. Horace Gregory, "Some Firsts," *Story* January 1937: 103. Recently, literary historians have challenged the view that politicized writers rejected modernist aesthetics in the 1930s; Alan Filreis, for example, asserts that "aesthetic left sectarianism . . . neither prevented experimental verse nor repudiated several basic elements of modernism" (*Modernism from Right to Left: Wallace Stevens, the Thirties, and Literary Radicalism* [New York: Cambridge UP, 1994] 3). It is quite true that by the mid-thirties some leftist magazines like *New Republic* and *Partisan Review,* reflecting the ecumenism of the Popular Front, were printing modernist poems by Williams, Stevens, and others. It is also true that *The Left* demanded (in its manifesto quoted above) that "new forms and techniques must be hammered out to express the fresh substance, the faster tempos and rhythms of the new world order, and [*The Left*] encourages experimentation." (The editors, however, were calling not for modern*ism* but rather for forms that expressed contemporary life for the working class.) But against these and other exceptions must be posited the continuous and widespread abuse of modernism in reviews by Mike Gold, Isador Schneider, Edwin Seaver, Edwin Rolfe, Stanley Burnshaw, Philip Horton, Granville Hicks, and Horace Gregory. Burnshaw's much-quoted depiction of Stevens's *Harmonium*—"It is the kind of verse that people concerned with the murderous world collapse can hardly swallow today except in tiny doses" (Burnshaw, "Turmoil in the Middle Ground," *New Masses* October 1, 1933: 42)—is only one of the most notorious of a steady litany of such attacks, e.g., "[T]he newer poetry is . . . no longer concerned with mere verbal experiment" (Horace Gregory, "Firsts: New Authors and Their First Books," *Story* January 1937: 103. For other examples dis-

cussed in this book, see Gregory's review of Cummings's *Collected Poems* (chapter 3) and Mason Wade's review of Williams's *Complete Collected Poems* (chapter 5).

14. Edwin Seaver, "Sterile Writers and Proletarian Religions," *New Masses* May 1933: 22.

15. Qtd. in David Madden, introduction to *Proletarian Writers of the Thirties,* ed. Madden (Carbondale: Southern Illinois UP, 1968) xxvii.

16. Arthur Koestler, *Arrow in the Blue: An Autobiography* (New York: Macmillan, 1961) 277–78.

17. Malcolm Cowley reports that in the early thirties "Amtorg, the Soviet trading corporation that served as an informal consulate . . . was receiving 350 applications a day from Americans eager to work for the Five Year Plan" (*Dream* 35).

18. *New Republic* January 18, 1933: 272.

19. Mencken quipped: "I am probably incurably opposed to communism. But I am also incurably opposed to denying Communists their constitutional rights" (qtd. in Klehr 74).

20. Qtd. and paraphrased in Aaron 214. Among the more prominent signers were Granville Hicks, Horace Gregory, Sidney Howard, Alfred Kreymborg, Isador Schneider, Edwin Seaver, Lincoln Steffens, Newton Arvin, Sidney Hook, Samuel Ornitz, Edmund Wilson, Malcolm Cowley, John Dos Passos, Sherwood Anderson, Theodore Dreiser, Matthew Josephson, Countee Cullen, Slater Brown, Henry Cowell, and Langston Hughes, fifty-three in all. Most were not professed communists. Hicks, Gregory, Schneider, Seaver, Cowley, and Wilson were, or became, leftist reviewers and critics (Klehr 80; Aaron 437n73).

21. Matthew Josephson, *Infidel in the Temple: A Memoir of the Nineteen-Thirties* (New York: Knopf, 1967) 151, 154.

22. *Daily Worker* May 17, 1932: 2, qtd. in Klehr 80.

23. Even terminology proved a problem. At the first American Writers' Congress (1935), when Kenneth Burke suggested substituting the phrase "the people" for "the workers," suggesting that the broader term enabled middle-class authors more latitude in writing about "all the aspects of contemporary effort and thought," he was viciously attacked by Mike Gold and other Communists as being elitist and fascistic (James Longenbach, *Wallace Stevens: The Plain Sense of Things* [New York: Oxford UP, 1991] 139).

24. In *American Writers and Radical Politics, 1900–1939: Equivocal Commitments* (New York: St. Martin's Press, 1986), Eric Homberger provides a concise background on the wrangles over "Prolecult" in the Soviet Union. Gold, "Towards Proletarian Art," *The Liberator* February 1921: 20–25, qtd. in Homberger 119.

25. Mike Gold, "A Letter to Writers' Art Groups," *New Masses* September 1929: 16, qtd. in Barbara Foley, *Radical Representations: Politics and Form in U.S. Proletarian Fiction, 1929–1941* (Durham: Duke UP, 1993) 87–88.

26. *New Masses* September 1930: 4–5.

27. *New Masses* June 1930: 22.

28. Listed in Max Eastman, *Artists in Uniform* (New York: Knopf, 1934), qtd. in Homberger 134.

29. V. F. Calverton, "Can We Have a Proletarian Literature?" *Modern Quarterly* 6 (Autumn 1932): 38–50.

30. Granville Hicks, "The Crisis in American Criticism," *New Masses* February 1933: 5.

31. Mike Gold, "The Keynote to Dos Passos' Works," *Daily Worker* February 26, 1938: 7. Politics, of course, affected this judgment: Dos Passos had recently broken with the Party over the Soviets' execution in Spain of his friend and translator, José Robles.

32. Granville Hicks notes that the term "proletarian literature" fell out of favor with the Party by the mid-thirties (*Part of the Truth* [New York: Harcourt, 1965] 134–35). It was replaced by socialist (or social) realism. Leftist poetry was similarly criticized by Phillips and Rahv: "[It] invoked the mythology of barricades and unfurled banners of insurrection. Its imagery was one of fire-sermons and leather-jackets, winds and tempests, marches and counter-marches . . . in sum, the inferno of exploitation and the paradise of Socialism. Its implicit premise was that we were on the eve of revolution. But as the eve was transformed into a long vigil, the banality of these poetic statements became correspondingly more manifest" (171). The emergence of the Popular Front had much to do with the demise of proletarian literature. As bourgeois writers and intellectuals now assumed increasing prominence in the Left (as evidenced by the American Writers' Congresses of 1935 and 1937), the concern with maintaining a "proletarian" focus inevitably diminished. Indeed, Rahv and Phillips's critique of the crudeness of much proletarian fiction and poetry shows that by the mid-thirties even the much-reviled exercise of "bourgeois intellectualism" was rearing its head—at least in *Partisan Review.*

33. William Stott, *Documentary Expression in Thirties America* (New York: Oxford UP, 1973) 21, 25, 26. Stott goes so far as to call this slanting "propaganda" (25).

34. "Seemingly" because Evans arranged, for example, items in his still lifes of rooms in the sharecroppers' homes to get particular effects. The pictures, nonetheless, convey a spareness, detachment, and objectivity that directly contrast Agee's subjective prose and have become classics.

35. Morton Zabel, "Recent Magazines," *Poetry* 45.3 (1934): 175; *Letters of Wallace Stevens,* ed. Holly Stevens (Berkeley: U of California P, 1996) 333, 309. Other leftist magazines were *The Symposium, PLUS, Westminster Review* (edited by T. C. Wilson), and *Story.*

36. It is interesting to note that in his memoir of the period, *The Dream of the Golden Mountains,* Cowley does not mention how he implicitly supported the Moscow Trials by criticizing in *The New Republic* those who attacked them. The trials are not even listed in the index.

37. Margaret Marshall and Mary McCarthy, "Our Critics, Right or Wrong, IV: The Proletarians," *Nation* December 4, 1935: 653.

38. Orrick Johns to Harriet Monroe, unpublished letter, ca. summer or autumn 1932, qtd. in Filreis 189.

39. Harriet Monroe, "Art and Propaganda," *Poetry* 44.4 (1934): 210–15.

40. Stanley Burnshaw, "The Poetry Camps Divide," *New Masses* July 31, 1934: 22.

41. Burnshaw's private letter to Monroe continues the same logic (or rather, illogic, since he assumes that the intermingling of politics and culture necessarily leads writers to a revolutionary "political awareness"): "Frankly, Miss Monroe, I find it almost unbelievable, that an intellect as unusual as yours finds it difficult to understand and condone the point of view expressed by those of us who feel the desirability and historical necessity of a proletarian revolution.... Don't you grant that the political awareness of revolutionary writers is nothing less than a logical necessity of intellectual awareness, since politics and culture are now proved inseparable?" (unpublished letter, July 26, 1934, qtd. in Filreis 198).

42. Of course, these categories are rather arbitrary. As noted below, critics often grew more radical in their views as the thirties progressed. Some reviewers, like Cowley, were less ideological in their reviews than in their political articles or editorials; hence their grouping. Generally, however, the difference between the two leftist categories is that those in the "radical to Marxist" group applied Marxist concepts and rhetoric more directly and explicitly in their reviews.

43. Stanley Burnshaw, "Wallace Stevens and the Statue," *Sewanee Review* 69 (Summer 1961): 355–66.

44. Granville Hicks, literary editor for *New Masses* at this time, confirmed Burnshaw's characterization of Marxian critical arrogance in his own memoir: "I was armored with self-righteousness.... My dogmatism in those years is something I cannot contemplate with pleasure and cannot fully explain. To be sure, I felt that the times were tough and that tough measures were demanded. When Communist sympathizers made jokes about meeting on the barricades, they were more than half serious, for we believed the line was being drawn more and more sharply and that the people on the other side of it were enemies.... The Party organizers, as I had come to know them, had a right to be belligerent, for most of them had been beaten and gone to jail for the cause, and they did not hesitate to risk their lives. I wanted, I think, to be as tough as they were" (*Part of the Truth* 122).

45. Eda Lou Walton, "Beyond the Wasteland," *Nation* September 9, 1931: 263–64.

46. Eda Lou Walton, "More Roses and Locomotives," *Nation* December 30, 1931: 729–30; Eda Lou Walton, "Beauty of a Storm Disproportionately," *Poetry* 51.4 (1938): 210–11.

47. Eda Lou Walton, review of *Ideas of Order, New York Times Book Review* December 6, 1936: 18.

48. Stanley Burnshaw, "Notes on Revolutionary Poetry," *New Masses* February 20, 1934: 20–22; Stanley Burnshaw, "'Middle-Ground' Writers," *New Masses* April 30, 1935: 19–21.

49. In his later years, Burnshaw would write a biographical study of Robert Frost, *Robert Frost Himself* (New York: George Braziller, 1986).

50. Cf. Williams: "Without the poem being a workable mechanism in its own right, . . . it will remain ineffective. And what it says regarding the use or worth of that particular piece of 'propaganda' which it is detailing will never be convincing." "The New Poetical Economy," *Poetry* 44.4 (1934): 221.

51. Stanley Burnshaw to Alfred Kreymborg, unpublished letter, qtd. in Filreis 296n26.

52. "'Middle-Ground' Writers" was, according to Filreis, "widely admired [and] served as a kind of popular-front primer for communist and fellow-traveling reviewers" (204).

53. Burnshaw, "Turmoil in the Middle Ground," rpt. in "Wallace Stevens and the Statue" 63–66; discussed in chapter 2.

54. Willard Mass to George O'Donnell, unpublished letter, July 6, 1937, qtd. in Filreis 58. Filreis rightly considers the judgment exaggerated.

55. Gregory, "One Writer's Position," *New Masses* February 12, 1935: 20.

56. Seaver, "Another Writer's Position," *New Masses* February 19, 1935: 21–22.

57. Le Sueur, "The Fetish of Being Outside," *New Masses* February 26, 1935: 22–23.

58. Gregory, introduction to *New Letters in America,* vol. 1 (New York: Norton, 1937), 14.

59. Gregory, "Highly Polished Poetry," *New York Herald Tribune Books* September 27, 1931: sec. 11, 28.

60. Gregory, "Poetry in 1937," *New Masses* "Literary Supplement," December 7, 1937: 13.

61. Gregory, "Adolescent Songster," *New York Herald Tribune,* December 13, 1931: 22.

62. Gregory, "The Collected Cummings," *New Republic* April 27, 1938: 368, 370.

63. Horace Gregory, *The House on Jefferson Street: A Cycle of Memories* (New York: Holt Rinehart, 1971) 211.

64. Alan M. Wald, *The New York Intellectuals: The Rise and Decline of the Anti-Stalinist Left from the 1930s to the 1980s* (Chapel Hill: U of North Carolina P, 1987) 3–24.

65. James MacGregor Burns, *Roosevelt: The Lion and the Fox* (New York: Harcourt, 1956) 266–67; T. H. Watkins, *The Hungry Years: A Narrative History of the Great Depression in America* (New York: Holt, 1999) 504–5.

66. Dos Passos joined with a number of other leftists disgusted by the Communists' tactics and published an open letter to *New Masses* (March 1934: 8–9) condemning the action. Co-signers included Edmund Wilson and James Rorty, enthusiastic fellow travelers just two years earlier (Wald 61).

67. *New Masses* April 1933: 11. Gold and the *New Masses* did not live up to this bold declaration.

68. Ironically, *New Masses* began the first John Reed Club in November 1929

not just to provide young writers an outlet but to make space in its pages for more commercial writers in order to save the magazine from bankruptcy (Homberger 128). Now the CPUSA was closing the clubs for the same reason: to court big names. But as Homberger points out, the closing also reflected the Party's shift to the Popular Front in 1934 and away from the sectarian class warfare common to the John Reed Clubs (139).

69. Waldo Frank qtd. by William Carlos Williams in letter to Louis Zukofsky, April 7, 1935, qtd. and paraphrased in Paul Mariani, *William Carlos Williams: A New World Naked* (New York: McGraw-Hill, 1982) 376 [hereafter cited as *New World*.]

70. Literary historians and poets differ sharply about *Partisan Review.* For James Longenbach, its editors represented intellectual tolerance and openness to modernist experimentation, e.g., "Phillips and Rahv set out to combat that dogmatism [of *New Masses*]" (140). He does not explain, however, how "the relatively even-tempered" editors called for "Sanctions against [William Carlos] Williams" in 1936 (138) and tried to humiliate him the following year (discussed in chapter 5). For Alfred Kazin, whose views seem tinged by the anti-Communist fifties, by the end of the 1930s "the inner group of *Partisan Review* did not value imagination. . . . Creative imagination they unconsciously disdained as simpleminded—except if it came from the Continent and thus could serve as an analogy to their kind of intelligence" (157). Philip Rahv, continues Kazin, "was inherently one of the narrowest men I knew, [but] he was vividly authentic and stimulating as a critic of literature in society. . . . He was already, in 1940, the Doctor Johnson of his small group of radical intellectuals" (160). In 1938 Wallace Stevens considered *Partisan Review* "the most intelligent [magazine] I know of" (*Letters of Wallace Stevens,* ed. Holly Stevens [Berkeley: U of California P, 1996] 332).

71. Mike Gold, "What about Dos Passos?" *Daily Worker* July 31, 1937: 7. As the title of the article indicates, it was Dos Passos that prompted Gold's exasperation, specifically, Dos Passos's praise of an America geographically remote from "European messes." Gold was prescient in wondering: "[H]as John Dos Passos swung around to the right?"

72. Hicks published his disaffiliation in *New Republic* October 4, 1939: 244–45. (*New Masses* would not print it.) In *Part of the Truth* he recalls: "Although it took me three weeks to reach a decision, I think I knew almost immediately [after the news of the Nazi-Soviet Pact] that I would get out of the Party. I realize now that I had had more doubts about the Soviet Union and about the Party, too, than I had ever admitted to myself, and, as always in a time of crisis, these doubts surged to the surface. . . . What confronted me at the moment was the simple fact that Russia was no longer in the anti-Fascist camp and therefore was not on my side" (176).

CHAPTER 2

1. Excluding one collectively published vanity press book in 1918, *Eight Harvard Poets.*

2. Van Doren, "Poets and Wits," *Nation* October 10, 1923: 400, 402, excerpted

in *Wallace Stevens: The Critical Heritage,* ed. Charles Doyle (London: Routledge, 1985) 39–40 [hereafter cited as *Critical Heritage*].

3. Stevens's daughter, Holly Stevens, writes in *Letters of Wallace Stevens* (Berkeley: U of California P, 1996) [hereafter cited as *Letters*] that "[t]he book was received rather indifferently by the public and the critics" (241). But the predominantly favorable reviews in *Critical Heritage* suggest the book was at least a critical success.

4. Edmund Wilson, "Wallace Stevens and E. E. Cummings," *The Dial* March 19, 1924: 102–3, excerpted in *Critical Heritage* 61–63.

5. Marianne Moore, "Well Moused, Lion," *The Dial* January 1924: 84–91, rpt. in *Critical Heritage* 48–55; Marjorie Allen Seiffert, "The Intellectual Tropics," *Poetry* 23.3 (1923): 154–60, excerpted in *Critical Heritage* 43–45; Allen Tate, review in *Nashville Tennessean* February 10, 1924, rpt. in *Critical Heritage* 55–57; Mark Van Doren, "Poets and Wits," in *Critical Heritage* 39–40; Matthew Josephson, review in *Broom* November 1923: 236–37, rpt. in *Critical Heritage* 41–43; Harriet Monroe, "A Cavalier of Beauty," *Poetry* 23.6 (1924): 322–27, excerpted in *Critical Heritage* 57–61; Louis Untermeyer, "Five American Poets," *Yale Review* 14.1 (1924): 159–60, excerpted in *Critical Heritage* 70–71; John Gould Fletcher, "The Revival of Estheticism," *Freeman* December 1923: 355–56, excerpted in *Critical Heritage* 46–47.

6. Gorham B. Munson, "The Dandyism of Wallace Stevens," *The Dial* November 1925: 413–17, rpt. in *Critical Heritage* 78–82. That this review was reprinted in 1928, in *Destinations: A Canvas of American Literature since 1900,* increased its influence (Alan Filreis, *Modernism from Right to Left: Wallace Stevens, the Thirties and Literary Radicalism* [New York: Cambridge UP, 1994] 308n24).

7. The poems dropped were "The Silver Plough Boy," "Exposition of the Contents of a Cab," and "Architecture." The poems added appear in *Wallace Stevens: Collected Poetry and Prose,* ed. Frank Kermode and Joan Richardson (New York: Library of America, 1997) [hereafter cited as *CPP*] 81–93.

8. Joan Richardson, *Wallace Stevens: The Later Years, 1923–1955* (New York: William Morrow, 1988) 77.

9. Raymond Larsson, "The Beau as Poet," *Commonweal* April 6, 1932: 640–41.

10. Horace Gregory, "Highly Polished Poetry," *New York Herald Tribune Books* September 27, 1931: sec. 11, 28. Larsson uses the same phrase: "His surfaces are polished" (641).

11. Eda Lou Walton, "Beyond the Wasteland," *Nation* September 9, 1931: 263–64.

12. Morton Dauwen Zabel, "The Harmonium of Wallace Stevens," *Poetry* 39.1 (1931): 148–54.

13. "Response to an Enquiry," *New Verse* October 1934, rpt. in *CPP* 771.

14. By contrast, Cummings seldom read newspapers, an avoidance that intensified his political isolation.

15. Unpublished letter qtd. in Filreis 16. "Real," as Stevens used it in letters, poems, and essays, refers primarily to the gritty reality of survival, e.g., "the lower class with all its realities" (*Letters* 291).

16. Latimer once wrote his assistant, Willard Mass: "Leippert is dead, you must forget you ever knew him—& Mark Jason has resumed his right name, Latimer. But Latimer must remain an unknown quantity—who he is, where he is, what he is—is a mystery. I love pseudonymity for its own sake" (ca. 1935, unpublished letter qtd. in Filreis 115).

17. Stevens did not save Latimer's letters; hence Latimer's questions can only be inferred from Steven's responses. As Stevens recalled a few years later to Hi Simons, "At one time [Latimer] wrote me a good many letters for the purpose of eliciting replies on the basis of which he said that he intended to write an analysis of my things" (August 8, 1940, *Letters* 359). Filreis cites an unpublished section of a Stevens letter to Latimer, dated September 25, 1935, apparently responding favorably to Latimer's request to ask Stevens several questions about particular poems and about his views on poetry in relation to life (121, 326n76).

18. The four issues of *Alcestis Quarterly* included poems by Stevens (12), Williams (3), Cummings (9), Elizabeth Bishop (4), and James Gould Fletcher (3), as well as those of younger, politically radical poets (Jack Wheelwright, Harold Rosenberg, Isador Schneider, Muriel Rukeyser, Ruth Lechlitner, and Willard Mass). Earlier incarnations of the magazine published (or received commitments from) Frost, Pound, Moore, Jeffers, Tate, MacLeish, etc. In addition to the two books by Stevens, Alcestis Press published two books by Williams (*An Early Martyr* and *Adam & Eve & the City*), Alan Tate's *The Mediterranean,* Elizabeth Bishop's *Minute Particulars,* and Robert Penn Warren's first book, *Thirty-Six Poems* (Filreis 118–19, 121).

19. In this difficult period for finding publishers, Stevens, quite surprisingly, retained his. Knopf published a trade edition of *Ideas of Order* in October 1936 and a revised version of *Owl's Clover* in *The Man with the Blue Guitar* in 1937.

20. Stevens expressed the same indifference two other times. Hand-carrying the typescript of *Ideas of Order* to Alcestis Press, he had lunch with its printer (the only staff member available), who said unpleasant things about Latimer. The following year he received a letter (unpublished) from William Carlos Williams, apparently complaining of Latimer's character. Stevens replied: "I agree that there is something wrong in the woodpile. But that is what people are like. My interest in making sure is to be able to act intelligently: or perhaps I ought to say cautiously. What Latimer is is nothing to me so long as he does not involve me. I am sending my [manu]script [for *Owl's Clover*] to him within the next few days. It is very easy to say of a man of this sort that he is a slop-over. . . . After all, if we go along with him knowing about the woodpile, we are no worse off than going along with almost anybody else" (May 13, 1936, *Letters* 311). He later recalled to Hi Simons: "I have heard various unpleasant things about him, but, for my own part, made up my mind long ago to speak nothing but good of him, since my own relations with him would not justify me in doing anything else" (August 8, 1940, *Letters* 359).

21. Stevens to Hi Simons, August 8, 1940, *Letters* 359.

22. James Longenbach makes a strong and valuable counter-argument that in *Ideas of Order* Stevens was "exploring the uses of ambiguity" (*Wallace Stevens: The Plain Sense of Things* [New York: Oxford UP, 1991] 152); but I think he pushes his thesis too insistently.

23. Stevens to Latimer regarding "Mozart, 1935," November 5, 1935, *Letters* 292.

24. Compare: "a slime of men in crowds" in the 1936 edition's opening poem, "Farewell to Florida."

25. These lines, and those following, urging the poet-pianist to absolve "this besieging pain" in "a starry placating," suggest Beethoven, particularly the choral movement of his Ninth Symphony.

26. Longenbach writes that "the poem searches for a mediation between a Marxist imperative to sing the present and a poet's desire to sing the sentiment of the marvelous" (147). But the imperative the speaker feels to play the present is not simply ideological: it reflects Stevens's own deeply troubled sense of the times (the body in rags carried down the stairs, the angry crowds) and of the poet's conflicted responsibility to them.

A very different reading comes from Milton J. Bates, who describes the "mobs of men" as having "been liberated from the oppression of the old social and economic institutions" and the speaker as choosing to continue playing Mozart (though adding clouds to the concerto), remaining in his "ivory tower," and braving "the hostility of the crowd, assured that this [aloofness] is ultimately the means 'By which sorrow is released'" (*Wallace Stevens: A Mythology of Self* [Berkeley: U of California P, 1985] 169–70).

27. Edward A. Filene, owner of a prominent department store in Boston, had urged a socially and ethically responsible capitalism, not unlike what Roosevelt envisioned in the New Deal, in which wealth and power were redistributed downward (Richardson 432n6).

28. Geoffrey Grigson, "A Stuffed Goldfinch," *New Verse* February–March 1936: 18–19.

29. Joan Richardson goes too far, I think, in calling Stevens at this stage "a naïve socialist" (95). One index of Stevens's contradictory politics was his opinion of Mussolini. In one letter to Latimer he describes himself as "pro-Mussolini" but adds that the "Italians have as much right to take Ethiopia from the coons as the coons had to take it from the boa-constrictors" (October 31, 1935, *Letters* 289–90). A few weeks later he attempts to clarify his comments, only to confuse them further: "While it is true that I have spoken sympathetically of Mussolini, all of my sympathies [regarding Ethiopia] are the other way: with the coons and the boa-constrictors. . . . A man would have to be very thick-skinned not to be conscious of the pathos of Ethiopia or China, or one of these days, if we are not careful, of this country. But that Mussolini is right, practically, has certainly a great deal to be said for it" (November 21, 1935, *Letters* 295). He never explains how Mussolini is "right, practically."

30. For this same reason, Stevens first sent "Mr. Burnshaw and the Statue" to Alfred Kreymborg's *Caravan,* where he "was likely to appear with a contingent of such reds as . . . Richard Wright, Meridel Le Sueur, [Ruth] Lechlitner, [Muriel] Rukeyser, and Kreymborg" (Filreis 186). "Of the 45 writers represented in the collection, no fewer than seventeen" were communists or fellow travelers (342n30).

31. Edwin Rolfe, "Poetry," *Partisan Review* 2.7 (1935): 33.

32. Babette Deutsch, "The Gaudiness of Poetry," *New York Herald Tribune Books* December 15, 1935: 18, rpt. in *Critical Heritage* 142–44.

33. Isador Schneider, "Order Limited," *New Masses* October 27, 1936: 24.

34. Theodore Roethke, review of *Ideas of Order, New Republic,* July 15, 1936: 305. As a promising poet himself, Roethke is surprisingly fuzzy when he writes: "The times and a ripened maturity have begun to stiffen Mr. Stevens' rhetoric." Did he mean it was acquiring a new rigor, or becoming arthritic?

35. F. O. Matthiessen, "Society and Solitude in Poetry," *Yale Review* 25.3 (1937): 603–7, excerpted in *Critical Heritage* 147–49; John Holmes, "Five American Poets," *Virginia Quarterly Review* 12.2 (1936): 294, excerpted in *Critical Heritage* 149–50; William Rose Benét, "Three Poets and a Few Opinions," *North American Review* 243 (Spring–Summer 1937): 195–97, excerpted in *Critical Heritage* 153–55.

36. Of more recent criticism I found only one example that entirely overlooks Stevens's recognition of contemporaneous pressures. Rejecting Burnshaw's assertion that in *Ideas of Order* Stevens is "in the throes of struggle for philosophical adjustment" (see below), Donald Sheehan writes: "[T]he 'philosophy' Stevens seeks to adjust in *Ideas of Order* is the poetics of *Harmonium,* and the 'struggle' is conducted wholly in the context of his individual search for . . . poetic forms" ("Wallace Stevens in the 1930s: Gaudy Bosh and the Gesture's Whim," in *The Thirties: Fiction, Poetry, and Drama,* ed. Warren French [Deland, FL: Everett/Edwards, 1976] 151).

37. Stanley Burnshaw, "Turmoil in the Middle Ground," *New Masses* October 1, 1935: 42, rpt. in "Wallace Stevens and the Statue," *Sewanee Review* 69 (Summer 1961): 363–66. It is noteworthy that *Ideas of Order* elicited two reviews in *New Masses:* Burnshaw's in 1935 and Schneider's a year later.

38. E.g., Sheehan's hyperbolic description of it as "the most celebrated encounter of poet and critic" (151).

39. Joseph Riddel, for example, calls Burnshaw's review the "coarsest kind of Marxian criticism" ("Poet's Politics—Wallace Stevens' *Owl's Clover,*" *Modern Philology* 56.2 [1958]: 118). Sheehan depicts Burnshaw "dismissing" *Ideas of Order* and quotes as evidence what Burnshaw said about *Harmonium* (151). Bates describes Stevens's response to the review as "at first irritated and defensive" (173).

40. See Stanley Burnshaw, "'Middle-Ground' Writers," *New Masses* April 30, 1935: 19–21. Chapter 1 analyzes this article in detail.

41. Burnshaw, "Wallace Stevens and the Statue," 355, 357–58, 360.

42. Stevens to Hi Simons, August 27, 1940, *Letters* 366.

43. Cf. Stevens's comment to Latimer on "A Fading of the Sun": "It is an old story that we derive our ideas of nobility, say, from noble objects of nature. But then it is an equally old story that we derived them from ourselves" (*Letters* 295). "Noble" appears often in Stevens's poems and essays, for example, in the title of his first essay in *The Necessary Angel:* "The Noble Rider and the Sound of Words."

44. Robert Emmet Monroe interprets the celestial paramours as being part of the statue itself, based on an actual statuary group in the Luxembourg Gardens of Paris ("Figuration and Society in 'Owl's Clover,'" *Wallace Stevens Journal* 13.2 [1989]: 128). In his letters explicating the poem, Stevens does not confirm this surmise or refer to any source for the statue.

45. Riddel interprets this passage quite differently: "[Stevens's] order is the 'poets' politics' which rule only in the 'poets' world.' The poets' politics can never be abstract [hence Marxist]; the poets' world is imaginative reality. . . . Stevens' politics precedes politics as we know them [*sic*], as systems of social order. They are not polemic. The poets of the 1930s who complained and prophesied were concerned with social abstraction, not man" ("Poets' Politics" 123). This reading, however, ignores that the futurity of Stevens's description ("a time in which the poets' politics will rule in a poets' world") is part of the mesdames' "radiant disclosure" of the future. That the "poets" are plural also suggests that Stevens is not simply referring to himself and his own aesthetics.

46. How strikingly this line anticipates, in ironic contrast, "The palm at the end of the mind / Beyond the last thought, rises / In the bronze décor" ("Of Mere Being," *CPP* 476).

47. Ruth Lechlitner, "Imagination as Reality," *New York Herald Tribune Books* December 6, 1936, 40, rpt. in *Critical Heritage* 156–60.

48. Eda Lou Walton, review of *Ideas of Order, New York Times Book Review* December 6, 1936: 18, excerpted in *Critical Heritage* 160–62.

49. Ben Belitt, "The Violent Mind," *Nation* December 12, 1936: 710, rpt. in *Critical Heritage* 162.

50. "His problem has been a curious one: moved to formal discourse in the quest for order and certitude, his art has not up to the present permitted him to pursue such discourse or his temperament to accept it."

51. Though *Owl's Clover* has attracted belated critical attention (e.g., Longenbach, Filreis, and, most recently, Angus Cleghorn, *Wallace Stevens' Poetics: The Neglected Rhetoric),* most Stevens scholars still consider the poem a failure. Thus Joseph Riddel: "At worst 'Owl's Clover' is contentiously defensive, impenetrably opaque, and gracelessly hortatory. At best it represents a poet facing with candor and passion the ugliness of a time so real that it virtually paralyzed the imagination" (*The Clairvoyant Eye: The Poetry and Poetics of Wallace Stevens* [Baton Rouge: Louisiana State UP, 1965] 134).

52. Cf. "The murmurous haunt of flies on summer eves"—Keats, "Ode to a Nightingale."

53. Cf. the description of the tinny present in "Mozart, 1935": "its hoo-hoo-hoo, / Its shoo-shoo-shoo, its ric-a-nic."

54. The line below that seems to contradict this line—"The sun no longer shares our works"—shows a sun "Detached from us, from things as they are"—detached from a world that, in Spain, is now at war: "And the earth is alive with creeping men, / Mechanical beetles never quite warm" (VII). In such a bereft world, the imagination, too, suffers: "The strings are cold on the blue guitar" (VII).

As examples of the many lines in Stevens's work that adulate the sun as a source and emblem of creative energy, consider the following:

Supple and turbulent, a ring of men
Shall chant in orgy on a summer morn
Their boisterous devotion to the sun,
Not as a god, but as a god might be,
Naked among them like a savage source. ("Sunday Morning," *CPP* 55–56)

                    what spirit
Have I except it comes from the sun? ("Waving Adieu, Adieu, Adieu,"
CPP 104)

Let this be clear that we are men of the sun
And men of day and never of pointed night ("Evening without Angels,"
CPP 111)

55. Joan Richardson credits this essay as a psychological breakthrough for Stevens, "the instrument he used to tear through the barriers he had set up [in *Owl's Clover*]" (133).

56. Cf. "crusted" as an ugly adjective in "Mr. Burnshaw and the Statue," in which the speaker, assuming the Marxian voice, belittles the statue: "a thing of the dank imagination, much below / Our crusted outlines hot and huge with fact." Here, "crusted" ironically suggests the Marxist's brittle, quickly stale world of fact and abstraction.

57. "The Noble Rider and the Sound of Words" (Princeton lecture, April 1941), in *CPP* 660–61.

58. William Carlos Williams, review of *The Man with the Blue Guitar, New Republic* November 17, 1937: 50.

59. Eda Lou Walton, "Wallace Stevens's Two Worlds," *New York Times Book Review* October 24, 1937: 5.

60. Ruth Lechlitner, review in *New York Herald Tribune Books* November 14, 1937, 2, excerpted in *Critical Heritage* 171–72.

61. Horace Gregory, "Poetry in 1937," *New Masses* "Literary Supplement," December 7, 1937: 13.

62. Dorothy Van Ghent, "When Poets Stood Alone," *New Masses* January 11, 1938: 41–46. The similarity of her views to Gregory's probably reflects the latter's influence as poetry editor of *New Masses*.

63. Selden Rodman, review of several poets in *Common Sense* January 1938: 28, excerpted in *Critical Heritage* 178. *Common Sense,* of which Rodman was co-editor, was a radical but anti-Communist magazine, somewhat akin to *Partisan Review.*

64. Samuel French Morse, "Man with Imagination," *Twentieth Century Verse* 8 (January–February 1938): 166–70.

65. Julian Symons, "A Short View of Wallace Stevens," *Life and Letters Today* 26 (September 1940): 215–24, rpt. in *Critical Heritage* 189.

66. Delmore Schwartz, "New Verse," *Partisan Review* 4.3 (1938): 49–52, rpt. in *Critical Heritage* 181–86.

67. Another leftist axiom gets the boot in this lecture: "Time and time again it has been said that [the poet] may not address himself to an élite. I think he may. There is not a poet whom we prize today that does not address himself to an elite. The poet will continue to do this . . . even in a classless society" (*CPP* 661).

CHAPTER 3

1. *E. E. Cummings: Complete Poems, 1904–1962,* ed. George J. Firmage (New York: Liveright 1991) 267 [hereafter cited as *CP*].

2. Milton A. Cohen, *Poet and Painter: The Aesthetics of E. E. Cummings's Early Work* (Detroit: Wayne State UP, 1987), 35–36.

3. The popular image of Cummings as rule-breaker is misleading. As Norman Friedman and many others have shown, his redefinitions of the conventions of writing typically respect the function of elements—his commas pause, periods stop, capitals emphasize, etc.—but expand their usage for expressive power and for visual and kinesthetic effects. Friedman, *E. E. Cummings: The Art of His Poetry* (Baltimore: Johns Hopkins UP, 1967).

4. E. E. Cummings [hereafter EEC] to Edward Cummings, May 22, 1920, rpt. in *Selected Letters of E. E. Cummings,* ed. F. W. Dupee and George Stade (New York: Harcourt, 1969) 71 [hereafter cited as *Selected Letters*].

5. E. E. Cummings, *i: Six Nonlectures* (Cambridge: Harvard UP, 1953) 31.

6. EEC to Edward Cummings, April 18, 1917, unpublished letter qtd. in Richard Kennedy, *Dreams in the Mirror: A Biography of E. E. Cummings* (New York: Liveright, 1980) 137.

7. Cummings's friend and fellow ambulance driver, Slater Brown, was arrested for having exchanged letters with antiwar socialist Emma Goldman about the hushed-up French mutiny. Cummings was arrested for good measure and, when interrogated, refused to distance himself from Brown by telling French authorities what they wanted to hear, i.e., that he hated the Germans, even though saying so would have released him. The French imprisoned him at La Ferté-Macé

for several months, until his father pulled strings to get him (and Brown) released (Kennedy 148, 156).

8. Malcolm Cowley, *Exile's Return: A Literary Odyssey of the 1920s,* ed. with introduction by Donald Faulkner (New York: Penguin, 1994); Harold Stearns, ed., *Civilization in the United States: An Inquiry by Thirty Americans* (New York: Harcourt, 1922).

9. Dos Passos, *The Best Times: An Informal Memoir* (New York: NAL, 1968) 82.

10. This circle included sculptor Gaston Lachaise, painter Edward Nagel, and soon-to-be publishers and editors of *The Dial* Scofield Thayer, Sibley Watson, and Stewart Mitchell.

11. The 1923 *Tulips and Chimneys* was a publisher's selection (and retitling) from the much longer 1922 manuscript, *Tulips & Chimneys.* The remaining poems went into *XLI Poems* (1925) and *&* (1925). In *CP,* Firmage uses the 1922 manuscript.

12. Paul Rosenfeld, "E. E. Cummings," *Men Seen* (New York: Dial P, 1925) 196–200, rpt. in *E. E. Cummings: The Critical Reception,* ed. Lloyd N. Dendinger (New York: Burt Franklin, 1981) [hereafter cited as *Critical Reception*] 37–38 [incorrectly attributed to "James Oppenheim"]; Harriet Monroe, "Flare and Blare," *Poetry* 23.4 (1924): 211–15, rpt. in S. V. Baum, ed. and intro., *E. E. Cummings and the Critics* (East Lansing: Michigan State UP, 1962) 22–23, 24; John McClure, "*Tulips and Chimneys,*" *Double Dealer* 6 (March 1924): 121–24, excerpted in *Critical Reception* 34; Mark Van Doren, "First Glance," *Nation* July 8, 1925, 72, excerpted in *Critical Reception* 43; Herbert S. Gorman, "Goliath Beats His Poetic Breast, Whilst Critics Gape," *New York Times Book Review* December 9, 1923, 5, excerpted in *Critical Reception* 28–29.

13. Edmund Wilson, "Wallace Stevens and E. E. Cummings," *The Dial* March 19, 1924: 102–3, rpt. in Baum 25, 27.

14. Gorham Munson, "Syrinx," *Secession* 5 (July 1923), rpt. in Baum 9–18.

15. Gorham Munson, "Studio Verse," *New York Sun* November 21, 1931, excerpted in *Critical Reception* 113–14.

16. R. P. Blackmur, "Notes on E. E. Cummings' Language," *Hound & Horn* 4 (January–March 1931): 163–92, rpt. in Baum 50–67.

17. In this five-year interval, however, Cummings published the play *Him* (1927), a book of nine "nonsense stories" (Kennedy 316) without a title (1930), and a book of black-and-white reproductions of his artwork, *CIOPW* (1931).

18. Malcolm Cowley, "The Last of the Lyric Poets," *New Republic* January 27, 1932: 299–300, rpt. in *Critical Reception* 119–23.

19. Babette Deutsch, review of *No Thanks, New York Herald Tribune Books* May 26, 1935: 14.

20. Horace Gregory, "Adolescent Songster," *New York Herald Tribune* December 13, 1931: 22.

21. Eda Lou Walton, "More Roses and Locomotives," *Nation* December 30, 1931: 729–30, excerpted in *Critical Reception* 116.

22. William Carlos Williams, review of *ViVa, Contempo* April 1, 1932: 1.

23. Christopher Sawyer-Lauçanno, *E. E. Cummings: A Biography* (Naperville IL: Sourcebooks, 2004) 341–42.

24. Cummings on *Eimi* in the introduction to *The Enormous Room* (New York: Modern Library, 1934) viii.

25. Cummings, *Eimi: A Journey through Soviet Russia,* ed. George J. Firmage (New York: Liveright, 2007) 215.

26. I am grateful to Michael Webster for helping identify characters in this passage (letter to author).

27. Unsigned review, *Boston Transcript* April 1, 1933, rpt. in *Critical Reception* 131.

28. Though Cummings attributes this opinion to "an anticommunist painter" in Paris, it is obviously his own view.

29. For Cummings's notes on verb versus noun and feeling over thinking, see his 1920 essay "Gaston Lachaise" in *E. E. Cummings: A Miscellany Revised,* ed. with intro. and notes George James Firmage (New York: October House, 1965) 12–24; and Cohen, *Poet and Painter,* chapter 1.

30. Yet, according to Sawyer-Lauçanno (368), Cummings was "stung" by the book's negative reviews.

31. Horace Gregory, "American Values in Moscow," *New York Herald Tribune Books* April 9, 1933: 6x, Gregory's emphasis.

32. Henry Seidel Canby, "The Great 'I Am,'" *Saturday Review of Literature,* April 15, 1933: 533, 536, rpt. in *Critical Reception* 136–38.

33. K. D. C., "Bookends," *Harvard Crimson* May 26, 1933: 4, 6, rpt. in *Critical Reception* 151–52.

34. Nathan Asch, "Descent into Russia," *New Republic* April 26, 1933: 314. Sawyer-Lauçanno comments on this charge: "Asch must have failed to read Cummings' account of his train ride to Odessa, or a good number of other passages in which Cummings describes, in detail, conversations with 'workers'" (367).

35. George Jean Nathan, "The Worst Book of the Month," *American Spectator* April 1933, qtd. in Sawyer-Lauçanno 366–67.

36. Paul Rosenfeld, "The Enormous Cummings," *Contempo* July 25, 1933: 1, 3, rpt. in *Critical Reception* 156–60; Ezra Pound, *New English Weekly,* ca. 1935, qtd. in Sawyer-Lauçanno 368; Marianne Moore, "A Penguin in Moscow," *Poetry* 42.1 (1933): 277–81, rpt. in *Critical Reception* 160–62.

37. The two-year gap between *Eimi* and *No Thanks* is illusory, since Cummings had finished the manuscript of *No Thanks* by January 1934 but could not find a publisher. Thus its poems are roughly contemporaneous with the Russian journal.

38. Although Cummings published both of these poems ("Ballad of an Intellectual" and "american critic ad 1935") in little magazines, it is interesting that he left them out of his books. He may have recognized their aesthetic weakness, but he also may have feared a lawsuit, since both are ad hominem attacks and their subjects might well have recognized themselves. In any case, his decision to exclude them recalls Stevens's excision of *Owl's Clover* from *Collected Poems.*

39. EEC to Hildegarde Watson, unpublished letter, December 28, 1935, qtd. in Sawyer-Lauçanno 407.

40. Willard Mass to Ronald Lane Latimer, February 5, 1935, unpublished letter qtd. and paraphrased in Alan Filreis, *Modernism from Right to Left: Wallace Stevens, the Thirties and Literary Radicalism* (New York: Cambridge UP, 1994) 64.

41. To be sure, most poets in the thirties had trouble finding publishers; and, most likely, the distinguished list of publishers rejecting *No Thanks* based their decision on the dismal economics of the book trade in 1934–35 and the fact that poetry books rarely made money, not on Cummings's politics.

42. Philip Horton and Sherry Mangan, "Two Views of Cummings," *Partisan Review* 4.6 (1938): 58–63, rpt. in *Critical Reception* 196–201.

43. *Nation* May 17, 1941: 591.

44. Isidor Schneider, "E. (i.o.u.) Noncummings," *New Masses* June 25, 1935: 26–27, rpt. in *Critical Reception* 167–70.

45. Lionel Abel, "Clown or Comic Poet?" *Nation* June 26, 1935: 749–50, rpt. in *Critical Reception* 170–71.

46. Babette Deutsch, "Some Rejected Addresses," *New York Herald Tribune Books* May 26, 1935: 14; Kenneth Burke, "Two Kinds of Against," *New Republic,* June 26, 1935: 192, rpt. in *Critical Reception* 171–73. The negative adjectives these two critics used to describe the satires are strikingly similar: "whim of the moment" (Deutsch) "personal moods" (Burke).

47. John Finch, "Two Spokesmen for the Man Alone," *Sewanee Review* 44 (January–March 1936): 122–25, rpt. in *Critical Reception* 174–76.

48. "Exit the Boob," *Esquire,* June 1935, rpt. in *E. E. Cummings: A Miscellany Revised* 286–91. Regarding the Left's belated view of communism and fascism as equal menaces, see my discussion of Sidney Hook's Committee for Cultural Freedom in chapter 5. Michael Webster has observed this same condemnation of left and right in a perceptive reading of another *No Thanks* poem (*CP* 403), "go(perpe)go" ("Cummings' Sinister Dexterity: Exercises in Meaning and Unmeaning," *SPRING* 13 [2004]: 90–103).

49. And as with the democracies, so with their "sit / isn'ts" (*CP* 548): they are "morons" (*CP* 466), "120 million goats" (*CP* 901), and "mrsandmr collective foetus" (*CP* 461).

50. Cf. Rousseau: "Man is born free, but everywhere he is in chains" (*The Social Contract,* chapter 1). "Shot" and "hung" might also refer to the lynchings of blacks in the United States, which increased during the Depression.

51. *Santa Claus,* scene 3, quoted in *i: Six Nonlectures* 107.

52. Michael Webster, " 'hatred bounces': Satire and Prejudice in the Poetry of E. E. Cummings," *SPRING* 7 (1998): 23–38. Webster provides a thorough historical background on the American presence of the two "poeds."

53. Robinson Jeffers, "May–June 1940," in *Modern American Poetry,* ed. Louis Untermeyer, new and enlarged ed. (New York: Harcourt, 1964) 371.

54. See Kennedy 382 and Sawyer-Lauçanno 420. Favorable reviews include

Paul Rosenfeld, "The Brilliance of E. E. Cummings," *Nation* March 26, 1938, rpt. in *Critical Reception* 189–91; Dudley Fitts, "Cummings's Poetry," *Saturday Review of Literature* March 19, 1938: 18, rpt. in *Critical Reception* 187–88; Peter M. Jack, "The Private Exercise of Poetry," *New York Times Book Review* June 26, 1938: 2; and S. I. Hayakawa, "Is Indeed 5," *Poetry* 52.5 (1938): 284–92, rpt. in *Critical Reception* 205–9. John Peale Bishop's "The Poems and Prose of E. E. Cummings" was published in *Southern Review* 4 (Summer 1938): 173–86, rpt. in Baum 99–109.

55. Horace Gregory, "The Collected Cummings," *New Republic* April 27, 1938: 368, 370, rpt. in *Critical Reception* 194–96; Edwin Seaver, "Books of the Day," *Daily Worker* March 10, 1938; Philip Horton (I) and Sherry Mangan (II), "Two Views of Cummings," *Critical Reception,* 196–201.

56. Rolphe Humphries, "Anarchist—Poet—Advertiser," *New Masses* April [12], 1938: 23–25, rpt. in *Critical Reception* 191–93.

CHAPTER 4

1. Introduction to E. A. Robinson's "King Jasper," in *Robert Frost: Collected Poems, Prose and Plays,* ed. and notes by Richard Poirier and Mark Richardson (New York: Library of America, 1995) 741 [hereafter cited as *CPPP*].

2. For example, "Bereft" in *West-Running Brook* was written in 1893.

3. Jay Parini, *Robert Frost: A Life* (New York: Holt, 1999) 248.

4. "Robert Frost," *Booklist* 25 (February 1929): 201.

5. G. H., "Robert Frost's Poems and Outlook on Life," *Springfield Union Republican* December 30, 1928: 7E. Lawrance Thompson identified the author of this review as Granville Hicks (*Robert Frost: The Years of Triumph, 1915–1938* [New York: Holt, Rinehart, 1970] 650–51n22).

6. Frederick E. Pierce, "Three Poets against Philists," *Yale Review* 18 (December 1928): 365–66, excerpted in Peter Van Egmond, *The Critical Reception of Robert Frost* (Boston: G. K. Hall, 1974) 8.

7. Mark Van Doren, "North of Eden," *Nation* January 23, 1929: 110, rpt. in Linda W. Wagner, ed., *Robert Frost: The Critical Reception* (New York: Burt Franklin, 1977) 76–77; Theodore Spencer, "*West-Running Brook,*" *New Republic* February 20, 1929: 24–25, rpt. in Wagner 77–78; Babette Deutsch, "Poets and Poetasters," *Bookman* December 1928: 471–72, excerpted in Van Egmond 8.

8. Granville Hicks, "The World of Robert Frost," *New Republic* December 3, 1930: 77–78, rpt. in Wagner 83–85; Frederick I. Carpenter, "The Collected Poems of Robert Frost," *New England Quarterly* 5 (January 1932): 159–60, rpt. in Wagner 110–11; Isador Schneider, "Robert Frost," *Nation* January 28, 1931: 101–2, rpt. in Wagner 95–98.

9. Genevieve Taggard, "Robert Frost, Poet," *New York Herald Tribune Books* December 21, 1930: 1, 6, rpt. in Wagner 86–88. It should be noted that Taggard had become a personal friend of Frost's (Thompson 388).

10. The best example is a slender volume by Peter J. Stanlis, a longtime friend of Frost's, *Robert Frost: The Individual and Society* (Rockford College and Peter Stanlis, 1973).

11. "Poverty and Poetry," talk given at Haverford College, October 25, 1937, rpt. in *CPPP* 765.

12. Frost writes to Louis Untermeyer a month after delivering this poem: "You ought to see some time my latest outbreak into political poetry delivered at Columbia a month since." *The Letters of Robert Frost to Louis Untermeyer,* ed. Louis Untermeyer (New York: Holt Rinehart, 1963) 225 [hereafter cited as *RF to LU*].

13. Malcolm Cowley observes: "Many radicals and some conservatives thought that the Bonus Army was creating a revolutionary situation of an almost classic type" (*The Dream of the Golden Mountains: Remembering the 1930s* [New York: Penguin, 1981] 85). President Hoover apparently thought so too, later ordering General Douglas MacArthur to clear out Anaconda Flats, where the veterans were encamped. Moreover, 1932 was an election year, and Frost's poem was delivered not long before the national parties convened.

14. Laurence Perrine argues that Frost's argument for curbing ingenuity is intended ironically ("The Meaning of Robert Frost's 'Build Soil,'" in *Frost: Centennial Essays,* vol. 1 [Jackson: UP of Mississippi, 1974] 232–33), but there is much evidence to suggest that he agreed with Tityrus. The excluded worker in "A Lone Striker" who ponders the other workers at their looms feels ambivalent about ingenuity: "Man's ingenuity was good, / He saw it plainly where he stood, / Yet found it easy to resist" (*CPPP* 250). Moreover, as Tyler Hoffman has shown, Frost wrote several unpublished poems depicting the abuses of industrialism in the mills and feared (correctly, as it proved) that mechanization of farming—another instance of "ingenuity"—threatened to plow under small family farms into agribusiness ("Robert Frost and the Politics of Labor," *Modern Language Studies* 29.2 [1999]: 109–10).

15. "[T]ariff walls" probably refers to the Smoot-Harley Tariff, passed by the Hoover administration in 1931 to protect U.S. industry, but which had the counterproductive effect of globalizing the Depression. Interestingly, "fences" positions Frost on the seemingly unenlightened side of the argument in "Mending Wall": "Good fences make good neighbors."

16. As early as 1916, Frost expressed similar views: "You can't be universal without being provincial, can you? It's like trying to embrace the wind." *Interviews with Robert Frost,* ed. Edward C. Lathem (New York: Holt Rinehart, 1966) 19 [hereafter cited as *Interviews*]. And Untermeyer quotes him as saying, "I am also a separatist. You can't mix things properly until you have separated them, unscrambled them from their original chaotic mixture and held them separate long enough to test their qualities and values" (*RF to LU* 211).

17. Interview in *Rural America* November 1930, rpt. in *Interviews* 77. The right relation between the individual and society interested Frost all his life. In a 1959 symposium titled "The Future of Man," Frost stated: "I like all this uncertainty

that we live in, between being members and being individuals. That's the daily problem: how much am I a member; how much am I an individual; how comfortable am I in my memberships" (*Interviews* 213).

18. Frost signed one letter to Untermeyer in this period (February 17, 1935) "Robert the Devil," playfully echoing the medieval story and the title of a Meyerbeer opera.

19. The early 1930s witnessed a number of literary symposia and forums, debating such topics as the New Humanism and, of course, proletarian literature. One journal of the time, in fact, was called *The Symposium*.

20. Harvey Klehr, *The Heyday of American Communism: The Depression Decade* (New York: Basic Books, 1984) 79.

21. E. E. Cummings, *i: Six Nonlectures* (Cambridge: Harvard UP, 1953) 31–32.

22. Stanley Burnshaw, *Robert Frost Himself* (New York: George Braziller, 1986) 63. Burnshaw speculates that Frost strove "so hard to make his views known to the world" partly because his father's strong political involvements left their mark: "[Robert] could never resist the excitement of parrying arguments" (67). Burnshaw also identifies the extreme anti–New Deal views of Frost's wife, Elinor, as pushing Frost further to the right.

23. Archibald MacLeish, "The Writer and Revolution," *Saturday Review of Literature* January 26, 1935: 441–42. The passage in MacLeish's article that riled Frost states: "[W]ith the revolution of the spirit from which, and from which alone, action can be born, . . . poetry has everything to do. True poetry is always destructive and recreative. But . . . its attack on the existing order takes place not in the minds of a people but in the minds of a few men and not at the time of the bomb-throwings but generations before" (442). MacLeish distinguished this revolution of the spirit from "[t]he current literary fashion . . . The Revolution." Publishers and critics, MacLeish felt, paid far too much attention to the latter at the expense of the former.

24. Newton Arvin, "About Poetry and Poets," *New Republic* January 8, 1936: 262. The line he quotes ("life [in America] goes so unterribly") is from "New Hampshire," *CPPP* 158.

25. Against these Darwinian throwbacks, the poem mentions "Heaven," "cloven rock [of ages]," and "God knows where"—all on the speaker's side.

26. Malcolm Cowley, "The Case against Mr. Frost," *New Republic* September 11, 1944: 312–13, and September 18, 1944, 345–47, rpt. in *Robert Frost: A Collection of Critical Essays,* ed. James M. Cox (Englewood Cliffs, NJ: Prentice-Hall, 1962) 41.

27. Robert Narveson's comment on these lines is instructive: "In his thoughts [the narrator] has, with more than a slight taint of self-satisfaction, loaded the dice in his own favor. He has left the 'common good' an empty category, while enjoying with full conscious satisfaction the solid experience of cutting the wood" ("'Two Tramps in Mud Time': Thoreau versus 'Poor Richard,'" in *Gone Into If Not Explained: Essays on Poems by Robert Frost,* ed. Greg Kuzma [Crete, NE: Best

Cellar P, 1976] 85). Other critics have also noted this self-satisfaction in the conclusion: Cowley calls it "a sound but rather sententious sermon" (42); Richard Poirier asserts that "the rhetoric at the end attempts to make the man's desire socially, morally, and politically acceptable" (*Robert Frost: The Work of Knowing* [New York: Oxford UP, 1977] 273).

28. Having to be approved by the FERA before he could rent a house on Key West also irked Frost. He describes it with mock-elation in a letter to G. R. Elliott: "You'll be exited to learn that after being kept in all this suspense, did we get a house from the authorities or not. We did, we did! . . . . I am saved now provided only I would pay my rent for the whole winter in advance. It makes me sick for home" (December 12, 1934, *Selected Letters of Robert Frost,* ed. Lawrance Thompson [New York: Holt Rinehart, 1964] 414; hereafter cited as *Selected Letters*). Hemingway, a permanent resident of Key West at the time, also disliked the FERA takeover of Key West; he made the FERA leaders look like fools in his novel *To Have and Have Not.*

29. Though Thompson identifies the stand's operators as Frost's own son and daughter-in-law, Carol and Lillian Frost, who sold such produce at Stone Cottage (to Frost's disapproval), the fact does not alter the poem's remote and generalized depiction of the poor (Thompson 438).

30. As Tyler Hoffman has brought out, the relocation of these indigent farmers alludes to the New Deal's Resettlement Administration's plan "to resettle urban slum dwellers in autonomous garden cities and submarginal farmers in new, productive farm villages." Three such cities were constructed. Frost was hostile to the plan and to FDR's agricultural reforms generally, believing they would "erase the distinction between the city and the country" and lead to the destruction of the small, family farm (Hoffman 125–29).

31. Compare this fanciful image of stones flying to the realistic one of the destitute hurling stones at the building where an artist practices arpeggios in Stevens's "Mozart, 1935."

32. Paraphrased in Thompson 427. If Frost did write the poem "a year or two earlier," it would still not rule out Roosevelt as the "thinker," since he had been in office well over two years by August 1935.

33. *Interviews* 83. The *Sun* also ran an editorial commenting on the interview. The next day, the august *New York Times* followed with an editorial (February 28, 1936). Neither of the editorials was especially critical of the poem or of Frost, though the *Times* does slip in a small jab: "If he implies Mr. Roosevelt's thought is pedestrian, the implication is a compliment. A statesman who has his feet on the ground can't very well have his head in the clouds" (*Interviews* 86).

34. James MacGregor Burns, *Roosevelt: The Lion and the Fox* (New York: Harcourt, 1956) 171–72, 179. Burns ascribes this flexibility not to Roosevelt's shallowness as a thinker but to his pragmatism.

35. Another oddity in this poem is that the set of examples Frost offers to show Roosevelt's oscillations has much more to do with poetry than politics:

From force to matter, and back to force,
From form to content and back to form,
From norm to crazy and back to norm,
From bound to free and back to bound,
From sound to sense and back to sound.

Has the poet himself flip-flopped, thinking not of FDR but of modernist poets with whom he fought a running battle about the need for content (not just
form alone), for boundedness (not free verse), and for sense in the sound of poetry? Frost was about to deliver the six Norton Lectures at Harvard (March 1936)
on the theme "The Renewal of Words," including such topics as "The Old Way
to Be New." His differences with formalist modernists and free-verse poets were
much on his mind then. Thompson even argues that the poem's notorious allusion and the newspaper interview were intended to drum up interest in the lectures at Harvard and in *A Further Range* (443).

36. Randall Jarrell, "To the Laodiceans," in *Poetry and the Age* (New York: Vin-
tage, 1955) 39. Other critics who express variants of this view are Reuben Brower
("In the last stanza . . . he manages to fuse wonder with irony and pathos in finely
distinct shadings of tone"—*The Poetry of Robert Frost: Constellations of Intention*
[New York: Oxford UP, 1963] 151) and George Monteiro ("the lightness of tone
conveys the poet's tenderness"—"Robert Frost's Liberal Imagination," in *Roads
Not Taken: Rereading Robert Frost,* ed. with intro. by Earl J. Wilcox and Jonathan
N. Barron [Columbia: U Missouri P, 2000] 165). A more extreme view is Robert
Pack's: "Frost's general attitude toward [the] people . . . is presented ironically yet
not without a measure of sympathetic identification with the possible implica-
tion that Frost himself must be numbered among the 'people' whom the poem
satirizes" (*Belief and Uncertainty in the Poetry of Robert Frost* [Hanover: Middlebury
College P, 2003] 185).

37. Poirier 269, his emphasis.

38. The collective title of "The Strong Are Saying Nothing" belies the poem's
emphasis on singularity: "Men work alone, their lots plowed far apart" (*CPPP* 272).

39. William Pritchard, *Frost: A Literary Life Reconsidered* (New York: Oxford UP,
1984) 208.

40. In turning "Abishag"—the poem's object lesson about the fall of the once-
great—into a washer woman, Frost also alludes to a strike by cleaning women
organized by Harvard leftists, an action he "had been outspokenly critical of"
(Thompson 436).

41. Jarrell's extravagant praise for this poem (and for "Neither Out Far nor In
Deep") has spurred other Frost critics to react. A few samples: Pritchard considers
"[t]he pleasures and satisfactions of both poems are more theatrical, less humanly
and morally profound than [Jarrell] claims" (209). Pack finds little of pleasure in
"Provide, Provide": "It is difficult to account for the speaker's unmistakable bitterness, with its clubbing effect of rhyme repetitions in each stanza as the speak-

er's irony becomes increasingly acerbic in offering his impossible advice" (187). Maxine Kumin supports Jarrell: "The lyrics illuminate unsparingly the terrible truth of man's nature. . . . What little comfort can be salvaged must be bought and paid for in full. But the poem transcends its bleak and stubborn honesty; it ends by delighting or at least gratifying us with its wisdom" ("A Note on 'Provide, Provide,'" in Kuzma, *Gone Into If Not Explained* 63).

42. Frost might be alluding here to the discovery (by Edwin Hubbel in 1929) that the universe was expanding, pushing galaxies further apart from each other and thus from Earth.

43. Brower reads the ending of this poem quite differently: "But the optimism has worn thin. 'Man's condition,' when one give close attention to an 'endless repetition,' is pretty terrible, and the piously hopeful prayer ["May my application . . ."] acknowledges something quite unbearable" (117).

44. Referring to this poem in his lecture "Poverty and Poetry" (1937), Frost explained why he couldn't "get in right with my radical friends": "the trouble with me [then] was that I was a lone striker; if I called it a 'collectivist striker,' that would be another matter" (*CPPP* 763).

45. In a letter to John T. Bartlett, Frost wrote that the narrative was "without prejudice to machinery industry or an industrial age" (December 5, 1933, *Selected Letters* 400).

46. Robert Penn Warren, who met Frost when the two attended the 1935 Rocky Mountain Writers Conference, recalls: "He had an interest in the Southern Agrarians, and he called himself a Yankee Agrarian" (interview, qtd. in Parini 298).

47. These fears comically exaggerated real ones Frost harbored in bucking the leftist tide. After he had called Rolfe Humphries a "bargain-counter revolutionary" in a lecture (see n. 50 below), a friend of Humphries threatened him that he might get a "fire-cracker" one day. Shortly afterward, a mysterious package arrived. Treating it like a bomb, Frost discovered: cigars. He told this story in his 1937 lecture "Poverty and Poetry," and his conclusion echoes the paranoid tone of "Not Quite Social": "So whatever's coming to me hasn't come to me yet" (*CPPP* 766).

48. Horace Gregory, "Robert Frost's New Poems," *New Republic* June 24, 1936: 214, rpt. in Wagner 132–33. Frost took especial glee in Bernard DeVoto's retaliation on Gregory in his broadside against Frost's critics (see n. 57 below). He confides to DeVoto: "I have never read a word of that ganglion's regrets about me in prose, but I suspected they are to be explained by his not unwarrantable if intuitive suspicion that I hate his obscratulations of the muse in verse. There is no baser form of hypocrasy [*sic*] than a false air of disinterestedness" (*Selected Letters* 441).

49. Newton Arvin, "A Minor Strain," *Partisan Review* 3.5 (1936): 27–28, rpt. in Wagner 123–25.

50. Rolfe Humphries, "A Further Shrinking," *New Masses* August 11, 1936: 41–42, rpt. in Wagner 134–36. To being called "counter-revolutionary," Frost retorted (in a lecture at the New School for Social Research in New York) that Humphries was a "bargain-counter revolutionary" (Thompson 463–64; see n. 47 above).

51. J. R., "Mr. Frost Ranges Further," *Christian Science Monitor* June 17, 1936: 14, rpt. in Wagner 128–29; "Frost: He Is Sometimes a Poet and Sometimes a Stump-Speaker," *News-Week* May 30, 1936: 40, excerpted in Wagner 118–19; Dudley Fitts, "*A Further Range,*" *New England Quarterly* 9 (September 1936): 519–20, rpt. in Wagner 136–37. Stanley Burnshaw continued this skepticism into the 1980s, opining that "Build Soil," "To a Thinker," and "A Lone Striker" were "undoubtedly *as poems* the worst in the book" (60, Burnshaw's emphasis).

52. Burnshaw does state that as late as 1935 he wondered "where Frost stood" politically ("No poet could be more elusive"), but he also acknowledges that such political poems as "Two Tramps in Mud Time" and "Neither Out Far nor In Deep" were readily available then and that he (Burnshaw) and friends concluded that "we were probably on opposing sides" (52). Burnshaw repeats Frost's "invitation" claim, without questioning it (60).

53. *Selected Letters* 431–32. Other factors contributed to Frost's depression. His wife's health had deteriorated markedly in 1936, and Frost himself suffered a serious attack of shingles in late summer. Then, too, Roosevelt's landslide reelection that November would not have cheered him, despite the equanimity he expressed about it in his letter to Untermeyer (quoted above).

54. Untermeyer's note, *RF to LU* 294; Parini 307–8.

55. *Saturday Review* January 1, 1938: 3–4.

56. Frost to DeVoto, January 20, 1938, *Selected Letters* 455, emphasis added. There is no question that Frost saw DeVoto as an attack dog, writing the invective that he, Frost, would have liked to write in this war against the critics. He tells DeVoto in May 1937: "You're there to lick em for us. To Hell with their thinking. . . . I wish I were any good. I'd go to the front with you. As it is—as I am—I must be content to sic you on. Results is all I ask" (*Selected Letters* 444–45). As Frost told G. R. Elliott about the same time, "I get a vicarious satisfaction out of seeing anybody's critic laid low" (*Selected Letters* 459).

57. DeVoto's idiosyncratic use of "proletarian" echoes Frost's own in his lecture "Poverty and Poetry," where he describes the head of the woolen mills in Lawrence as a "genuine proletarian, because he came up from nowhere" (*CPPP* 760).

58. Louise Bogan, "Verse," *New Yorker* March 4, 1939: 68–70, rpt. in Wagner 151–52.

59. "The Muse; Collected Poems of Robert Frost," *Time* May 15, 1939: 83–85, 87, rpt. in Wagner 154–57.

60. Muriel Rukeyser, "In a Speaking Voice," *Poetry* 54.4 (1939): 218–24, rpt. in Wagner 158–61.

61. He wrote to Frederic Melcher on September 1, 1930: "I'm not afraid of the radicals I should be thrown in with nor of the Jews. I may be a radical myself" (*Selected Letters* 367).

62. I take issue, therefore, with Thompson's view that in the political poems Frost "was more and more inclined to strike out poetically in self-defense . . . [against] those who criticized him for his laissez-faire attitudes and his belief in

the old doctrine of 'every man for himself'" (438). Defensiveness was certainly a factor, but less so than a desire to assert his own counter-philosophy.

63. Arvin, "A Minor Strain," rpt. in Wagner 125.

64. "Introduction to Robinson's *King Jasper,*" rpt. in *CPPP* 744.

CHAPTER 5

1. Among the groups Williams joined, attended meetings of, signed petitions of, or wrote essays for in the 1930s are the communist-sponsored League of American Writers, the American Federation of Writers, the American Writers' Congress, the Committee for Cultural Freedom, the League for Cultural Freedom and Socialism, and the Committee of 400. He also organized and chaired the Bergen County Committee Medical Board to Aid the Spanish Democracy.

2. William Carlos Williams [hereafter WCW] to Louis Zukofsky, February 10, 1933, unpublished letter qtd. in *New World* 337, 361.

3. Stevens was a notable exception to this generalization, since Knopf stayed with him. Frost's poetry made money for Henry Holt.

4. Anonymous review of *The Knife of the Times, New York Herald Tribune Books* June 19, 1932: 7; Gertrude Diamant, "Mr. Williams in His Clinic," *New York Post* June 25, 1932: 7, rpt. in *William Carlos Williams: The Critical Heritage,* ed. Charles Doyle (London: Routledge, 1980) 118–20 [hereafter cited as *Critical Heritage*].

5. Though Williams, by request, was not officially listed as an editor, he gave Johns advice, wrote a manifesto, and solicited manuscripts for the magazine.

6. "Manifesto," *Pagany: A Native Quarterly* 1.1 (1930): 1. Williams's article on Gertrude Stein in this issue similarly praised "pure writing."

7. "Announcement," *Pagany* 1.1 (1930): 1, emphasis added.

8. "Comment," *Contact* 1.1 (1932): 7.

9. "Comment," *Contact* 1.3 (1932): 131.

10. According to Mariani (*New World* 328), Williams intended this as an "Open Letter" on the state of contemporary poetry for the first issue of *Contact* (February 1932). It is ambiguously dated "1932" in *The Selected Letters of William Carlos Williams,* ed. John C. Thirlwall (New York: New Directions, 1957) 129 [hereafter cited as *Selected Letters*].

11. Note the striking similarity between this "coincidental reflection of the times" and the view that Wallace Stevens came to adopt in 1941: "That [the poet] must be contemporaneous is as old as Longinus and I dare say older. But that he *is* contemporaneous is almost inevitable" ("The Noble Rider and the Sound of Words," in *Wallace Stevens: Collected Poetry and Prose*, ed. Frank Kermode and Joan Richardson [New York: Library of America, 1997] 659).

12. *The Collected Poems of William Carlos Williams,* 2 vols. (New York: New Directions, 1986, 1988) 1: 370 [hereafter cited as *CP-WCW*].

13. Williams, "The New Poetical Economy," *Poetry* 44.4 (1934): 220–25.

14. "The sun-beams that shine / They're yours. They're mine," in the song "The Best Things in Life Are Free" (from the 1930 movie *Good News*).

15. About fifteen of the poems in *Collected Poems* date from 1930 and later, but only "The Sun Bathers" alludes to the Depression.

16. Probably the most political poem Williams wrote in the twenties, "Impromptu: The Suckers," about the Sacco and Vanzetti executions, was not published until 1941. Like many other writers who became leftists, he was incensed by what he saw as the railroading of the two immigrants: "I believed that they had been double-crossed, that New England was ganging up on them" (*CP-WCW* 1: 513n).

17. Babette Deutsch, "Heirs of the Imagists," *New York Herald Tribune Books* April 1, 1934: 16, excerpted in *Critical Heritage* 130–31.

18. Phillip Blair Rice, "William Carlos Williams," *Nation* March 28, 1934: 365–66, excerpted in *Critical Heritage* 129.

19. Charles Henry Newman, "How Objective Is Objectivism?" *Dynamo: A Journal of Revolutionary Poetry* 1.3 (1934): 26–29.

20. Geoffrey Grigson, "Two Poets," *New Verse* April 1934: 18–19.

21. Raymond Larsson, "Recent Verse," *Commonweal* January 18, 1935: 351. Regrettably, Larsson does not develop this insight in the short space he devotes to Williams.

22. Conrad Aiken, "The Well Worn Spirit," *New Republic* April 18, 1934: 289–91.

23. Marianne Moore, "Things Others Never Notice," *Poetry* 44.2 (1934): 103–6, rpt. in *Critical Heritage* 131.

24. Wallace Stevens, preface to Williams's *Collected Poems, 1921–1931,* rpt. in *Critical Heritage* 126.

25. C. G. Poore, "The Poetry of William Carlos Williams," *New York Times Book Review* February 18, 1934: 2. Cf. Newman (see n. 19 above): "Williams has made a definite contribution to American poetry" (29).

26. Among the leftist magazines Williams published poems or essays in during the mid-thirties were *Smoke, Westminster Magazine, New Verse, New Tide, Alcestis Quarterly, New Democracy, Direction, New Republic, Programme, New Directions in Poetry and Prose, Partisan Review and Anvil,* and, by late 1937, *New Masses.*

27. Like so many little magazines of the period, *Blast* had a short life span: five issues from September 1933 to November 1934.

28. Williams, "Art and Politics: The Editorship of *Blast*" (1933), rpt. in *A Recognizable Image: William Carlos Williams on Art and Politics,* ed. Bram Dijkstra (New York: New Directions, 1978) 75.

29. Williams, "Social Credit as Anti-Communism," *New Democracy* January 15, 1934, paraphrased in *New World* 348–49.

30. For a more complete discussion of Latimer's politics, personality, and publishing contributions, see chapter 2.

31. WCW to R. L. Latimer, February 25, 1935, *Selected Letters* 152, Williams's uppercase.

32. In December 1934, Latimer had asked Williams to describe Marianne

Moore; Williams obliged with a paragraph-long description (qtd. in *New World* 394).

33. To Gorham Munson: "[T]he American Communists, poor deluded radicals, didn't even have the sense to work out an intelligent attack to be achieved by stages; no, it had to be revolution emerging out of the shambles of bloody street fighting. But what he [Williams] wanted was a bloodless revolution.... And he didn't want communism and Social Credit combined" (March 5, 1934, unpublished letter paraphrased in *New World* 353).

To Fred and Betty Miller: "[A] new revolution would not last more than a week before special interests moved in to carve up the country. The problem with the American Communists was that they still had no idea of what they were really up against in this country. They were too naïve.... What the Communist intellectuals ought to do ... was ... something pragmatic, in the American tradition and then talk about the revolution. You didn't 'make a cake by reading a book [Marx] either'" (July 1934, unpublished letter paraphrased and qtd. in *New World* 360–61).

To Kenneth Burke: "It's too far into the distance to pray for a pro-literary Communism.... Hell, we act like a lot of lost sheep. Yet I have no answer. Are we so impotent that we can't do anything but yell for a Lenin or else go pantsless?" (May 7, 1935, unpublished letter qtd. in *New World* 378).

34. WCW to Louis Zukofsky, January 29, 1936, unpublished letter qtd. in *New World* 388.

35. "Correspondence," *Partisan Review* 3.4 (1936): 32.

36. Mariani, e.g., asserts "the editors were *calling for* 'Sanctions Against Williams'" (*New World* 389, emphasis added).

37. *I Wanted to Write a Poem: The Autobiography of the Works of a Poet,* ed. Edith Heal (New York: New Directions, 1958) 57 [hereafter cited as *IWWP*].

38. William Carlos Williams, *The Autobiography of William Carlos Williams* (New York: New Directions, 1967) 299.

39. WCW to R. L. Latimer, December 28, 193, unpublished letter qtd. and paraphrased in *New World* 382.

40. *IWWP* 56; David Frail, *The Early Politics and Poetics of William Carlos Williams* (Ann Arbor: UMI Research P, 1987) 132. Williams corresponded with Coffey and published an opinion piece on the trial, "A Man versus the Law," in *The Freeman* June 23, 1920: 348–49.

41. Another poem about a persecuted proletarian, "Item" (*CP-WCW* 1: 379), describes a woman whose face looks like "a mashed blood orange" from being roughed up by the police: "the young men / who with their gun-butts / shove her // sprawling." Williams read about the incident in a newspaper—"a note / at the foot of the page."

42. Note the similarity between Chief One Horn's speech ("You big fool!") and Pound's Kung (Confucius) in canto 13. Confucius addresses a Taoist priest who, like the prospector, sits inactive:

And Kung raised his cane against Yuan Jang,
Yuan Jang being his elder,
For Yuan Jang sat by the roadside pretending to
be receiving wisdom.
And Kung said
"You old fool, come out of it,
Get up and do something useful."

The themes are identical: get up and do something for yourself.

43. The poem's original title (published in the 1934 *Galaxy: An Anthology*) was "Study for a Figure Representing Modern Culture" (*CP-WCW* 1: 540n).

44. Depicting these pleasurable moments, however, does not mean the poem "aestheticizes poverty, sensualizing the old woman," as Bob Johnson argues ("'A Whole Synthesis of His Time': Political Ideology and Cultural Politics in the Writings of William Carlos Williams, 1929–1939," *American Quarterly* 54.2 [2002]: 19). "The Poor" is a better candidate for this claim (see below).

45. Robert Von Hallberg, "The Politics of Description: W. C. Williams in the 'Thirties," *ELH* 45.1 (1978): 145.

46. WCW, notes, July 27, 1955, quoted in *CP-WCW* 1: 541n.

47. *CP-WCW* 1: 541n. Williams also described the yacht race as a metaphor for Roosevelt's struggle against wealthy Republicans trying to block his New Deal programs, while the poor would ultimately be the losers (August 25, 1935, unpublished letter to Ezra Pound, paraphrased in *New World* 370–71).

48. WCW to R. L. Latimer, January 26, 1936, unpublished letter qtd. in *New World* 386.

49. There is a curious disagreement among Williams scholars regarding reviews of these two books. Charles Doyle writes: "Nor were the books reviewed [he cites one exception: T. C. Wilson's review], so there is little critical notice of Williams in the mid-1930s" (*Critical Heritage* 16). But Paul Mariani, in *William Carlos Williams: The Poet and His Critics* (Chicago: American Library Association, 1975), correctly points out that "both volumes received wide and favorable notice" (48) and lists several reviews.

50. T. C. Wilson, "The Example of Dr. Williams," *Poetry* 48.2 (1936): 105–7. An interesting sign of changing times for *Poetry*, this review appears in a special "Social Poets Number" (edited by Horace Gregory).

51. Robert Lann, review of *An Early Martyr*, *New Republic* July 15, 1936: 304.

52. Eda Lou Walton, "New Poems by William Carlos Williams," *New York Times Book Review* November 15, 1936: 3.

53. Robert Fitzgerald, "Actual and Archaic," *Poetry* 49.2 (1936): 94–95.

54. Ruth Lechlitner, "Ahead of His Time," *New York Herald Tribune Books* January 19, 1936: 13. Lechlitner was somewhat less enthusiastic about *Adam & Eve & The City*, whose long title poems "are less effective" because "the precise tools and limitations of objectivism are not adapted to [their] subject-matter" ("To the Mind as to the Eye," *New York Herald Tribune Books* November 22, 1936: 14x).

55. "Image and Purpose" [review of Sol Funaroff's *The Spider and the Clock*], *New Masses* August 16, 1938: 23–25 (Williams's emphasis).

56. "A Twentieth Century American," *Poetry* 47.4 (1936): 227–29.

57. According to Reed Whittemore, the editors also cited the version in *Poetry* as a reason for rejecting the article (*William Carlos Williams: Poet from Jersey* [Boston: Houghton Mifflin, 1975] 256–57). That Lewis's submission smacked of self-promotion may also have been a factor.

58. *Partisan Review* to H. H. Lewis, February 4, 1936, unpublished letter, Beinecke Library, Yale University, qtd. in Whittemore 257.

59. "Ripostes," *Partisan Review* 4.2 (1938): 61–62.

60. Cary Nelson quotes this passage of Williams's review to support his (Nelson's) argument that excluding poets like Lewis from our "cultural memory" impoverishes and falsifies our poetic history in its culturally determined bias against political poetry (*Repression and Recovery: Modern American Poetry and the Politics of Cultural Memory, 1910–1945* [Madison: U of Wisconsin P, 1989] 49). Interestingly, Nelson finds no uneasiness in Williams's praise and even echoes some of the same contradictions in commending Lewis for "recovery": "[H]e is . . . willfully crude and polemical. . . . In his playful 'Thinking of Russia,' America's whole history collapses for a moment under the pressure from the merciless, willfully childish pun ["Uncle Sham"] . . . ; it is as if the country is not worthy of a better conceit" (48)—or Lewis was incapable of conceiving one. If, for Nelson, "literariness" is itself culturally determined and therefore suspect, it not only existed for Williams but was of primary importance, the bedrock underlying his expanding recognition of political poetry. Hence, the mystery of his praise for Lewis.

61. For this reason, I disagree with Bob Johnson's view that this essay marked a major shift in Williams's aesthetics: "During the 1930s, Williams came to see that 'pure poetry' often emanated from the emotional intensity of political commitment . . . to radical social causes. . . . In his reviews of Lewis . . . we see the early modernist urge to renovate language joined to and displaced by the Depression faith in political causes" (10–11). By the mid-thirties, Williams was not one "to see the rejuvenating possibilities in the Russian Revolution" (11); nor, despite his momentary enthusiasms, did his skepticism permit him to maintain an uncritical "faith in political causes."

62. *Letters of Wallace Stevens*, ed. Holly Stevens (Berkeley: U of California P, 1996) 296; Stanley Burnshaw, "Wallace Stevens and the Statue," *Sewanee Review* 69 (Summer 1961): 359.

63. "Muriel Rukeyser's 'US1,'" *New Republic* March 9, 1938: 141–42; "Sermon with a Camera," *New Republic* October 12, 1938: 282–83; review of Stevens, *New Republic* November 17, 1937: 50.

64. WCW to Robert McAlmon, July 18, 1939, unpublished letter, Yale Collection of American Literature, Beinecke Rare Book and Manuscript Library.

65. Whittemore asserts that the magazine which strongly supported the CCF, *New Leader*, was at this time attacking the "Stalinoid" League of American Writers (258), to which Williams belonged at the time. But in his letter to Williams

(discussed below), Hook stated that he had "nothing to do with *The New Leader*" (Whittemore 257).

66. Both Hook and co-founder Eugene Lyons state that the CCF was founded to oppose "crime[s] against cultural freedom" from the Far Left (e.g., the Moscow Trials) as well as from the Nazis and fascists on the Far Right (Sidney Hook, *Out of Step: An Unquiet Life in the Twentieth Century* [New York: Harper & Row, 1987] 259; Lyons, *The Red Decade* [New York: Bobbs-Merrill, 1941] 342). Hook scholars and historians of the period generally confirm this as the group's aim. Christopher Phelps notes that originally the group was to be called the League against Totalitarianism (*Young Sidney Hook: Marxist and Pragmatist* [Ithaca: Cornell UP, 1997] 202).

67. WCW to James Oneal, July 11, 1939, unpublished letter, Beinecke Library.

68. WCW to Norman Macleod, October 31, 1939, in Norman Macleod, "Literary Intelligence," *Pembroke* 6 (1975): 154.

69. *Partisan Review* 6.4 (1939): 126.

70. WCW to Norman Macleod, November 6, 1939, in Macleod 154–55.

71. WCW to R. L. Latimer, December 17, 1937, unpublished letter qtd. in *New World* 407.

72. Alfred Kazin, "William Carlos Williams Applies the Insight of a Poet to a Novel of Unusual Quality," *New York Times Book Review* June 20, 1937: 7, rpt. in *Critical Heritage* 140–42.

73. Sol Funaroff, "Everyday America," *New Masses* September 21, 1937: 27. Williams returned the compliment in his 1938 review of Funaroff's poetry (see n. 55 above).

74. Fred R. Miller, "With a Kick to It," *New Republic* July 7, 1937, 257.

75. Willard Maas, "A Novel in the American Grain," *New York Herald Tribune Books* July 11, 1937: 4.

76. Philip Rahv, "Torrents of Spring," *Nation* June 26, 1937: 733, rpt. in *Critical Heritage* 143–45.

77. Eda Lou Walton, "X-Ray Realism," *Nation* March 19, 1938: 334–35, rpt. in *Critical Heritage* 150–52; Fred R. Miller, "Passaic River Stories," *New Republic* April 20, 1938: 341, rpt. in *Critical Heritage* 153–54.

78. Cf. a doctor's "stenographic" analysis of characters in *The Knife of the Times* (Gertrude Diamant, in *Critical Heritage* 118–19).

79. Two stacks can be seen at the far-left background of Sheeler's painting, but they are too distant to be William's king- and queen-like figures. Henry Sayre also observes these differences between painting and poem but concludes that "[i]f there is any connection to Sheeler's painting at all, it is only in Williams's [ironic] use of the word 'classic'" (*The Visual Text of William Carlos Williams* [Urbana: U of Illinois P, 1983] 69n24).

80. Babette Deutsch, "Poet in a Barrel," *Nation* November 19, 1938: 542–43. Deutsch's and Miller's praise of "American" English and rhythms in Williams's writing hints at a larger trend among leftist writers in the late 1930s: a rapproche-

ment with America, as political freedom was become a scarce commodity elsewhere. Dos Passos best exemplifies this trend.

81. Horace Gregory, "Fresh, Impudent Poems," *New York Herald Tribune Books*
February 5, 1939: 20.

82. Horace Gregory used the same phrase against Cummings and his generation the same year: "The Collected Cummings," *New Republic* April 27, 1938:
368, 370.

83. Mason Wade, "The Poems of William Carlos Williams: A Volume That
Places Him with Our Best," *New York Times Book Review* July 23, 1939: 2, 12. Mariani takes this "just below the first" assessment as typifying all the reviews (*New
World* 424). But the strikingly positive tone of most of them, Untermeyer's mention of the Pulitzer, and even Winters's unexpected prediction of Williams's future fame (see below) argue against this generalization.

84. Louis Untermeyer, "Experiment and Tradition," *Yale Review* 23.3 (1939):
612–13.

85. Philip Horton, "Anthology of a Mind," *New Republic* December 21, 1938:
208, rpt. in *Critical Heritage* 156–58. Elsewhere in the review, Horton compares
Williams to Cummings: both are "aggressive individualists."

86. What really irked Williams was Horton's vacillation in gauging Williams's
achievement: "I'm not important but I'm not insignificant. Boy! that's pretty ca-
gey shootin'." He concludes: "To hell with him. If he hadn't had Stevens to teach
him how to look crookedly [i.e., using the "anti-poetic" tag] he wouldn't have
had anything at all to say. Tell him to go wipe his nose" ("Reviewer on the Spot,"
New Republic January 11, 1939: 289).

87. Ruth Lechlitner, "The Poetry of William Carlos Williams," *Poetry* 54.6
(1939): 326–35.

88. Lechlitner's accurate description of Williams's plans for *Paterson* leads me
to suspect that the two had corresponded about it. Her name, however, does not
appear in his *Selected Letters* or as a correspondent in Mariani's biography.

89. Yvor Winters, "Poetry of Feeling," *Kenyon Review* 1.1 (1939): 104–7. Winters was later to make this infamous judgment of Williams in a postscript to the
reprinting of this review: "To say that Williams was anti-intellectual would be
almost an exaggeration: he did not know what the intellect was. He was a foolish
and ignorant man, but at moments a fine stylist" (*William Carlos William: A Collection of Critical Essays* [Englewood Cliffs, NJ: Prentice Hall, 1966] 69). Cf. Paul
Rosenfeld's antithetical view of Williams as "an intellectual poet" ("Williams
the Stylist," *Saturday Review of Literature* February 11, 1939: 16).

90. R. P. Blackmur, "Nine Poets," *Partisan Review* 6.2 (1939): 114. As if answering Blackmur's objection to the "run-down" humanity populating Williams's
poems, Mason Wade writes in his review (see n. 83 above): "Unavoidable human misery gives his lyricism a sharp edge, but for the most part he finds beauty
in things and people deemed too wretched for notice by more squeamish souls"
(2, 12).

91. Apart from the communists' special use of "confusion" (discussed in chapter 1), one sample of this descriptor appears in Lillian Symes's 1936 discussion of *The Nation* and *The New Republic*: "When the social historian of the future seeks to epitomize in a chapter heading the intellectual atmosphere of the decade between 1930 and 1940, he will undoubtedly hit upon some such phrase as 'The Great Confusion'" ("Our Liberal Weeklies," *Modern Monthly* October 1936: 7).

CONCLUSION

1. *Letters of Wallace Stevens,* ed. Holly Stevens (Berkeley: U of California P, 1996) 294–95.

2. Wallace Stevens, "The Irrational Element in Poetry," lecture at Harvard University, December 1936, rpt. in *Wallace Stevens: Collected Poetry and Prose*, ed. Frank Kermode and Joan Richardson (New York: Library of America, 1997) [hereafter cited as *CPP*] 788.

3. *E. E. Cummings: Complete Poems, 1904–1962,* ed. George J. Firmage (New York: Liveright, 1991) 438 [hereafter cited as *CP*].

4. For example, Joseph Carroll's *Wallace Stevens' Supreme Fiction: A New Romanticism* (Baton Rouge: Louisiana State UP, 1987).

5. Regrettably, one subject I must omit here is Stevens's World War II poetry as a reflection of his still active social sensibility. Both Alan Filreis (*Wallace Stevens and the Actual World* [Princeton: Princeton UP, 1991]) and Jacqueline Brogan (*The Violence Within, the Violence Without: Wallace Stevens and the Emergence of a Revolutionary Poetics* [Athens: U of Georgia P, 2003]) have written insightfully on the topic.

6. How similar this theme and its images are to Cummings's depiction of disbelievers in "Jehovah buried, Satan dead": "go dreamless knaves, on Shadows fed" (*CP* 438). But where Cummings expresses contempt, Stevens conveys pity.

7. "We" might be seen here as simply a rhetorical device (the editorial "we") except that in many other late poems it refers specifically to the speaker and his beloved, e.g., "and there [tomorrow] they'll scarcely find us(if they do,/ we'll move away still further:into now" (*CP* 579)

8. "freedom from freedom" may allude to Erich Fromm's recent book, *Escape from Freedom* (1941). Cummings did not publish this poem until after Roosevelt's death: first in *Quarterly Review of Literature* (spring 1946), then in *XAIPE* (1950). I am grateful to Michael Webster for providing the date of the magazine publication.

9. Richard Kennedy notes that Cummings was not well informed about the war (he seldom read newspapers) and that his political opinions—like most people's—tended to be based in emotion rather than rational argument (*Dreams in the Mirror: A Biography of E. E. Cummings* [New York: Liveright, 1980] 388). For a critique of Cummings's moral logic in "why must itself," see Milton A. Cohen, "The Po-

litical Cummings: Iconoclast or Solipsist?" *SPRING: The Journal of the E. E. Cummings Society* ns 6 (October 1997): 70–80.

10. For discussion of Cummings's obtuseness about the offensiveness of these poems, see Kennedy 432–33 and Milton A. Cohen, "From Bad Boy to Curmudgeon: Cummings's Political Evolution," in *Words into Pictures: E. E. Cummings' Art across Borders,* ed. Jiri Flajsar and Zeno Vernyik (Cambridge: Cambridge Scholars P, 2008) 24–25.

11. *Robert Frost: Collected Poems, Prose and Plays,* ed. and notes by Richard Poirier and Mark Richardson (New York: Library of America, 1995) 324 [hereafter cited as *CPPP*].

12. *Interviews with Robert Frost,* ed. Edward C. Lathem (New York: Holt Rinehart, 1966) 146 [hereafter cited as *Interviews*].

13. Qtd. in Reginald L. Cook, *The Dimension of Robert Frost* (New York: Rinehart, 1958) 39.

14. March 12, 1920, and May 24, 1916, *The Letters of Robert Frost to Louis Untermeyer,* ed. Louis Untermeyer (New York: Holt Rinehart, 1963) 97–98, 32.

15. "Harrison" may have been modeled on Granville Hicks, who was "a Puritan Yankee" and had shifted from Freudianism to Marxism in the early 1930s. If so, Frost probably wrote the poem in that decade.

16. Lisa Seale estimates, for example, that between 1950 and his death in 1963, Frost gave 310 public poetry readings. This number does not include numerous public lectures and newspaper interviews ("War and Peace: Robert Frost and the United Nations Meditation Room," *New England Quarterly* 77.1 [2004]: 108).

17. See Mark Richardson's fine explication of this poem in "Frost and the Cold War: A Look at the Later Poetry," in *Roads Not Taken: Rereading Robert Frost,* ed. with intro. by Earl J. Wilcox and Jonathan N. Barron (Columbia: U Missouri P, 2000) 55–78. Frost's trope of orgasmic explosions owes something to Robinson Jeffers's "dive-bomber's screaming orgasm" in the poem "May–June 1940."

18. Lawrance Thompson and R. H. Winnick, *Robert Frost: The Later Years* (New York: Holt, Rinehart, 1976) 320.

19. *The Collected Poems of William Carlos Williams,* 2 vols. (New York: New Directions, 1986, 1988), 2: 63–65 [hereafter cited as *CP-WCW*].

20. On October 20, 1952, the *Chicago Daily Tribune* ran an article titled "Poet Assailed as Unfit for His Praise of Reds," in which Mrs. Virginia Kent Cummins of the Lyric Foundation cited this poem as "the very voice of communism." *CP-WCW* 2: 473n.

21. Williams's comments on this poem at first appear contradictory regarding his attitude toward organized religion. To Babette Deutsch, he confides shortly after he wrote it that "the poem is anti-Catholic, anti all that the Bible damnation theorem symbolizes. It is . . . [against] anything that postpones the perfectibility to 'heaven' and all that heaven implies" (*CP-WCW* 2: 477n). Having mellowed somewhat in his recollection of the poem in *I Wanted to Write a Poem: The*

Autobiography of the Works of a Poet (ed. Edith Heal [New York: New Directions, 1958]), he states: "It is a Christian poem, very definitely. The Pink Church stands for the Christian Church. . . . My conception of Christ as a socialistic figure related to a generous feeling toward the poor, also confused many. . . . I am not at all convinced that communism in its original meaning is any more communistic than Christ's own doctrine" (76). In fact, though, his opinions are consistent: admiration for Christ's "socialistic" treatment of the poor; contempt for the church as a repressive institution that offers paradise only in the next world.

22. Williams envisioned the poem set to music and sent it to Celia Zukofsky for that purpose. It was published with her score in *Briarcliffe Quarterly* (October 1946) (*CP-WCW* 2: 478n).

23. In his letter to Deutsch, Williams was explicit about this parallel: "I particularly detest Eliot, the Catholic church and the Dictatorship not of the proletariat but of such rats as Stalin and all his kind" (*CP-WCW* 2: 477n).

24. According to Paul Mariani, Williams was twice appointed to the position "Consultant in Poetry" to the Library of Congress, but never served. His first appointment (1952) was stalled by the Library of Congress's Librarian, Luther Evans, who, because of the Virginia Cummins flap (see n. 20 above), demanded that Williams first pass a loyalty investigation. When Williams's lawyer interceded, Evans revoked the appointment, citing not Williams's loyalty but his ill health (a recent stroke). The following year, he was reappointed by the Library Fellows, but Evans again required "loyalty and security procedures" be met (666) and then simply shelved the appointment. Evans's successor later wrote Williams that the Library of Congress had not even evaluated the FBI report and that, in any case, Williams's security status was not in question. Williams published that letter to clear his name (*New World* 651–55, 658, 666–67).

25. T. S. Eliot, "The Metaphysical Poets," in *Selected Prose of T. S. Eliot,* ed. with intro. by Frank Kermode (New York: Harcourt, 1975) 64.

Index

—prose: *The Autobiography of William Carlos Williams*, 247n38, 253n21; *I Wanted to Write a Poem*, 166, 247n37, 247n40; *Kora in Hell*, 183

—relations with Wallace Stevens, 77, 159–60, 177, 229n20, 233n58

—reviews of: *Adam & Eve & the City*, 149, 172, 248n49; *Collected Poems, 1921–1931*, 158–60; *Complete Collected Poems*, 149, 186–90, 251n86; *An Early Martyr*, 32, 148, 171–72, 197, 248n49; *Life Along the Passaic River*, 182–83; *The Knife of the Times*, 150, 250n78; *White Mule*, 181–82

—Social Credit theory, interest in, 161, 246n29

—and Spanish Civil War, 148, 162–63, 196, 245n1

—and warring factions on left, 149, 172, 173, 174–75, 178–79, 190

—working class and poor, empathy for, 3,

4, 7, 148, 157, 181, 185–86, 195, 196, 198, 216, 217

—*See also* comparison of Cummings, Frost, Stevens, Williams; Latimer, Ronald Lane; Lewis, H. H.

Wilson, Edmund, 14, 18, 21, 42, 46, 97, 98, 120, 223n20, 226n66; *The American Jitters*, 25–26; "An Appeal to Progressives," 10–12, 13, 17, 221nn3–4; review of Cummings's poetry, 90, 235n13; review of Stevens's poetry, 48, 228n4

Wilson, T. C., 32, 41, 224n35; review of Williams's poetry, 171, 248n50

Winters, Yvor, 32; reviews of Williams's poetry, 189, 251n83, 251n89

Wright, Richard, 14, 26–27, 44, 231n30

Zabel, Morton, 29–30, 32, 224n35; review of Stevens, 51, 228n12

Zukofsky, Louis, 154, 163, 164, 245n2, 247n34